The Courage to Be Happy

To get access to free interactive material to accompany this book please visit

www.couragetobehappy.ie

The Courage to Be Happy

A New Approach to Well-Being in Everyday Life

Colm O'Connor

Newleaf

Newleaf
an imprint of
Gill & Macmillan Ltd
Hume Avenue, Park West, Dublin 12
with associated companies throughout the world
www.gillmacmillan.ie

978 07171 4833 2

Typography design by Make Communication
Print origination by Síofra Murphy
Printed in the UK by MPG Books Ltd, Cornwall

This book is typeset in Linotype Minion and Neue Helvetica.

The paper used in this book comes from the wood pulp of managed forests. For every tree felled, at least one tree is planted, thereby renewing natural resources.

A CIP catalogue record for this book is available from the British Library.

5 4 3 2 1

Contents

Preamble

An acorn seed can sit as motionless and silent as stone on a shelf in your garden shed for years. You can take this acorn seed and place it, where there is no light, in the damp, dark soil. Then, as if by magic, the seed awakens from its eternal sleep and begins to move. In time the acorn breaks open, and the first tentacles of life break through its surface. Soon afterwards the early shoots of an oak tree begin to emerge into the light. It is quite an astonishing miracle that this dead pebble of a seed can hold such dormant power. Without fanfare, this patient and persistent growth transforms into an oak tree.

> Your happiness and well-being lie dormant within you.
> They are like seeds waiting for you to turn over the soil of yourself.

The title of this book, 'The Courage to Be Happy', may seem strange. One would not normally think that happiness requires courage. However, one of the central threads running through this book is showing how natural happiness is more a consequence of courage than of good fortune. How can happiness require courage? You will hopefully discover that natural happiness and well-being flowers as a consequence of such things as self-discipline, overcoming adversity, living a spiritual life, and engaging in a range of activities that require an application of the self in overcoming everyday anxiety. There is courage required in assuming the moral responsibility of taking care of one's life and well-being. Courage is essential for looking at oneself, for inhabiting the vulnerability of life, for acting in accordance with virtue rather than self-interest, and for having a passionate self-discipline in the application of oneself towards noble goals.

The use of the word courage acknowledges, at the outset, that life itself is an ordeal that demands a heroic response. The purpose of life, from an evolutionary perspective, is simply to overcome adversity—whether small or large. In doing so, we survive and thrive. Happiness does not arise from putting on a happy face or from sticking a smiley face on the lapel of our everyday life. It is something deeper. It requires backbone. It is the courage to be. It is the courage to live the life that is living you. It is the courage to be well—to be happy in a joyful and sorrowful world.

Whatever you are experiencing in your life, you must start from a position of self-acceptance and respect. Whatever worries, relationships, stresses or uncertainties are affecting your well-being, you must inhabit the unhappiness that has descended upon you. Your unhappiness is the stuff of life, and, if you can inhabit it fully and trust yourself, it can be transformed. Your unhappiness can be converted. However, if you reject your unhappiness by trivialising or demonising it you will regress even further.

We live in an age in which unhappiness, depression, stress and anxiety are everywhere. Depression is among the top five illnesses diagnosed in the Western world. We struggle with such things as bad relationships, job stress, self-rejection, low self-esteem, worry, anxiety and helplessness. The list is actually endless, because everyone is unhappy for different reasons.

Whatever the causes of your unhappiness, this book will lay out a way of looking at yourself that can transform your psychology, your behaviour and your theology! You can achieve this not by starting with your unhappiness and trying to eliminate it but by starting with your natural happiness and cultivating it. They represent very different paths.

For example, you can approach your life by identifying what is wrong with it and trying to eliminate it. Or you can try to find what may be right with your life and nurture and expand it. This book will try to help you with the latter—to help you awaken your innate happiness, strengths, purpose and well-being.

Amazingly, you often repress happiness and at times even banish it from your inner life. The repression of well-being and natural joy is a largely undocumented but very pervasive phenomenon. Who would want to repress their happiness? you ask. That seems a bit odd. Well, what happens in life is that as we get older we replace natural, relaxed joy with anxiety and worry. We inhibit our freedom, suppress our spontaneity and become preoccupied with the four Ss: status, security, significance and safety. As these take priority in life we have to turn away from our natural selves, from natural joy. There are times in life when you realise this—when you are shocked into seeing that you are living your life as if half asleep. This may be as a consequence of a loss, an illness, a bereavement or some other life-changing event. You are shocked, then, into seeing that your life is indeed wonderful, that your lover is indeed beautiful and that you are indeed blessed. Many of these moments are often epiphanies forced by tragedy, loss or trauma. These are occasions when the curtains of your preoccupied life part and you see a greater meaning.

Or else you are disturbed from the slumber of your life by what I call 'post-traumatic joy'. This is the happiness that emerges after being overcome by a positive experience that awakens you to the bliss and well-being of your own life. This may be the birth of a child, an uncomplicated grief, a loving relationship, a breakthrough in one's personal development or the breaking free of a toxic relationship. Just as negative events can cause post-traumatic stress, positive events can trigger post-traumatic joy!

This book will reintroduce you to the dormant self within you that remembers joy, happiness and contentment, once banished to the corners of the self and replaced by anxiety.

After thirty years working as a psychologist and psychotherapist I have realised that therapeutic intervention is only one way that change can be facilitated. Change is not brought about by insight alone but also by such things as discipline, emotional commitment, out-of-character behaviour, habit formation, loving encouragement, self-emancipation and spiritual ritual.

Hopefully you will feel supported by what I write. I can, through the wonder of writing, be with you and support you in achieving what you want and need. In all of this,

> As your courage grows,
> May the forest part before you,
> May your step be sure underfoot and
> May invisible hands come to support you.

Acknowledgments

This book is dedicated to my late father, Cormac, whose scholarly inspiration, artistic vision and poetic heart have cleared a path before me. His kind-heartedness, courage and character have inspired me throughout the writing of this book. To my dear Mom, Phyl. You live every page of this book and are the embodiment of courageous joy. You are my hero.

To my beautiful wife, Jean. Your love and encouragement throughout the inevitable vicissitudes of writing this book have been the standing stones of my well-being. You have been the sweet wind beneath my wings.

My three children, Brendan, Christine and Ciara, have been such a source of joy and love for me. You have each given my life a meaning and purpose that lies beyond the depth of words. Brendan, with your positivity and hope, Christine, with your wit and gentleness, Ciara, with your simple and sublime joy. You have, as always, been teaching your father how to walk.

Gerry, Una, Mary and Joe: you have been my home and the secure base from which I have ventured and to which I will always return.

A very special word of thanks to Don Hennessy, who has been my friend and colleague for twenty years. Without your gentle encouragement towards this end I doubt I would have made it. Thank you.

To my friend, colleague and fellow-psychologist Declan Aherne, who has been a thorn in the shoe of my complacency, forever reminding me of my Buddha nature.

In addition, my lifelong friend Stephen, who has kept my head plugged into reality and sustained me with many hours of pints and laughter over the years.

To my 'supervision group', who have, for more years than we care to measure, shared a sacred space with me every two weeks and have been a deep well from which I have drawn so much.

My thanks to Breda for helping me in the eleventh hour when I wondered if I would get there. You were great!

A special word to Eoin and Jean: your empathies and imagination have been such an inspiration to me over so many, many years. Bless you always.

Fergal Tobin, for seeing in my manuscript what I doubted was there. And to all the staff at Gill & Macmillan, who have been delightful to a person.

Finally, I need to acknowledge the outstanding work of the key researchers in the field of happiness and well-being listed in the select bibliography. I relied on the compiled research presented in these texts, particularly the summaries of Martin Seligman in *Authentic Happiness*, Sonja Lyubomirsky in *The How of Happiness*, Ed Diener and Robert Biswas-Diener in *Happiness*, Jonathan Haidt in *The Happiness Hypothesis* and Daniel Gilbert in *Stumbling on Happiness*. I have also been influenced by the work of many scholars and writers who have helped me find the words to write what I wrote.

Chapter 1

The art, science and discipline of happiness

Have you ever noticed that when you get good advice it can sustain you for a day or two but then fades into the background of your everyday life? Have you not found that your good intentions remain only good intentions and that, month after month and year after year, you promise yourself the change that never happens? Have you not read wonderful books that you thought would change your life but then been disappointed in your inability to convert wisdom into action? Or have you been inspired by a film, a story or an epiphany that at the time felt life-altering and lasting only to find that its effect dissolved quickly into the watery greyness of your life?

If these experiences are familiar to you, you will hopefully find comfort in this book. You will recognise the three forces that you need to convert good intention into meaningful action: knowledge, spiritual desire and self-discipline.

Much of your happiness will rise or fall on self-discipline. The book will challenge you to see that the absence of a passionate self-discipline in important areas of your life has been your greatest weakness.

At the same time, self-discipline itself is not enough. You need to have a *feeling for* your life and to act with *right feeling*. The way of happiness and well-being is also the way of the human heart. The landscape of your happiness includes the wonder, beauty, tenderness, love and inspiration you have known. It is a landscape that is also shaded by your experiences of grief, sorrow, trauma, tragedy and worry. Therefore, you will need more than good thoughts and good deeds. You need an open heart that is touched by the poetry, music and art of life. This 'heartfulness' gives feeling and meaning to your life. It is the window of a compassionate heart through which the fresh wind of well-being can blow through you. We will, hopefully, open this window together.

You also know the reliability of science, of needing to step outside your inner world to know what is real and what can be counted on. As a scientist-practitioner I believe passionately in the need to build our knowledge in accordance with sound research. I will give that to you. So, when it comes to well-being, I will tell you what contributes to happiness, according to what current research tells us. I will convert that into the twenty-one things you can do that have been proved to enhance your well-being.

Therefore, this book will outline for you how to understand and change your happiness and well-being based on psychological research, traditional wisdom and the under-appreciated art of self-discipline. The book will reveal how ancient spiritual disciplines and modern psychological research intersect to offer a deeply meaningful and radical way of living in the world.

What I know about you

In picking up this book you are already telling me something about you. I know that you are like me, someone interested in being a better human being. You want to feel better about yourself, to break down your fears and insecurities, to experience the natural happiness, joy and contentment that you know lies within you. Be assured that they are there, like sleeping giants within you.

You probably know what brings you comfort and temporary pleasure but are less sure of what brings lasting happiness. Therefore, you are always searching, always taking yourself apart and examining yourself. We are all trying to be happier but are not quite sure how to capture this elusive butterfly.

I also know that you are somewhat confused; that you have conflicting goals that you don't know how to resolve; and that you struggle at times with depression, anxiety and stress. I know these things because you are human. Everyone has conflicting needs that create inner tensions and stress. Most people are in perpetual states of inner conflict—they want both security and adventure, safety and unpredictability, separateness and connection and dependence and independence.

Therefore, you want to be yourself and, at the same time, other than yourself. You are always at war with yourself.

The human species has survived over the past hundred thousand years because each individual was programmed to adapt and survive in order to maintain the species. This serves the species well, but at a cost to the individual person. You therefore reflexively do things that are good for Homo Sapiens but often bad for you as an individual.

Therefore, to develop your happiness and well-being you will need to change things you do that are reflexes and habits that do not serve a useful purpose for you, such as excessive worry, stressful over-activity, status seeking, seeking compulsive control and dreading your future.

The development of the idea

I wanted to write this book not just as a psychologist but also as a man, as a father, a son, a failure, a lover and a poet. I have wanted to write this as someone who has been searching for happiness but who has at times struggled to find it. I have always had that buzz of potential and excitement for life, but I have equally been disappointed in my ability to fulfil myself and overcome my self-doubt and insecurity. A thin membrane has always stood between me and the life I could be living.

You may think that, as a clinical psychologist helping unhappy people for thirty years, I might be a tad happier than most. It was a bit of a blow to my pride to admit, over the past decade or so, that this was not always the case. Though I was able to help most people I worked with, I was not always doing so well myself. Reluctantly, I realised that I was not very happy. My life was becoming overcast and grey. I knew that blue skies lay behind, but the clouds began to part less and less. I was no happier with my life than some of my patients. So I took steps to deal with it—to feel better about myself and life.

However, a second blow to my pride came when I had to admit that I initially failed in my attempts to improve! I floundered around in my own well-intentioned self-treatments. I expected that I could think my way out of trouble. I over-estimated this strategy! I discovered how impotent thinking could actually be when it came to emotional issues.

Though 'Physician, heal thyself' was my daily admonition, I couldn't get a grip on what was wrong or how to deal with it. I needed to do something different. So, without being despondent, I decided to explore the issue of personal happiness with curiosity and determination. That was when I began to turn the corner.

You and I need these critical moments in life when the tide turns and when we know we need to change our lives. This turning of the inner tide doesn't provide the solution, but it marks a turning point when we begin to move slowly or quickly in a new direction. I had to confront those elements in myself that prevented me from being true to myself and aligned with my true nature. I was depressive and controlled more by guilt, perfectionism and fear than by confident self-belief. A cocktail of negative attitudes, states and dispositions contributed to a vague state of 'unhappiness'. I decided I had to change.

I am glad to say that the process of self-exploration and change I undertook reinvigorated my life. I discovered a number of dramatic things about how to improve one's well-being and how to understand one's unhappiness. These lie at the heart of this book. I will present an understanding of happiness and well-being that I trust will not be another impotent programme for change but will be an inspirational and scientific appreciation of your own well-being. Despite the false promises of popular psychology, self-improvement is difficult.

My personal struggles coincided with my interest in positive psychology. This is a new field that has been conducting research into happiness and well-being. It developed as a reaction to the preoccupation of psychology with human disorders, deficits and disabilities to the neglect of all the other human attributes that are reflective of humanity at its best.

I felt this moral responsibility to examine and understand how my psychological wellness could be enhanced. So I studied the work of Martin Seligman, Sonja Lyubomirsky, Jonathan Haidt, Ed Diener and Robert Biswas-Diener, Matthieu Ricard, Tal Ben-Shahar, Daniel Gilbert and others, expecting to discover the optimal path towards well-being. Though the research didn't provide all the answers I sought, what I did find was exciting and fascinating, and this will form part of this book.

Seminar

In order to share my discoveries I organised a public seminar in Cork in May 2009 entitled 'The Science of Happiness and Well-Being', at which I presented the core findings of the research on what enhances well-being and happiness. People were very interested in the workshop. I got a great thrill from the enthusiastic feedback it received. It helped me to clarify what causes happiness and psychological wealth.

However, despite this new knowledge, I wasn't making any substantial changes in my own life, and I wasn't much happier. I needed to challenge myself further. Yes, I had the ideas and research, but its impact on my life was mainly an intellectual one. I hope you can identify with this yourself: those many times when you learn something new, acquire new insights about yourself or read a great book that appears revolutionary, only to find that the knowledge has little effect on your emotional life. You know what you *should* do, but that is a lifetime away from doing it.

Well-being group

I went on to set up what I called a 'well-being group' with eight professional colleagues who were interested in enhancing their well-being. We attended regular meetings, in a structured way, to see if we could put into practice a number of our personal goals regarding our well-being, and we based this on what works, according to the research. This was not a problem-focused group but a health and well-being group devoted to the setting of specific goals. Each member had to report on their changes and was required to remain accountable to the group for that. A core principle was the belief that it's all very well knowing what you would like to do but that it's far more difficult to remain focused and disciplined in putting those aspirations into practice, even if you know that these things will be good for you.

After a number of weeks it was obvious that the meaning and effectiveness of the group was quite dramatic. In some cases it resulted in significant life changes, and in every case it resulted in a dramatic sensitivity to, and awareness of, the patterns of well-being. The feedback was hugely encouraging, and in this book I want to share much of this learning with you. We realised a few simple things very quickly, which I present as seven initial realisations about happiness.

SEVEN INITIAL REALISATIONS

These will kick-start our examination of happiness and present an outline of what is to follow.

Realisation no. 1

The first simple but rarely appreciated realisation was that *you cannot think yourself happy!* This may seem obvious, but most of us operate on the subconscious assumption that we can think our way out of problems and towards wellness. It's somewhat disappointing to discover that this really is not the case! If you are like me you will think and think and think about your problems, and you will come up with many helpful thoughts, ideas and strategies that you believe will solve your problems. In your head these sound great, but unfortunately they regularly collapse like a tent. This is one of the illusions I examine in this book. (An extension of the assumption that we can think ourselves happy is the popular belief that we can talk our way out of relationship problems).

Realisation no. 2

A second realisation was that *knowing what causes your unhappiness will not, of itself, make you any happier!* Information and understanding, while necessary, are usually insufficient to create change. There are two reasons for this. Firstly, though you think you know what will make you happier, you are probably wrong about it. (I show you why later). Secondly, even if you are right in your assessment, knowing it makes little difference. Information is dead if it isn't coupled with the motivation to change, with the knowledge of what exactly to change and with the self-discipline to sustain a programme of action. It has to be converted into experience, emotion and action. Your relationships don't improve just because you think you know what the problem is. Knowing something doesn't mean that it can be translated into everyday experiences of well-being. Knowledge, in and of itself, is entirely dead.

Many people actually become addicted to getting more information. They operate on the assumption that if they just get the next book—such as this one—they will make that breakthrough. However, more information, in this age of abundant information, is not what we need—we also need desire and discipline.

Realisation no. 3

A third realisation was that *eliminating unhappiness does not make you happy.* Or, to put it another way: plucking the weeds from your garden does not cause flowers to grow! One of the great errors of psychology, psychiatry and some popular thinking has been the belief that if you get rid of what is bad then what is good will automatically come in to replace it. We now know that this is not the case. Sometimes we have to do the opposite of what we might think. We need at times to sideline the bad things in our life while we cultivate the good. This can make all the difference. In other words, what this book is about is not weeding out the bad but how to plant and cultivate that which is good.

Therefore, one of the most dramatic realisations within the group was that, despite our ability to set goals, converting informed good intentions into immediate, observable action was still very difficult. This was fascinating to me. I was intrigued. Others shared the same experience, and this became a powerful motivator in the group: that it's so easy to talk the talk of good intentions when it comes to change.

Realisation no. 4

The fourth realisation, therefore, was that *developing one's happiness and well-being has to stand on the three legs of knowing what to do, why one should do it and how to do it.* This is summarised here as:

(1) *the what:* knowing specifically what you need to do
(2) *the why:* having the inspiration and purpose to do it
(3) *the how:* having the self-discipline to sustain it once the inspiration has faded.

These three elements represent the layout of the book. Let me explain them a little more.

(1) *The 'what'*

In this section of the book I present the science of happiness—a summary of what psychological research suggests that one should and should not do to improve well-being. This section presents the myths about happiness that have been discovered through empirical research. More importantly, it presents the twenty-one things that the research says we must do in order to enhance our well-being. We also need to understand the necessity and benefits of enhancing our well-being. Scientific research has some compelling things to say about this.

(2) *The 'why'*

It's not enough to know what one should be doing. One needs to understand and develop a solid base of inspiration and motivation to change. I will invite you to consider your own personal 'theology'. This is the purpose, the meaning and the virtues that can help you live life more fully—that can open the windows to joy and happiness. When you awaken your life with issues of meaning, purpose, existence and mortality your happiness is more deeply felt and consolidated. This aspect of your life is critical because so many of the solutions to the problem of how to live a happy life lie beyond psychology, at the burning-point of life: how we find happiness and hope in a life of suffering and mortality.

(3) *The 'how'*

Most of the universal models of learning and change involve intense self-discipline, practice and habit formation. No new skill or artistic ability is learnt without going through the tedious repetition that is practice. This simple and self-evident principle is applied successfully to a range of things, such as mastering a craft, learning a musical instrument, developing athletic prowess, improving physical fitness, rehabilitating after injury or trauma, learning something intellectually, losing weight or learning how to meditate. Whether you are an alcoholic committed to AA or a music student learning to be a pianist, building a new self or a new skill requires the bricks and mortar of self-discipline.

This is rarely applied to emotional well-being and happiness. Interestingly, it's a principle applied with universal diligence in parenting. Most parents try to teach their children self-discipline because of the intuitive awareness that self-discipline is the key to a fulfilling life.

From this viewpoint, this book shows that happiness is a consequence of what you do more than what you think. The activities and disciplines presented in the book are supported by psychological research, inspired by passionate purpose and made effective by perseverance. There are two parts to this: the first is knowing how to develop new habits; the second is knowing what one should practise. These will be explored.

Realisation no. 5

However, having a list of what to do is not sufficient in itself. The 'what to do' must be integrated with the 'why you do it'. This brought me to the fifth realisation: *Activities are at their most powerful when they are part of a spiritual discipline that integrates that activity with one's purpose in life.* Happiness in its richest sense is achieved through the practice of spiritual discipline. Having examined the research carefully I summarised the things that improve well-being in the twenty-one things to do.

However, I knew this was not enough—there was something missing. What the research presented was a kind of technology or list of techniques and strategies. But they had no soul or heart. While they satisfied my wish for rigour and evidenced-based practice, they did not inspire me. However, I discovered eventually that all the things that made a difference to a person's happiness had a spiritual quality to them. Each strategy was not only a simple technique but also an activity that had a symbolic meaning. Each activity seemed to symbolise and ritualise a person's place in the world and the meaning of that place.

It was possible, then, in a very simple but elegant way to present the following four spiritual disciplines:

(1) the disciplines of the mind
(2) the disciplines of the heart
(3) the disciplines of the body
(4) the disciplines of the soul.

In the final chapters the powerful impact of integrating one's goals and activities into spiritual discipline is presented. Here our activities and things to do have the potential to become passionate activities that can awaken the imagination and the soul.

This book shows that being happier requires more than intelligence, insight and motivation. All the activities that enhance happiness and well-being are, in essence, core spiritual disciplines. That is, they are disciplines that are integrated with our measure of our self-worth and our purpose in life.

A form of moral courage and determination sustains spiritual disciplines. This book shows how we are at our happiest when we find the courage to live for something larger than ourselves and to persevere against the winds of self-doubt and self-indulgence.

Realisation no. 6

The sixth realisation was that *to understand ourselves and our happiness we must see ourselves in the round, that is, within the full arc of our human condition.* This book presents a programme for change that sees you in the round: as a rational thinker willing to change; as a spiritual and symbolic person who searches for meaning and purpose in life; and as a mortal, transient creature who has no control over their ultimate fate in life.

The meaning of your life is inspired by the conditions of existence: by the essential mysteries of life, by the miraculous and magnificent and by the traumatic and tragic. How you live, how you find and understand happiness, will be influenced in a fundamental way by your unspoken 'theology' about life. I will help you to clarify what this is and how you can use it effectively.

You are also a person who lives in the real world and knows the value of practice and perseverance—who appreciates the ancient virtue of self-discipline. When it comes to your happiness and well-being, soft optimism or positivity will not be enough. You will need to identify the adversary within yourself and do battle with your inner demons and dragon.

Seeing you in the round is to see both parts of your humanity: the part that needs to live in your body, to inhabit the life you have; and the part that needs to imagine your life and self in ways that enable you to give meaning and purpose to that life.

Both parts of your humanity are experienced in the conflict between your imaginative spiritual self (that can infuse your life with meaning, purpose and joy) and your physical self that washes dishes, brings children to school and worries about the little things in life.

All the great poets, writers and religions have wrestled mightily with this tension. So, to see you in the round is to see you as a spiritual as well as a psychological person. You don't just want to feel happy—you want to feel worthy of that happiness, to have a sense of purpose and to feel confident in your ability to overcome adversity.

To achieve this we have a real need for focused self-discipline, for determined happiness and for a kind of dogged and courageous joy.

Realisation no. 7

I have realised by virtue of this journey that *happiness is a natural cellular consequence of overcoming obstacles and adversities.* By that I mean that happiness and well-being is a physical state as much as it is an emotional one. It's nature's reward for overcoming the endless stream of small (and large) obstacles that obstruct the path towards our destiny. It's nature's way of encouraging us to endure.

Secondly, I also discovered that 'deep happiness' is experienced when we overcome obstacles and adversities by *engaging in actions that symbolise a meaning and purpose that is larger than ourselves.* In other words, when our deeds have an emotional meaning and a particular purpose we experience deep well-being. The idea that overcoming small adversities or challenges is related to happiness and well-being is not new. It's a motif of all ancient mythologies about how to live a meaningful life. How to fully embrace and understand that life is not meant to be easy—it expects that there is something heroic about how you live.

Thirdly, *a constant symphony of joy plays through our lives. It's the background music that scores life, but it goes unheard in the din of everyday stress and mental chatter. There is a sublime impulse in humanity and in all of nature to enjoy just being itself!*

What I hope this book helps you to do is to remember who you are at the deepest level and to remember that happiness and joy are very much part of your actual physical existence. It behoves you to overcome the stress and anxiety that covers this deeper joy.

SELF-DISCIPLINE, HAPPINESS AND CHANGE

No matter how often you decide to lose weight, get fit, be happier or improve your marriage, nothing shifts unless you have the motivation and self-discipline to persevere with certain behaviour—especially with that which doesn't bring immediate results!

In reading popular self-help books you will have felt certain that you were going to put a dramatic new idea into action, only to discover that by the end of the week you have forgotten the very idea that enthused you so much. You may find yourself going back to the book to remember what it was you felt so strongly about in the first place. Sounds familiar?

Have you ever assumed that you were about to start a new chapter in your life and make some lasting changes only to find that, once the initial euphoria had worn off, the water level of your self returned quickly to its former position?

Have you not made countless efforts to do certain things in your life, such as losing weight, getting fit, being happier, improving your relationship, being a better parent, increasing your work performance, managing your time or maximising your efficiency? And, despite all these honest and genuine efforts at change, have you not experienced the inevitable disappointment of discovering that you have failed in your efforts? 'I know it looks like I am moving, but I am standing still,' sang Bob Dylan on a recent album.

I am hopeful that the reason you have purchased this book is that you realise that the kinds of changes you need require more than good intentions. Don't you waste a lot of your life dwelling on but never fulfilling your good intentions? You keep yourself going with the wishful 'Some day I will . . .'

Why we avoid emotional self-discipline

A critical question, then, is: If you know that practising good habits and disciplining ourselves to be psychologically healthy is good for you, why do you not do it? How do you let yourself off the hook, as it were? In fact, in your desire for the easy life you may believe that if happiness is dependent on the rigours of self-discipline there is something seriously wrong. Our consumerist culture and popular psychologies have us hoping that there are shortcuts to happiness.

There are four reasons why you don't bring appropriate self-discipline to bear on your happiness and well-being:

(1) lazy narcissism
(2) self-rejection
(3) spiritual cowardice
(4) cognitive flooding.

(1) *Lazy narcissism*

Narcissism is that self-important quality in you that makes you feel entitled to get what you want just because you want it. There are two simple beliefs that sustain this attitude:

- The belief that life should give you happiness
- The belief that life knows what you need.

The first is your childish and narcissistic belief that you are in some way special. This belief suggests that happiness is something you should get just by virtue of being you! Your childhood belief, which you still carry with you from infancy, is that the world will provide for you, that other people and the world are there to serve you and that life should give you happiness. When this expectation goes unfulfilled it can, as you can imagine, make you resentful and frustrated. The truth is that you are not so special that life makes exceptions for you. You have to be willing to discipline the self to achieve what you want.

The second belief you may have is that not only should life make you happy—like a good mother—but that it should also give you exactly what you need to be happy. Again, you have this hard-wired, childlike expectation that the world will figure out what you need and give it to you. You assume subconsciously that you won't have to work too hard to figure out what you need. So you become passive. You hold on to this sense of royal entitlement. However, it's not long before this unfulfilled expectation grows into cynicism, depression or anger at your life, your spouse, your children or God.

Therefore, when it comes to self-discipline and practice the narcissist in you says: 'It shouldn't have to be this hard. I shouldn't have to do these things in order to be well. Something is wrong. I deserve to be catered to. I am the person in need, so why should I have to be making the effort?' Now, you may not think these things, but you may feel them!

When you indulge your narcissism you are in denial about the fact that you are responsible for yourself. Being self-responsible is difficult because it means that you are willing to carry the burden of being yourself. In denying your self-responsibility and mortality you turn your face away in a sulk, preferring to blame others or the world for your fate. There is a kind of sulky refusal to realise that you must work hard in many areas of your life—particularly at being emotionally well and happy.

(2) *Self-rejection*

This reason involves our guilt and self-worth. Deep in our being we have this feeling that we aren't quite worthy of happiness and the good things in life. There is a part of us that has already decided to accept our lot and that feels that we don't really deserve much more. We may reject and blame ourselves and feel that we have made our miserable bed and that it's our duty to lie in it. We reject our natural rights, our human responsibility and our obligation to mind the life we have. Though we are worth so much more than we give ourselves credit for, we mentally abuse ourselves with persistent assaults and rejections.

You too have this toxic belief that you will become a better and stronger person if you blame, attack, put down, doubt, ignore and reject yourself. You have this kind of self-bullying belief that 'if I create enough upset and distress for my inner self, my inner self will change for the better.' This is disturbing and flawed and is the source of most of your suffering in life. It's your greatest impediment to happiness.

Rather than needing self-doubt, self-rejection and self-neglect you need self-encouragement, self-acceptance and self-emancipation. You need a healthy narcissism that helps you realise that you are *entitled to happiness*.

(3) *Spiritual cowardice*

Spiritual cowardice refers to the fact that we all have a tendency to hide, to be afraid of facing up to the bully within us and standing up for the small child of our promise and dreams. Unfortunately, we let anxiety and self-doubt bully our passionate and vulnerable self into the corners of our heart. This is when fear rules our emotional life. Therefore, change takes courage, the pursuit of happiness takes courage, and accepting that your responsibility in life is to be happy takes courage.

(4) *Cognitive flooding*

Cognitive flooding explains why we fail to change. We fail because we are literally flooded with information, problems, stresses and multiple tasks. They keep us preoccupied with the urgent but unimportant demands on our time. People we meet are rushing here and there, trying to get things done. Our calendars get filled with tasks, errands and family responsibilities. Our 'head-space' is usually so flooded with a range of tasks, responsibilities, feelings and regrets that we find it almost impossible to figure out what we want in life or how to get it. We become mentally stressed and worn out. We get so flooded that we make poor decisions, engage in infantile problem-solving and are unable to focus for any length of time on a non-urgent but vital aspect of our humanity and life. This is the disease of false urgency. This is the excuse we use for self-neglect.

So, these psychological reasons influence your emotional well-being. They inhibit your ability to take yourself seriously and to become more disciplined and principled about your happiness. This is why most people struggle with being consistent and with applying themselves to personal development. It's difficult.

THE FOUR FALSE MYTHS OF POPULAR PSYCHOLOGY

Popular psychology books

I am both attracted to and suspicious of books in popular psychology that promise easy solutions to many of the difficulties of life and living. I too would like to change my life in seven days, to find the eight steps to effective living, to follow the nine steps to relationship passion and to take ten minutes to manage my life. Such promises are most attractive, but they make many false promises about the ease with which personal transformation can occur. (All the great philosophies and religions have addressed the problem of self-improvement and conclude that the ordeal of self-discipline is one of the most important ingredients to personal transformation).

People whose success has been in the corporate world write many of these books and transfer many of the immediate, success-oriented, go-getting, corporate American-style attitudes to the area of personal growth and development. 'How to change your life and make a million dollars—guaranteed,' promises the headlines. Popular psychology promises, like the used-car salesperson, that 'This will radically transform your life, or your money back!' It does this very successfully.

I do enjoy looking at these books, and I speed-read them to see what simple truth is wrapped, perfumed and sold as a cure-all in them. Many of these products are not unlike the tonic sold in the Wild West by the travelling salesman as the cure for everything, from psychoses to pneumonia, from arthritis to anxiety.

While these kinds of books promise a great deal and offer much common sense and wisdom about the principles of personal change, they appeal to all of us who long for relief from the realities of living. To the degree that such approaches offer us hope they often lack a courageous heart. While you can be attracted to many of these approaches you will be disappointed to find that the batteries of self-discipline and inspiration are not included!

We are all influenced, then, by simple myths that prevent us from doing the work we need to do.

(1) The information myth

A myth of the popular psychology movement is that what you need to make yourself happier is more information.

The thing about advice and information is that very often it's the last thing we need. In fact, we are flooded with information. We have too much of it. The more information we get the less focused and persistent we become in life. Every day we encounter more advice and more information, more solutions and more strategies. In our post-modern age, new information is presented to us at an exponentially increasing rate that overloads us with data and opinions.

Good advice or knowledge is dead unless it's transformed into lasting action. Most of the information you collect melts like ice on the warm floor of your good intentions. Fritz Perls, the founder of gestalt therapy, considered most intellectual insights to be little more than what he called 'aboutism'. Having great ideas 'about' how to be happier would, in his mind, have been as useful as a fishing rod with no line. Too much information impedes us. People like me who spend a lot of time in their heads are, by necessity, spending very little time in their bodies. Therefore, we can easily live a fantasy life detached from the flesh and blood of joy. Happiness, as we will find, is a physical activity that is activated more by the senses than by the intellect and more by passionate and self-disciplined action than by thinking.

(2) The relief myth

This myth is that we can find relief from the unavoidable burdens of life.

The hope of finding relief from self-responsibility and the conditions of mortality is a kind of magical wish we all have. We nurture the idea that deep life-satisfaction can be achieved in an easy and magical way rather than through work and virtue. It's quite natural to think this way. We all have this childlike wish.

Everyone seeks some relief from the burden of being themselves, because sometimes it feels too much. We just get tired of the constant worry and striving to find the answer to our problems. Who doesn't want relief? So you will pick up a book like this hoping—maybe imagining—that it will provide you with the solution, the relief and the answer to the anxiety and distress of living.

(3) The transference myth

We all have a tendency to look to outside authorities, such as institutions, symbols, leaders, flags, religions, other people and marriages, to provide us with some relief from the burden of being ourselves. Freud called this transference, that is, transferring onto someone or something else the expectation of saving us from self-responsibility for our own happiness. So if we are unhappy we find things outside of us to blame—our parents, our spouses, our society, our children, our jobs and so on. This blame is a consequence of the transferring onto people or things outside of us the responsibility to make us happy. You and I do this all the time because the ordeal of being self-responsible seems too much at times. It's easier to out-source our happiness to others!

(4) The myth of keys, steps and rules

It's not difficult for people to sell the idea that there is an easy path to happiness. This promise is usually sold using three common metaphors: the key to happiness, the steps to happiness and the rules to happiness. Each metaphor contains a myth that appeals to our wish for psychological relief from life's difficulties.

The myth of the key

This is the myth that there is a key to happiness. What is sold is the notion that if you have the key you will be able to unlock the door to easy happiness and success. The salesperson tells you they have the key. Of course you want it. Who doesn't? If I offer you the key to happiness all it takes is to turn it once in the locked door of your self and hey presto!—happiness. I find myself picking up books to see what the key being sold is only to find that by the tenth page the key only gets you past the first door in a labyrinth of a thousand other doors!

The myth of the steps

This myth tells you that there are, say, eight steps to the kingdom and that if you take these steps you are in: if I present the eight easy steps to transformation all you have to do is find out what the steps are and take the eight steps. *Note that it's not* 800 steps, or 133 steps, but 8. It's hard not to want to take the few steps as an alternative to the many thousands you have already taken in your life.

The myth of the rules

This myth states: 'I can offer you the rules to successful happiness.' This, of course, requires no insight, awareness or creativity. All you need to do is to follow the rules, which relieves you of the burden of self-responsibility and self-doubt. It appeals to your naïve longing for some outside authority to just tell you what to do. I want this rulebook, please!

The hero's journey

Our preferred myth is that of the hero's journey, described so well by noted depth psychologists such as Joseph Campbell, Otto Rank and Carl Jung.

Here we don't use business, sales or other corporate metaphors to describe the human purpose. We look to ancient myths and spiritual traditions. They are the great stories of the hero who, in the service of a higher purpose, overcomes adversity to find joy. Great world literature gives us the clues as to how to live a full and meaningful life: by taking the heroic path. These sources are solid—they have stood the test of time. The myth of the heroic journey, as a model for how to live our lives, shows that great courage is necessary to follow the path of human transformation and transcendence.

Corporate and business models of living are obsessed with success and with a desire to master and control one's world. Rather, we must be inspired by those sources that do not demand that we seek more and more control but by sources that help us to let go—by the ocean rather than the city, by the monastic rather than the corporate, by the West of Ireland rather than the 'big smoke', by silence rather than words, by natural landscape rather than artificial reality.

> My wish is that you might walk with me
> across the landscape of the heart,
> the wilderness of the soul
> and the meadows of the imagination.
> In these places one experiences
> The wound of life and the fragility of happiness.

Come with me on this journey through
the wild, the frightening and the beautiful.
Walk with me and let's look into your heart,
the tender unseen places where joy blossoms.
Come with me through the Stations of the Cross,
the joyful and sorrowful mystery that is life.

Desire

Desire is the fuel for action. However, you must understand what you desire and know what gives your life purpose. For example, what desire has you reading this book? Is it that somewhere in your hidden life you have heard a call to something deeper? Is it that you want more from this passing urgent life that seems to slip through your fingers as you try to hold it?

You may not be as happy as you wish, you may be struggling with depression, you may feel a certain emptiness in your life or you may have become entangled in a dysfunctional relationship. Whatever your struggles, you have a hunger in you, a calling in you, a desire in you for more life, a desire to change and to experience your life more fully. You want to grasp this life with more passion and meaning. If that is the case you are just like me: this book aims to help us both.

THE BURNING-POINT OF LIFE

There are almost 7 billion people on the planet. You are one of them. You represent one seven-billionth of humanity. If all of them, you included, were to march past God's front porch it would take about a thousand years. Your appearance would represent one second out of that thousand years! I emphasise this for one simple reason: for us to remember that we are both part of a much larger project than our private search for status or happiness. We need to open our hearts to our place in this larger story. We need to cultivate a sensitivity to the emotional effects of inhabiting this wonderful mystery.

Your spirituality arises from a deep sense that there is a breath that is breathing you, that there is a life that is living you. Your heartbeat and your breath sustain you, yet they are not yours. They are the living rhythm of life itself, as it has pulsated through the history of the universe. You are a part of something that is so much bigger than who you think yourself to be. The natural state of all life is a state of wellness and acceptance. You will know from the inherent fragility and vulnerability of life that you are almost obliged to live in a state of gratitude. What this book invites you to do is to access the essential fire and inspiration of your life, to sustain it through self-discipline and then to drive it by the revelations of research.

Universal suffering and unhappiness

The larger life project of which we are a part ensures that we experience certain things. I can state for certain that every single one of the 7 billion people on our planet knows what it is to experience stress, unhappiness, anxiety and depression. Why is that? Because the human condition places us directly into an anxious and self-conscious existence that makes such experiences inevitable. So there is nothing remarkable about the fact that you feel stressed, worried and at times hopeless. Join the 7 billion-strong queue waiting to register a complaint with God! However, the corollary of this is that these 7 billion people also know what it is to experience bliss, joy, peace, happiness, hope and awe.

Our problem with emotional suffering and unhappiness is that we don't want to experience these things. We try to get rid of them. We create an internal battle with ourselves that can last a lifetime. We are always trying to be more secure than we are, more important than we are, more competent than we are and less vulnerable than we are. In our efforts at being more than we are we often create unhappiness with ourselves. We are then caught in a conflict and paradox, and we realise that

trying not to be unhappy causes it;
being able to be unhappy relieves it.

Mortality

Before we can talk meaningfully about happiness, what causes it and how to nurture it we must begin at the burning-point of all life: the point at which you live most intensely and are in touch with the essentials of life. It's that place where you are acutely aware of both your frail mortality and the aching beauty of life. It's the place where you are most fully alive.

At this point life is revealed to us in both its majestic beauty and its haunting tragedy. These places are where the Buddha and the Christ lingered. It's where the lovers, poets and musicians gather to dance.

The great taboo in modern Western cultures and societies is not sex, money, status or one's private indiscretions but our mortality. In fact, many aspects of society and culture are built around the shared agreement to keep the truth of our human condition in the shadows—to deny the fact and effects of death. This is the source of great distress and unhappiness, as I show, because it involves a crude rejection of our very selves.

However, the fact of our mortality is at the heart of both our happiness and our unhappiness. When we learn to inhabit ourselves rather than to seek a migration to some other manufactured self we will find ourselves looking towards the sun and the moon.

The sun will reveal the majesty of creation, the wonder and possibility of our precious life, the gifts that have been laid at our disposal, our inherited sense of worth and the tender heartbeat of love within us.

When we look towards the moon we will remember our destiny and fate, we will recognise that we have but a brief moment to shine, that we are inadequate in the face of the majesty of creation, that we are afraid and that we feel despair because of our helplessness.

I look forward to your company as we cut back the briars and branches of self-doubt and create a clearing through the forest. Because of the nature of your difficult life and your unavoidable limitations, you are called to live a heroic life. You have no option. But along the hero's path you will find joy.

The source of our unhappiness: The existential octet

Every single one of the 7 billion people referred to above experience the following eight emotional conditions:

Anxiety
Inadequacy
Helplessness
Insignificance
Vulnerability
Isolation
Woundedness
Shipwreckedness

I will refer to these as the existential octet, and we will revisit them from time to time throughout the book. You can't be human and live without experiencing these emotions intensely, because, very simply, they are the symptoms of mortality. These are eight raw experiential conditions of life that settle on the floor of your emotional world. Various cocktails of these experiences represent our unhappiness. For example, when you feel anxious and inadequate you feel unhappy. When you feel helpless and insignificant you feel unhappy.

The thing is, we can't escape these experiences. We can't escape a lot of what we call unhappiness. Why is that? We will come back to this later.

The source of joy

However, that is not all. While all these experiences are familiar to you, their corollaries are also part of life. To the degree that the octet of emotions is a symptom of your mortality the following set is a symptom of your enduring life, and they are even more accessible to you if you follow the right path. These are:

Peace
Competence
Influence
Openness
Connectedness
Confidence
Transcendent hope
Self-worth

You are, therefore, simultaneously a joyful and a grieving person. However, happiness and joy are your birthright and inheritance.

THE VALUE OF A RESEARCH-BASED APPROACH

The research section of the book summarises what scientific research says makes a difference to well-being. The activities presented in this book have been examined in robust ways and represent a fairly good summary of what has been found to improve happiness. These, of course, are not the only things that are influential, but they do represent a good guide for what you need to consider doing with the time available to you in life.

If you are to take your self-improvement seriously it behoves you to consider what the research shows. Science, as I have noted, has to be one of the legs on which our conclusions stand. It's not sufficient that I just present to you philosophical opinions and theories. Scientific research holds us accountable and asks that we support what we present with some evidence.

Creating a reliable map

The other reason for being familiar with scientific research is that when it comes to your personal growth and development it's essential to have a place from which to start your journey of transformation. What I present will show you where to start. Because of the ease with which we can become confused about what to do, the research findings provide us with an excellent base camp from which we can make our journey into the mind and heart. It's important to be grounded in something more substantial than intuition or personal preference.

Therefore, the research presented identifies crucial locations for emotional sustenance on the rough map of our emotional well-being. These might be considered our oases or watering holes: proven locations of sustenance. They provide us with some essential markers and survival aids on our journey.

I invite you to metaphorically mark down the locations listed in the research section of this book on the internal map of your emotional well-being and happiness. They may be places you only rarely visit, but they are places that you know for sure can help sustain you.

Science challenges your complacency

The emphasis on research complements and challenges the duality of our nature. One part of us relies too much on our own opinions, preferences, inclinations and personal theories. Most of us like to stay in character and only do what fits with our preconceived ideas about life. Even the most intellectual and rational of people only make decisions and choices that are consistent with their emotional schema about life.

Putting it simply, no matter what information you pump into the adult people in your life they will still hold on to their broad general conclusions and preferences. The conservative will always be conservative, the liberal always liberal. My hope, therefore, is that both sections of this book will rattle your cage a little and shake you out of some of the complacency you have about your life.

I know that research findings, no matter how convincing, will have little effect on us without motivation and discipline. Consider, for example, how difficult it is to reverse the habits of smoking, substance abuse, overeating, lack of exercise, cynicism, negativity, obsessiveness, worry and so on. Therefore, I am not naïve enough to think that readers will change because of the facts presented. The chances of that are close to nil. My conviction, however, is that, coupled with your theology, self-discipline and inspiration, you can rely on sound research to motivate you to continue on the path you have begun.

You are a mental miser

Research in social psychology shows that most human beings are what is termed 'cognitive misers'. In everyday life we are naïve scientists. We are naïve because we have a need to attribute causes to certain effects based on simplistic assumptions. We all do this in order to render the world a meaningful place. We try to figure out what causes certain things based on the evidence we have. We are naïve because the research we use to come to our conclusions is weak. Despite this, we tend to think that we are rational in coming to our conclusions about complex things. What determines our conclusions is not our ability to reason but our motivation. Social psychology shows us that we are more like motivated tacticians than rational and logical operators.

Science and art

Research needs to be humanised. We have dual sensitivities and concerns that arise from the fact that we are physical mortals and imaginative symbolists. We have physical, psychological and existential needs. We need science to help us negotiate the physical world, but we need such things as music, literature, inspiration and the varieties of human expression to help us negotiate our psycho-spiritual world. Your well-being is inspired by the latter but can be lived with the guidance of the former. The science of happiness is not the answer, but it's part of the solution, and it's a really good place from which to start!

The trinity of science, art and discipline

I will not tell you what science says that you should do and expect that you will do it. You must have the motivation to turn the maintenance of your emotional well-being into a rounded discipline. As I mentioned at the outset, most self-help books and prescriptions for change fail to appreciate that inspiration, self-discipline and existential purpose are our real areas of concern.

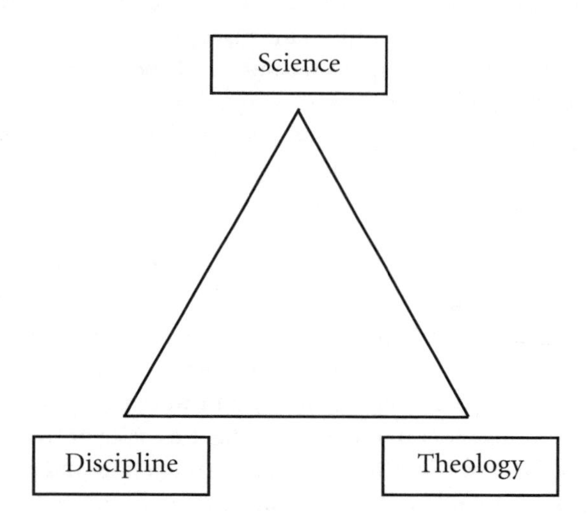

Symbolic

One of the most important discoveries for me has been that to live a richer and deeper life the activities you engage in must have symbolic importance and meaning. Then you are living at the highest psychological level. You are living the symbolic life, where the small, ordinary and deliberate activities of your life are imbued with extraordinary meaning.

In this way, work may be vocational, caring for an ill family member may be sacramental, being a parent may be sacred, personal development may be redemptive, life change may be a form of atonement, exercise may be a prayer and daily rituals may be a form of thanksgiving. What I mean by these examples is that one's life can have a theological and existential meaning that is passionate, inspirational and peaceful.

In truth, all human activity serves a symbolic purpose. Each activity serves an existentially transcendent function as well as a literal, physical one. What we do can have a meaning at the highest and the lowest of levels.

DEFINITIONS AND CAVEATS

Defining happiness

Our concept and definition of happiness is not a smiley face posted on top of life's ordeals, not a patronising 'cheer up' uttered to the bereaved and not a 'think happy thoughts' as life places its heavy burdens on us. No, I am talking about a happiness and a well-being that is rich and courageous. A happiness that can embrace the inevitable suffering and natural joy. I am talking about well-being in the sense of a rich and fulfilling experience of life. Happiness is not a soft, cheesy, superficial falsity but a gutsy, earthy, heroic acclamation. A Hallelujah!

Pleasant feelings are very much part of being happy; but happiness, in the round, represents a life-satisfaction that is rich and fulfilling and that, above all, has a sense of permanence. While permanence can't be guaranteed, there is a rich happiness and inner confidence about the future. The happy person anticipates the future in an optimistic and hopeful way. So the goal in life is not to have a series of never-ending pleasant experiences but a sense of inner conviction and confidence about the future and a deep satisfaction with the meaning and purpose of one's life, including one's suffering.

At the same time, I will also speak of that uncomplicated natural passing happiness that we all feel, which is neither superficial nor deep but part of the simple pleasure in being alive. When happiness is associated with 'having a nice day,' smiley faces and Helen Steiner Rice-type theology, it quite rightly becomes diminished.

Happiness can be understood simply as a measure of the intensity and duration of positive feelings, without having to define exactly what those feelings are. If you tell me that you are happy today, I don't need to know the causes and constituents of that happiness to have a general understanding of what you are feeling: that you are in good mood and have a hopeful and positive disposition!

Each experience of happiness is a weaving of different threads of positive emotion regarding the past, present and future. It includes such emotions as freedom, flow, bliss, competence, influence, pleasure, belonging, passion, anticipation, hope, faith, compassion, tolerance, joy, wonder, awe, love and self-belief. Just as none of your experiences of happiness are exactly the same, no two people experience it in exactly the same way.

Defining unhappiness

I will use unhappiness to refer to that summarising experience of life that is the background colour, as it were, of one's daily existence. Momentary distress, acute stress reactions or passing negative emotions do not really constitute unhappiness. Rather, I will refer to unhappiness as a general low mood that one experiences from time to time and that endures over a substantial period of time—say, three months or so.

At the same time, I will often refer to the language of unhappiness in terms of stress, anxiety and depression. The general unhappy feelings one has in life will very often be summary terms for a cocktail of these three common symptoms.

I will also speak of unhappiness as a general summary term for our experience of the primary negative emotions of guilt, frustration and grief that arise from existence itself.

Unhappiness can also be understood very simply as a measure of the duration and intensity of negative emotion. As with happiness, I don't need to know its causes or constituents to have empathy for what one may feel. It's not always helpful to distinguish between the many different negative emotions, because emotions are never pure: they are always a cocktail of many feelings.

Because unhappiness and happiness are general terms, my experience of them will be different from yours. It's important, therefore, to appreciate the wide spectrum of emotional feelings and life situations that constitute both unhappiness and happiness.

Finally, it's my impression that the term 'unhappiness' is often misused. There are times in your life when you conclude that you are unhappy but when a more detailed exploration and reframing of experience can turn it around towards something meaningful. For example, many of us engage in negative self-talk about the amount of stress we are under and about how unhappy we are with things. However, in many instances one can discover that the stress one is experiencing is meaningful, purposeful and an integral part of one's chosen life. But when one begins to forget and lose touch with this chosen purpose, one can begin to feel unhappy. What is needed is not to get rid of the stress but to realign and remember one's chosen values and priorities, for example one's virtues of service and vocation.

We can lose touch with a deep contentment that lies dormant within us. When we lose touch with our existential choices and with how we choose to live life we forget who we are; and when we do that our experiences of unhappiness increase. It's for this simple reason that one of the most important recommendations embedded in this book is that we must develop the self-discipline of emotional realignment precisely because we forget who we are.

Some caveats before we begin

1. The approach, exercises and disciplines in this book are *not designed for the psychologically cynical.* They are for the contemplatives in life who are committed to personal growth and development. The spiritual disciplines are for ordinary people living ordinary lives.
2. The disciplines of happiness should *not be thought of as a dull drudgery aimed at eliminating spontaneous joy and happiness* but as disciplines that liberate us from the stifling slavery of our own self-interests and self-rejection.
3. *The disciplines of happiness are not hard.* The difficulty is that the things you need to do to improve your well-being are not, in and of themselves, complex or extremely difficult. What is hard is being committed to them and experiencing them as meaningful and necessary.
4. Discipline needs desire. The primary requirement for living a happy life—for living a content life—is desire. Desire is recognised by all the spiritual traditions as a longing for meaning, for, if you will, an imagined God. Though you may not be as happy as you wish and may feel a certain emptiness in your life, you still have a hunger in you, a calling in you, a desire to change and to experience your life more fully. Because you are aware of your own mortality and the brevity of life, you want to grasp on to this life with passion and meaning. If that is the case you are just like me: *you want to live this life more fully and to experience a well-being that gives a resonance to your life.* This book aims to help us to do that.
5. In facing the disciplines of happiness and well-being you will have *to reject the notion of getting immediate relief or gratification.* I will ask you to study your own well-being with a rigour and a commitment that you would give to anything in your life. I won't ally myself with your desire for a magic pill. Hopefully the book will confront your narcissism and the impediments to your personal growth.

6. You will have found that with most books, as with most experiences in your life, you get the idea, you get the concept, but *converting that into a way of being and acting that can become ingrained in your life is a real challenge.* It's for that reason that we speak of discipline: the disciplines of joy.
7. *Many people recoil from the word 'discipline'* because they associate it with rigorous, righteous or right-wing ideologies. That is not what this is about. It's not just about changing habits and engaging in daily discipline: it's about the deep, inner psychological life. To the degree that you live a meaningful life you can integrate that in a rigorous discipline that is sure to effect powerful changes.
8. Lest you are *fearful of the term 'spirituality'* as possibly being a soft or weak leg in all of this, let me reassure you that I am speaking here of what the philosopher Kierkegaard referred to as *'the spirituality of the shipwrecked', that is, that sense of heroic purpose and passion that arises from having to face the suffering and adversity of life.* We inhabit a life in which we have to deal with trauma and tragedy. How we deal with this is very much part of how we live in the world. Equally, we inhabit a life in which we encounter the miraculous mystery of life that inspires passion and awe. So when it comes to examining our spirituality it will be a kind of working-class spirituality that will confront us with some essential questions that represent the fire of our life.

For exercises related to this chapter please check out the book web site at

www.couragetobehappy.ie

Chapter 2

Happiness in the round

THE ANCIENT ARCHETYPAL IMAGE OF THE CROSS

The recent films starring Tom Hanks, *The Da Vinci Code* and *The Secret*, refer to him as being a symbolist. The films illustrate the importance of symbols in the psyche. Because the conditions of human life and our place in the universe are such an immense mystery to the human being, we need symbols and symbolic communication in order to give expression to what lies beyond the power of reason or words. Language, music, emotions, signs, symbols, art and all forms of human gesture are symbolic communications and representations of an inner world and awareness that is beyond and beneath everyday life. We are a symbolic people, and therefore we respond to symbols.

Take your own national flag, as a simple example, and consider what it means and evokes for you. It symbolises so much more than the particular geographical borders of a country. People have died for that flag, and all over the world people stand before their flag at sporting, political and social events and can be moved to tears because of what it means to the human psyche. Symbols are, in many ways, reminders that we are more than our own private little lives—that we are part of something bigger than ourselves. When we experience that connection to something larger than ourselves we are moved by deeper emotions than we are typically aware of.

For that reason I will start with symbol of the cross. I will use it not as a Christian symbol but as a universal one. It is an archetypal and universal image that symbolises both the horizontal and the vertical dimensions to life. It is a universal symbol that the analytic psychologist Carl Jung said we would lose at our peril.

The horizontal line of the cross is symbolic of our anxious life and everyday preoccupations. These are the things that cause us stress, worry, anxiety and the responsibilities we attend to daily. The horizontal dimension serves to distract us from a vertical life of depth and transcendence. We live on the shallow horizontal level most of the time, as we are distracted with the worries of everyday life and our attempts to secure our status, safety, survival and significance. The horizontal line might be represented like this:

STRESS ANXIETY

The vertical dimension symbolises our spiritual existence. At the top of the vertical axis is the spirit, and at the base is what we would call the soul. The spirit refers to all those transcendent experiences that enable us to rise above our horizontal condition and bring a lightness of heart, joy and hope. The soul refers to the deeper experiences of grief, loss and suffering. At the level of soul we are aware of our mortality and the earth from which we have emerged.

The vertical dimension of life is where we embrace the opposites of suffering and hope, mortality and transcendence, death and birth, joy and grief. On this dimension we are attuned to both the beauty and the fragility of life. On this dimension we see our horizontal stresses and worries for what they are: preoccupations and distractions from the essentials of life. When we bring the horizontal and vertical dimensions together we get the image of a cross as a simple symbol of human existence.

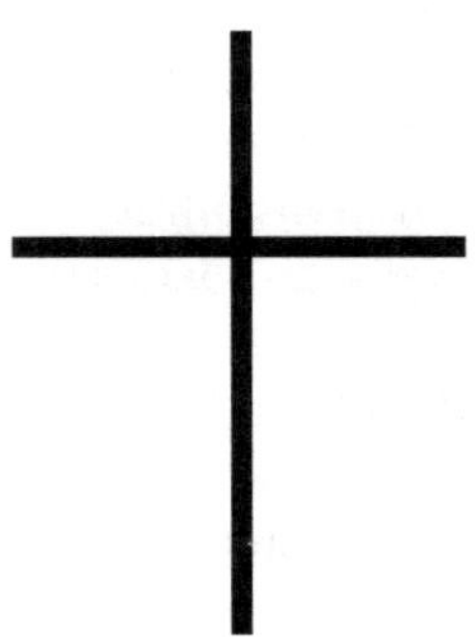

Now, if we seek to integrate the horizontal with the vertical we can introduce a circle at the centre of this image to symbolise the integration of horizontal and vertical living. Our symbol then takes the wonderful form of the Celtic Cross. There is a legend of how St Patrick, when conversing with a Celtic community, was shown a sacred standing stone that was marked with a circle that was symbolic of the moon goddess. The legend goes that Patrick made the mark of a cross through the image of the moon and blessed the stone, making the first Celtic Cross. This legend implies that St Patrick integrated ideas of the ancient druids in Christian practices. This is more folklore than fact, but it's appealing in its integration. The moon, as a symbol of our mortal frailty and connection with natural creation, is the circle within which we stand, from which we see life in the round and from which our vertical and horizontal lives emerge.

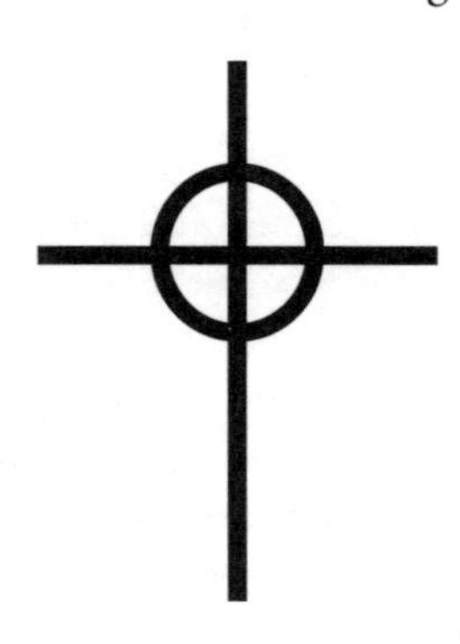

This, then, is a symbol for this book. It is as a symbol of where we must locate ourselves if we are to live a rich, spiritual, soulful and, at the same time, ordinary, everyday life.

> We must live within the circle, at the burning-point of life where our horizontal preoccupations intersect with our soulful and spiritual existence. At the burning-point ordinary life is lived in the context of an extraordinary existence.

Our life is then a life of integrity and integration. We can rise above our stress and distress to experience joy and hope. We can enter our stressful life with the heart and imagination of the vertical. We are rooted in the soil while we look to the sky. We are ordinary people with unavoidable stresses who can open our hearts to the vertical movement of joy and grief that attends all living things. At the burning-point of life we know happiness and the lightness of heart that comes to those who embrace the passionate ordeal of living.

Your tear-point

When I work with people in counselling I often work intensely at what I call the 'tear-point'. Your tear-point is that point when tears come to your eyes. Tears are an extraordinary thing in human beings. Unlike any other creature, human beings cry. Our tears are the outward sign of our hidden emotional world. Our tears are a quite extraordinary revelation of our hidden vulnerability, sorrow and joy.

> Genuine tears come to us particularly at the burning-point of life, at the centre of our Celtic Cross, where our horizontal and vertical lives intersect, when we simultaneously experience the blissful joy and the unavoidable grief of life.

These tears reveal the sorrow of knowing that our joy cannot last. Tears come to your eyes when you experience an intense love for someone or something along with the grief that recognises that they are not yours to hold.

Tears of joy are shed at exactly this point. The joy is the intense love and delight you experience in some exquisite moment like watching your child succeed at something, holding a newborn baby or expressing a heartfelt love for someone. The grief is in knowing that you will never be able to capture that love, and that every beautiful thing in life comes to pass and dies. You can't capture and hold forever the love that you have and feel for any part of life.

So, as you watch your little daughter leave your side and skip her way to school, tears come to your eyes as your love for her wells up, and you realise that, despite this love, you can't protect her from all the sufferings of life that awaits her, that you will not be able to protect her. Your heart breaks with such love, a love at the burning-point of life. The tear point is where our horizontal life is pierced by the sublime joy of living and the anticipatory grief of knowing that it's not ours to hold.

An exciting journey lies ahead for you. Don't be afraid. Many people have walked this forest path before you. They have left clues in the grass and trees to help you on your adventure.

HEROISM AND HAPPINESS

We live in a time when we want easy solutions to life's problems. We want easy-to-understand directions for finding guaranteed happiness. We want simple explanations for how to live. Yet to have a fulfilling life we need to be able to tolerate complex understanding and difficult challenges. To understand why it's hard to be completely happy we must avoid simplistic solutions and address the deeper conflicts that inhabit the human heart. Ultimately, these knots can be unravelled with a poetic simplicity, but it comes only after honest struggle. Whatever paths we find to happiness, they should be recognised by their deep humanity, their toleration of mystery and their elegance.

The heroic urge

It's unlikely that you think of yourself as a hero. Your self-assessment is probably that you have done 'the best you could' and have 'tried to live a good life.' If you have lived a normal life you have had periods of darkness and light, of dawns and dusks. However, you are unlikely to consider yourself a heroic individual. 'I wish,' says you.

However, let me invite you to reflect on this. You will tend to equate heroism with mighty deeds performed by great figures. You will tend to associate it with courageous acts that have saved people's lives or inspired multitudes. You will think of such people as Mahatma Gandhi, Martin Luther King Jr and Nelson Mandela. Or maybe someone in your life who has been a role model or mentor has been a hero to you. They are inspirational characters because they have overcome great adversity and courageously remained true to their beliefs in pursuit of a noble goal.

Heroes are inspiring to us because we constantly struggle with adversities. We seek inspiration to endure with self-belief and hope. We are faced with many obstacles and feel that life is sometimes an uphill battle. We know how hard life can be. The hero who faces these things and still emerges victorious therefore inspires us. The integrity of the effort, in the face of difficult odds, is inspirational.

The stories of heroes are an inspiration to anyone struggling honestly with life. For this reason, myths, religious texts, ancient stories, legends, plays and films all tell the same story.

The story of every great hero is also your private story exaggerated and embellished by character and plot. Your life, no matter how small, is, by necessity, a heroic one.

It's apparent in modern cinema that we are inspired by stories of heroism, by characters who overcome adversity in pursuing their goals. Almost every film you watch is a story of someone surviving against the odds, overcoming obstacles, staying true to their heart and succeeding on a mission. We must not look at successful millionaires, recovered celebrities or happy hypnotists for our clues about how to live. We must look a bit closer to home!

The hero in these films usually goes through a challenge and transformation that inspires us because *our lives are the same.* We cheer, applaud and weep with the hero, because in the smaller intimacies of our own life we know *exactly what it's like to struggle against the odds, to strive, to fail, to strive again and yet to succeed.* Maybe you fail more often than you succeed, but the heroism is in your persistence. So you are moved to tears by Marcus Aurelius's courage, by Christy Brown's defiance or by Kevin Costner's character in the film *Field of Dreams,* because you face these challenges and opportunities every day in the great ordeal that is life. Your life asks big questions of you. It asks for bigness in return. It's in this 'field of dreams' that we will seek the clues to living a rich and fulfilling life.

Trying

In your life you have struggled with many adversities, both in your exterior and interior life. Only you know how hard you have tried. You have tried your best to work with whatever life has set before you—be it growing up, maintaining relationships, living a virtuous life, being a good parent or succeeding at work. You have responded to what life has set before you with a uniquely heroic response. You have had no real choice in many instances. In fact, life has demanded it from you.

The psychological and spiritual truth from which we start our discussion about happiness is that life demands this heroic response from you. To the degree that you are equal to this call the gates of well-being open for you.

For this reason, one of the conclusions I come to in this book is that *the purpose of life is the overcoming of adversity*. This may seem like a somewhat negative view, but it's right here that one uncovers life's hidden jewels.

From here we go on to discover that *happiness is the deep satisfaction that results from that earnest endeavour*. Happiness is the joy that is inherent in the honest application of the self. From this joy a lightness of heart follows.

Your call to heroism is evident in your everyday life. Look at how hard you strive. Look at how you seek to overcome whatever inhibits your progress. Look at how, in even the smallest of your endeavours, you are always trying to be better, to be different, to succeed and to master your life. Though you may even feel you are a failure in some aspects of your life—broken relationships, depression, stress and anxiety, self-doubt—even in the midst of these struggles you have always been *trying*.

Though almost defeated on many occasions you persist in the life that at times hardly sustains you. Though you may wander in the valley of darkness your wandering speaks of your longing. In every moment of every day you exert some effort to maintain a course, to rise above, to cope with, to come to terms with and to be equal to the challenge before you. All for what? To taste the bliss of being alive, to give meaning and to refuse defeat. This quality in you, and in all human nature, is awe-inspiring.

Such great thinkers as Friedrich Nietzsche, Joseph Campbell, William James, Carl Jung, Ernest Becker and Sigmund Freud have spoken inspirationally about the heroic struggle that is your life. It's heroic because the forces and conditions you have to deal with are indeed awesome, while the resources you have at your disposal have seemed to be meagre by comparison. However, while you are bound by the limitations of your mind and body you are blessed with imagination, freedom and the ability to live a rich, symbolic life. These blessings make your life magical.

Finding happiness in life has to be achieved not in spite of one's heroic challenge in life but because of it. In other words, deep happiness is so because of the joy that is experienced in the passionate ordeals of life. We must not look for easy solutions or shortcuts. No, the only way round is through!

Life demands a heroic response because it doesn't give us answers to its great eternal mysteries, because it makes us powerless in the face of our mortality and because it doesn't offer us refuge from danger. We have to live with a considerable amount of existential ignorance and helplessness. You might say we are shipwrecked. We wake up on the shore of an enchanting and frightening life with just a rough map and a determined heart.

The heroic quest is natural. All of nature seems to pulsate with this will to survive. Natural organisms instead of dying away seem willed to adapt to difficult environments and to find new ways to survive and overcome. Nature seems to enjoy this surging ahead into the unknown. The entire process of evolution is characterised by growth and yearning. It's in your defiant persistence in the face of life. At these times you can feel your wordless connection with nature. It's your common source.

Working-class spirituality

I have worked for the past twenty years as a clinical psychologist with a non-profit community agency that provides counselling and psychotherapy. The majority of my clients have been poor or working-class people in need of guidance, counselling, encouragement and support in dealing with individual, marital and family problems, including abuse.

In working with these families I have encountered an inspirational working-class spirituality. It's a spiritual courage, hope and resilience that is not born of privilege but of character—the character of people who heroically find joy through the integrity of honest endeavour, old-fashioned virtue and good humour. Our notions of happiness must remain connected to the reality of everyday adversity and the conditions of life and living.

Working-class spirituality is found in the determined single mother on social welfare, the unemployed married couple who want to work on their relationship, the parents of teenagers living in deprived communities who want to give them a good life, the battered woman planning her night-time escape with her infant children, and the young man who was abused as a child and now wants to protect his children from himself.

There is something about suffering and integrity. There is integrity in finding success or happiness the hard way. There is a sense of having earned one's good fortune. Integrity comes with such bravery.

You could, in truth, write a novel about your own life in heroic terms. You are called to heroism every day. It may just mean getting out of bed in the morning to face a boring and thankless job; it may mean bringing some good cheer into the family home. There are countless small everyday achievements that give fulfilment, integrity and purpose to an ordinary life.

What you are doing in the ordinariness of your everyday life is establishing a sense of meaning and self-worth. You can, through your sense of imagination, give your life a noble and heroic purpose. How you experience yourself and your life is an act of rich imagination and symbolic living.

To know who you are you must see yourself in the full round of your existence, not in the limited arc of your worries about yourself.

> You don't find happiness by looking more closely at your problems but by looking more expansively at yourself.

There is so much more to you than meets your inner eye!

HAPPINESS IN THE ROUND

In ancient Ireland the gods of the people were found in the natural world. Their gods were not distant beings residing in another universe but were close and ever-present. The gods of the land, sea and sky were primary. To know who you were you had to look around at the landscape before you, at the earth holding you up, at the sky above you and at the sea surrounding you. The Celts had many gods to represent the many and varied sources of sustenance in their lives.

When you look at ancient people, who had exactly the same brain as we have, you get a sense of what you would be like if you were stripped of the social codes, roles and comforts that define your life. For this reason it's fascinating to examine the beliefs and practices of ancient people, because they reveal so much about who we are—who we are beneath the protective veil of modern life.

As I identified earlier under 'Realisation 6', to understand and develop your happiness you must understand it in the round. You must strive for something holistic. You must see yourself not from the viewpoint of your problems or symptoms but as if from above—to see yourself set in the context of the wide expanse of your humanity rather than in the narrow corridor of your small and stressful life. We must see humanity from the viewpoint of psychology *and* religion, of science *and* art, of philosophy *and* literature, of the specific *and* the general.

Trauma and tragedy

Before we consider the positive emotions and the meaning of happiness we must be conscious of the broader context of the human condition. We must be willing to take in the full picture. We can't avoid the three Ts: the traumatic, the tragic and the terrible—the distressing events that are an intimate part of life on earth. Understanding happiness in the round has to be big enough to acknowledge the suffering of life. Such suffering is actually what gives meaning to happiness and human joy. Celebration derives its purpose from the background of these distressing inevitabilities in life. We celebrate because we have survived. Joy and grief are sisters. Therefore, inhabiting your human condition and experiencing deep happiness in life means that you are big enough to know that trauma and tragedy are inevitable. There is no escaping this. All great novelists, playwrights, poets, artists, sages and spiritual leaders have illustrated that the joy of life is married to the tragedy of death. Our systems of denial don't want to look at this and at times can't quite bear it. In fact, there is a personal and social taboo against bringing this truth into consciousness and social awareness.

The general taboo is against contemplating the inevitability of our own death. We recoil from it. We are castigated if we mention it: 'Oh, don't be so morbid!' is the inevitable response. There are blankets of modern superstitions cast over our right to speak about our death or the death of those we love. We also dare not speak of its offspring: human suffering and grief. We find it distressing to be reminded of these things. Even the word 'suffering' can distress us. Unfortunately, happiness is not an escape route from these inevitable experiences.

In fact, this reflex to escape certain aspects of life is at the root of our anxiety, stress and depression. Each of these symptoms is caused by our desire to live not in the full round of our human condition but in the circumscribed arc of control and certainty. However, our striving for too much control and too much certainty creates distress within us.

Is there not some lack of courage in wanting to turn our face away, to escape into the positive things too quickly? 'Don't dwell on that!' your mind prompts you in response to 'the D word'. Yet it's our ability to savour mortal life that creates the reflex for all that is inspiring and beautiful. We are able, then, to experience its magic.

'Look at how old you're getting, Grandma'

During lunch with my mother-in-law my little daughter remarked how old her grandmother was looking, as little children often do! For her this was as simple an observation as her comments about the crumbs on her grandmother's lap. (At another point during lunch she also pointed out to her grandmother that the reason her mouth looks funny when she talks is that she talks too much! But let's leave that aside, for now!) When my daughter commented on her grandmother looking so old there were immediate comments from my wife and myself. 'You don't say that to people,' we corrected. This triggered my thoughts about what that instruction really meant.

Later I joked with my wife about what would happen if I were to say to one of her female friends—now almost fifty—that she was looking so much older than when I had seen her previously. The taboo against such comments, which would be taken as an insult, was quite clear. My older daughter (aged eighteen) pointed out that it's all right to say to children that they are looking older, because for them it's a compliment; but we agreed that once someone gets into their early twenties comments about them looking older become increasingly taboo.

You don't need to be a psychologist to figure out that it's taboo, because to say it is to remind people of their decay and of their helpless attempts to prevent it. To point out the ageing process to someone is to confront them with, very simply, their physical deterioration and death; and the insult is to point out their failure to hide it—to hide their mortality. Billions are now spent by people on cosmetic surgery in the hope of *looking* younger, of looking *as if* they are defeating the decaying process of ageing.

At one level this is the subject of animated exchanges over coffee. At another it's intriguing to observe how it exposes our frail nature and helplessness. It's frightening to consider the degree to which we deny our inadequacy and helplessness in trying to hold back the tide of ageing.

The pervasive denial of our condition is disquieting in itself. It's as if there is an enormous elephant in the room of our lives that must not at any cost be acknowledged. Even the mental health and medical professions avoid it. The elephant is our existential helplessness and anxiety. Your dread is that you can't be well if you admit to the truth. You fear that it spoils the party, spoils the delusion and unmasks God!

Magic and miracles

However, the truth of life is that anxiety and grief represent only part of what we are. Inhabiting the full human condition means that there are also the three Ms of magic, mystery and miracles, which are also an intimate part of life. I am not talking about magic in the sense of illusion or trickery but of the magical quality and magical potential in life. Something is happening beneath the surface of your life that is awe-inspiring, gratitude-evoking and sublime. The sense of the magical is ever present. Poetry touches this magical interiority that is inherent to all created things. Your spiritual wisdom reveals this to you. In the midst of suffering an inner transformation can occur that transcends everyday distress.

You inhabit an extraordinary mystery: a majestic, beautiful and passionate world. You are blessed with the magic powers of an extraordinary imagination. The gift of life has been given to you. 'The beauty of the world hath made me sad,' wrote Patrick Pearse. What is miraculous is that the universe works with you and co-operates with your deepest longings. The universe provides for you and holds you with invisible hands. What seems impossible to your thinking mind is made real by your imaginative heart.

Now, the scientist may feel somewhat queasy at these sentiments. However, the artist, lover, sculptor and poet know the language of the heart—the tragic beauty of life, the bitter-sweet romance, the seasons of a person's life. I mention art and poetry because, as a psychologist, I must acknowledge the limits of psychology itself. It can take us only so far.

THE LIMITS OF PSYCHOLOGY

It's no coincidence that the influence that psychological research, psychotherapy and psychiatry have had on modern social life has been largely negligible. The ability of counselling, psychology and psychiatry to help society to understand life, come to terms with suffering, foster happiness and develop mentally healthy societies has been small indeed. While they have been of benefit to a great many isolated individuals they have not contributed too much to humanity. Though the pioneering fathers of psychology have contributed significantly to modern philosophy regarding our mental life, beyond this psychology has just nibbled at the edges of life's great questions.

So why is this? Why so little effect? Well, for one simple reason:

> When it comes to the essential questions about our existence, psychology dumps humanity on the doorstep of theology.

Thus wrote the wonderful and neglected anthropologist Ernest Becker.

Mystery and immensity

In other words, psychology and psychiatry are mute when it comes to the big questions of existence; they have little to say. In the face of the immensity, magnificence and great mystery that is our individual existence, modern science has to be modest. None of the human sciences is equipped to address the biggest questions about life, such as: What part does my individual life play in the infinite project of Creation? How do I measure my personal value and worth? What meaning do I draw from my inevitable death? How do I find happiness? Whose hand created me? Who am I serving? Is it worth believing in a personal god? Am I related to something infinite or not? What is my purpose in life? How am I supposed to live? Why am I afraid? Why was I not born happy? Why do I have to suffer? Why do horrible things happen to people I love? Why is life difficult? How do I cope with my inevitable illness, decay and death? Why do I have to search for meaning? Am I utterly alone?

We can bring these questions closer to home, like the parents who had to ask the unbearable questions: 'Why has my little five-year-old child been run over by a car and killed? Why has life visited this unspeakable grief upon me?' Like the young man who asks, 'Why was I left by God to be sexually abused by my father for twelve years?' Like the battered woman who asks, 'Why does my husband treat me with such cruelty, hatred and contempt? Do I deserve this?'

Why such pain? What should be my source of inspiration for living, and why?

The problems of suffering, mortality and meaning are addressed more by religion than by psychology or psychiatry. Whether their handling of these questions is acceptable to you or not is less important than the recognition that big questions rumble away in the basement of the self and affect how we live. For this reason religious and spiritual approaches to life will have an immediacy, vitality and imagination that the human sciences don't possess. I include literature, art, poetry and music in these aesthetic approaches to existence.

These essential questions relate to our awareness that, in living life, in inhabiting our bodies, we are part of a Creation project that is so much bigger than we are. We are subconsciously aware that there is an immensity around us that we are unable to grasp and that seems too big for our thinking to embrace.

The images of the Hubble Space Telescope have illustrated how infinitesimally small our galaxy is, only one among an infinite number of galaxies stretching out into an infinite universe. Our galaxy is smaller in the universe than one grain of sand is in the Sahara Desert. We experience this immensity when we look up into the stars, when we look at the beauty of Creation and when we sense the extraordinary intelligence behind it.

Our sources of inspiration

To get the inspiration to live happily we turn to relationships, family, society, religion, music, sport, art, literature and all sorts of other activities to sustain us. It's by means of these that we experience an emotional purpose that enables us to correct our sense of isolation. It's by means of these that we find hope, happiness and consolation—though never finding intellectual answers. Our sources of inspiration, consolation and meaning are not found in academic science but in such things as beautiful music, the face of a little child, human creativity, the touch of a lover and the anticipation of joy.

Happiness as a theological and existential question

'How can I find peace and happiness in life?' is both a psychological and a theological-existential question. The only answers that can give us deep satisfaction are ones that resonate with our deepest longings and intuitions. Psychology and psychiatry can never give a person what great art, literature and religion can give them. They can never provide the wisdom that romantic love, personal bereavement, suffering and child-rearing can. Because they can only attempt to answer a small number of questions about life, they can never provide a full framework for understanding or changing it.

Therefore, your approach to developing your happiness has to be theological as well as scientific; it has to be emotional as well as rational; it has to be symbolic as well as literal. Our solutions or suggestions must have a *feeling* for the symbolic. Anything you do to improve your well-being has to symbolise the purposes of your life and the possibilities you have yet to realise. Happiness is not just created by doing what you think is the right thing or by doing what science says is the right thing. It's created by doing things with the *right feeling*. The right feeling is one of integration: you feel this when small everyday acts symbolise what you are striving for in life. This is the simple heroic impulse.

The theological and existential issue is that we are caught in a life in which meaning is not given to us. We must search for it and create it. These are the spiritual wings on which happiness flies!

Symbolism and right feeling

When you see a stonemason work on a wall outside a country house you see him step back and admire his work from a distance; you see him adjust some blocks here and there; you watch him tidying up his work with a sense of pride at his creation; you see the pleasure he gets in having applied himself to a difficult task; and you see his satisfaction in achieving this simple challenge. What you see is how someone can make something quite ordinary into something special. You see how someone can infuse the mundane with a sense of the sacred. It's this spiritual virtue, this sense of the symbolic, that makes us all 'men from La Mancha.'

> We alone inject into the black-and-white pictures of life the full colour of feeling and imagination.

When my six-year-old daughter comes to me with another little painting she smiles with such delight when I praise her work. The ordinary things we create or do in life are symbols of our interior life, are indications of our worth and are stepping-stones to happiness.

Love

Love is the feeling of connection and compassion. If there is any feeling or experience that comes close to resolving the big questions of life, it's love. I don't mean love in the romantic or personal sense but in the sense of connecting with the larger project of which you are a part, the sense of compassion you feel for all of life. Love is not an intellectual answer.

> Love doesn't give you the meaning of life, nor does it explain suffering. What it does is give you that feeling for life. What it provides is an experience of being alive that soothes your anxious heart.

It also gives us some relief from life. When a mother holds her baby in her arms she knows that she has an answer to something that is beyond words. When a father swells with pride at his children's successes he feels right in himself. The experience of honest love has a resonance that is soulful, that connects us to a larger purpose and that joins us experientially with all of nature. Something feels right, but you don't quite know what it is. This is the sweet mystery. Maybe we can unravel it together.

However, lest we lose the run of ourselves and forget our purpose here, we must stay the course and return to you—to looking at yourself with a fearless honesty, to placing your search for joy on the map of yourself. Let's take a look.

For exercises related to this chapter please check out the book web site at

www.couragetobehappy.ie

Chapter 3
The 'who' of happiness

Fearless self-knowledge

To explore the way of happiness and well-being your starting point has to be you as a person. All the great philosophers have suggested that self-knowledge is the prerequisite for integrity and happiness. In this section I place our search for happiness in the context of the unavoidable struggles of our existence and our humanity. I also ask you to be fearless in assessing your commitment to your emotional well-being, and I will hopefully inspire you. In that regard we look at how taking care of your well-being is a moral responsibility. I emphasise how important it may be to know what is out of character for you, and that to realise this may be the avenue for your own changes. We conclude this exploration by examining the way you treat yourself and how your patterns of self-rejection can eat away at your well-being.

YOUR MORAL RESPONSIBILITY TO TAKE CARE OF YOUR LIFE

An té a bhíonn amuigh, fuarann a chuid.
The meal of the person outside goes cold.

Happily ever after

The language and feeling of happiness are things that children know well. While the concept might be scientifically too big for research purposes it's not too big for a child. Children intuitively know, without intellectual analysis, what makes them happy and what is important in life: a safe place, love, belonging and fun. Every child knows a happy heart—a heart that lets them curl up in bed at the end of the day with a smile, feeling delight in the love of their family, regardless of their life circumstances.

Every child loves the line at the end of the story that says, 'And they lived happily ever after.' The child knows that that is all that matters for the future. Knowing that the characters in the story will be happy soothes a child's little heart. They sleep peacefully in that knowledge. They are relieved that there is no need to be afraid, that the terrors have been overcome and that happiness is what lies ahead. The stories don't end with 'They lived wealthily ever after,' 'physically well for ever after,' 'as important people forever after' or even 'as heroes forever after.' No, what is implied is that the happiness is a consequence of the hero's courage in staying true to some noble virtue, such as love or loyalty.

As adults we long for the same feeling. Don't you long to be able to say that what lies ahead for you and for your children is that you will 'live happily ever after'? Is that not your simplest and deepest wish? What the traditional fairy stories teach children is that it's not going to happen without courage. The ancient stories teach you that unless you have a heroic impulse to save your self, to embrace all that is sacred and to confront your fears, you may fall short.

The hook

Have you gone through life thinking that your happiness and well-being would take care of itself? Have you believed that your good intentions, good personality and good life would, of themselves, make things work for you? Or have you felt that, if you devoted yourself to making other people happy and to taking your responsibilities seriously, somehow life would pay you back? Or have you had this sense that there is a natural justice in the world and that the more you give to others the more you will get back from life?

If you are answering 'Yes' to any of these, maybe you need to think again. Such an answer suggests that you may assume a somewhat passive attitude towards your happiness in life. Maybe this has let you off the hook of having to take more direct responsibility for your emotional well-being. Let's see.

The thesis of this book is that in order to deal with stress, anxiety and depression, or in order to feel better about yourself, you can and must take an active approach to your emotional well-being. Rather than emphasising the benefits of this for you I want to dwell on the responsibility you have to do this. There is an ethic at issue here that is vital for us to consider before undertaking our journey. Taking care of yourself is more than a lifestyle choice: it's a moral responsibility.

We carry an enormous responsibility to take care of the life we have been given. It's not something you like to think about too often, because when you do you realise that there is so much more you should be doing for yourself. Part of this responsibility is not just to yourself but to those close to you: your children, partner, friends and family.

We need to mind the only life we have. We need to awaken from the treadmill of life-stress and micro-management. We must not trivialise ourselves. We must, as the poet Mary Oliver put it, save the only life we can save: our own. It's all we have.

Existential terror and responsibility

Your responsibility to take care of your mental health and happiness is awakened when you face the brute facts of your human condition: you grow and blossom for a short time and then pass away. However, your subconscious denial of your mortality allows you to carry on regardless. It's almost as if you imagine that you are an immortal little god running the little kingdom of your own life, which stretches out before you. In being able to deny the truth of your vulnerable and mortal life you dilute the responsibility you have of caring for it.

What causes you to ignore your responsibility to care for your own emotional life is fear. This is the terror of squaring up to the certain and unavoidable facts of your life: it's beautifully sacred and terrifyingly brief. If these simple truths were to remain at the forefront of your consciousness you would shudder at your self-neglect, you would be shamed at your avoidance and you would be outraged at your complacency. If you could capture the brief, burning intensity of your life you might carry that responsibility with a greater sense of honour.

Instead, you trivialise your self-responsibility. 'Forget that,' you think to yourself, 'I have more important things to take care of, like proving and justifying myself through approval, recognition, status and certainty.' Your list of things to do becomes your theology for life.

You read your list like it's your own daily office or scripture. It becomes the ruler with which you measure your effectiveness as a person.

It's strange to think that it takes courage to take care of yourself and to experience this moral ethic to mind your life. It's frightening to experience how quickly your life is slipping away. It's even more distressing to realise how casual you have been about it. The courage is in facing up to these simple but profound truths.

Your true responsibility is to be happy and to cherish your emotional well-being, because it's all you really have. That is your purpose: to experience the delight that is inherent in all mortal life—to dance.

Narcissism versus grace

Why might you avoid taking your happiness seriously, learning what to do about it and then doing it?

Firstly, because it's actually easier to blame others, luck or circumstance for your emotional state of mind. This is a universal defensive mechanism called projection. It occurs when you project onto the world the responsibility for you being the way you are.

Secondly, you have a certain hidden arrogance that allows you to disrespect yourself. This inner arrogance allows you to neglect and trivialise yourself. It allows you to feel more important than you are. It's morally wrong.

Thirdly, there is also a narcissistic belief that you shouldn't have to carry the burden of minding your own life. There is a narcissistic self-important belief that life should take care of you. This is the belief that you are entitled to happiness and emotional well-being simply by being alive. This is a long way from gratitude and grace: the sense that you and those you love have been gifted with life and that you have an obligation to appreciate the full round of life.

If you approach your well-being with a sense of responsibility and gratitude, and not with projection, arrogance and narcissism, you can build a spiritual discipline that orients you towards what is important in life and not towards the escape hatch of relief.

Passive suicide

Rather than choosing an active and responsible life, many people take the path of passive suicide.

While we become distressed by active suicide, we support all forms of passive suicide: the gradual killing of oneself by way of neglect.

Examples of passive suicide include eating the wrong food, ignoring one's happiness and well-being, not wearing a seat-belt, neglecting one's health, smoking, becoming addicted to anything, putting oneself down and persisting with self-rejection and self-doubt. We overwork, develop stress and anxiety and ignore our unhappiness. 'It will pass away.' 'It's not important.' 'Time is on my side.' But it doesn't pass away. And it is important. And time is not on your side at all.

Passive suicide arises from our narcissism. So we may think to ourselves, 'There are no consequences for neglecting myself. I am the only one who suffers. I am a little god, and I will, when I *feel like it*, change my ways.' This is the epitaph.

Your happiness flutters like a candle, straining to stay alight and needing shelter from you. To value your inner happiness and well-being is a spiritual responsibility. It emerges out of compassion for the transience of all beings. Christ spoke of love as the major path. Buddha spoke of acceptance. For this reason, what will sustain you in the long run is not a set of techniques or gimmicks but courage, fearlessness and responsibility.

Hygiene and health

Let me give you an interesting comparison. Consider, if you will, how much time you spend every day in taking care of your personal hygiene and grooming. How much time do you spend on these things? If you are really honest your average won't be too far off thirty minutes per day.

You probably know where I am going with this, but think it through a little more. You take care of your personal hygiene and grooming for thirty minutes per day, seven days a week—something that adds up to a total of about two working days per month—for two reasons: to feel well physically and for social approval and acceptance. This is normal and healthy. However, it does highlight a psychological priority. As one of Billy Crystal's vain comic characters used to say: 'You know, darling, it is better to look good than to feel good!'

What if you were to spend the same amount of time very specifically on your emotional well-being? What if you were to spend that time engaged in very specific and disciplined activities that guarantee a reduction in the stress, anxiety and depression in your life? Or, more positively, that helped you cultivate positive emotions, confident attitudes and softer feelings? I trust that you would accept that if you knew exactly what to do and how to do it, and if you could invest thirty minutes on your well-being each day for three to six months, it *would have a dramatic effect.* While I am not presenting this as our prescription at this point, I want to tickle your unconscious with a *feeling for* what is possible on an everyday level if you had the inspiration, know-how, motivation and self-discipline to care for your 'mental hygiene' every day.

Imagine that you had a 'bathroom for your soul' in your house devoted not to physical grooming and self-care but to the care of your emotional self! A place where you looked in a mirror and saw your inner self and made adjustments based on what you saw! A place where you spent ten minutes each day 'detoxing' from the debris of your stressful day or practising techniques that ensured that you were emotionally aligned. You would of course argue that you couldn't afford the time. Yet you spend such time on your grooming!

This might sound a bit ridiculous to you, but I hope that the point being made doesn't. A core objective for self-improvement is to convert good intentions into concrete action.

Given the decline in traditional religious practices over the past fifty years, we need concrete symbols and rituals to give expression to our inner anxieties and hopes. Crude though it may have been at times, formal religion at least got people to acknowledge that there was more to life than security and status. For Christians, Jews, Muslims, Buddhists and Hindus one hour a week invested in prayer, devotion or ritual serves a hugely important function in realigning the self. The clear prioritising of the need for some form of discipline in living a good and virtuous life has been the practice of people since the dawn of humankind.

However, for all the deeper reasons mentioned above, we avoid the responsibility we carry as individuals, couples, families and communities of treating our emotional life with the same reverence as our physical life. We just say, 'Ah, sure I'm grand.' Yet the rates of depression, stress and anxiety in everyday life today are rising. Equally, the social care of children, couples and families coping with abuse, disability and illness still lag far behind our obsession with physical health and appearance.

So you get by with just enough. You learn to tolerate mental anguish and distress. You get used to it, imagining that it's your lot in life. You are ashamed of yourself. You feel impotent because you just don't know what to do. You and I wander the wasteland of our emotional life somewhat lost. Issues relating to our personal worth, self-doubt and spiritual guilt are let rest. We let sleeping dogs lie.

Happiness is not a luxury. It's not lightweight. It's not the 'icing on the cake' or the dessert at the end of the meal. It's not just feeling good. Enhancing our well-being and happiness is not enhancing a comfortable and easy life. Rather, it's at the core of our humanity and responsibility. It's an imperative. It's our noble call. It's an investment in our life. It enables better functioning and relationships. It must be at the heart of every family. It flows from the conditions of love, sacredness and spirituality. Its achievement was, according to Aristotle, our main purpose in life. To Captain Picard in *Star Trek* it would be a 'prime directive'!

Therefore, taking care of your happiness and well-being is probably the most momentous thing you can do with your life.

And there are so many benefits that can be gained if you do.

A FEARLESS MORAL INVENTORY OF YOURSELF

Is í ding di féin a scoilteann an dair.
A wedge of itself splits the oak.

The first step on this journey of transformation is to be truly honest with yourself about who you are. To be a happier, more content person, and to overcome the symptoms of depression, anxiety and stress, you must be willing to look in the mirror of your emotional self—to admit to good and bad habits, personal strengths and weaknesses and your positive and negative emotions. I am borrowing the phrase 'fearless moral inventory' from Alcoholics Anonymous, who use it as a key step in recovery. It's a step we must all take. Have you ever conducted a self-assessment that has all these characteristics: that it's fearless, that it's moral and that it's a full inventory? No, I didn't think so.

To the degree that you can be fearless in your self-assessment you express a willingness to take full responsibility for your failings. To the degree that you can assess yourself on scales of basic morality you are willing to look at your integrity as a person. I don't mean moral in a pious sense but in the sense of living in accordance with good virtue. To the degree that you can allow this to be an inventory that is a detailed stocktaking of the self, you will not take shortcuts in how to become a happier and more fulfilled person. Therefore, we will not start with false optimism, wispy affirmations or 'follow your dreams' inspiration. We will start with a pep talk.

When rugby coaches wish to motivate their teams to enter the arena they challenge their players to confront their fears and doubts. Players are challenged to look in the mirror to see the fears that inhibit them and to build up the inspiration to defeat them. In order to motivate yourself to take big steps in life sometimes you need an adversary with whom you can do battle. Quite honestly, if you want to live a more fulfilling life, a richer life and a more passionate and meaningful life, you will need to take on a few of your inner demons. It's not sufficient to try to be a better person or to think happy thoughts. No. Real change is accompanied by a battle with the inner characters who sabotage, undermine and repeatedly defeat your efforts to change. It's not always easy to identify who exactly your inner adversary is. Nevertheless, we can be confident that they lie within.

When addicts and alcoholics have to do a fearless moral inventory on their AA programme they have to look into the dark shadows of the self. They have to bring to light their past bad, abusive and irresponsible behaviour. They must take full and complete responsibility for themselves. There is no hiding place, no excuse-making—just the challenge to accept full responsibility for oneself.

In completing a fearless moral inventory there is no room for 'poor me'. There is no tolerance for suggesting that you are the way you are because of what was done to you. There is no room for 'me as victim', no self-pity or blaming everyone else. There must only be gutsy and honest self-responsibility. The willingness to say, 'I am fully and totally responsible for myself. No excuses.' This of course evokes your fear of isolation. *To carry the full burden of responsibility for your own life is actually not an easy thing to do.*

Are you willing to look at yourself, to assess yourself and to take full responsibility for your emotional life and well-being? Are you willing to admit to your bad habits, your lazy shortcuts, your self-indulgence, and your self-absorption? Are you willing to look fearlessly at how badly you treat yourself at times? If you can say 'Yes' to some of these we can begin.

Self-defeat

We continually fall into states of helpless unhappiness because of the same well-worn, self-defeating patterns. You doubtless find yourself back in unpleasantly familiar places, with familiar feelings and thoughts. Like me, you end up repeatedly making the same mistakes.

You continually convince yourself that you are different from what you were, but you end up back at the starting-line. You may blame others or 'the world' for your bad feelings, but, though you change your life, you still end up standing helpless in the forest of yourself. You probably make excuses and exceptions for all the mistakes you make, telling yourself that the next time things will be different; but the next time you still end up frustrated by the familiarity of your failures.

You engage in a lot of positive-self talk and positive thinking. You make a big change in your life, such as moving house; but, despite the change, you end up lying awake at night with different worries but the same feelings. It's as if your body doesn't listen to your head, and you end up defeating yourself.

Confronting the enemy within

All the major religions and philosophies have addressed the need for people to confront the self within that leads to destructive behaviour. They have recognised humanity's dual nature: we do good and bad things! By identifying and defeating the inner enemy, 'redemption' and 'salvation' were achieved. Therefore, it will be very important that, as part of this exploration, you are willing to fearlessly identify your own self-defeating patterns. We all have predictable negative patterns that are familiar and even reassuring for us. We tend to cling to them and nurse them, because they are soothing. They protect us from a confrontation with our responsibility.

Your disfigured self

Many of us feel emotionally disfigured. Many of you reading this will feel that your very self is *flawed, disfigured or ugly*. You may hide this behind guilt, self-doubt and self-hatred or obsess about trying to 'improve yourself.' You may feel that you have some horrible emotional characteristics that no-one could enjoy, love or accept. You can feel profoundly handicapped with this ever-present feeling that 'there is something wrong with me.' You may feel deep shame about who you think you are. And herein is the root problem for so many of us. If you are engaged in self-rejection, if you don't like who you are, then this is where both the problem and the solutions lie.

An image of yourself determines how you feel. The plans for your self are drawn more from your imagination than from reality. At best they are rough sketches based on a negatively biased selection of memories. This 'blueprint of the self' is not based on accurate measurements but on a sketch on the back of the envelope of your life, drawn from hazy memories and misinterpreted experiences.

The solution to the problem of your unhappiness is not the 'plastic surgery' of the self. This doesn't reconstruct the image on which one's actions are based. The problem is not with *who* you are but with the *image* of who you think you are. Don't trust it!

When we attack, mutilate, disfigure and misrepresent our deepest self we commit a great violence. When we doubt, reject and ignore our self we do ourselves a grave injustice. We inhibit and assault our talents, potential and natural joy. We annihilate the divine that is within us. We lock ourselves on to the horizontal plane and measure our lives in coffee spoons and television channels.

The energy of Creation has a life of its own. Our job is to plough the land of ourselves, to plant the seeds of happiness, to discipline ourselves in our preparation, to have faith that divine Creation will do its work and that the life energy of 13 billion years wants us to be fully alive. Creation will co-operate with everything you do that aligns you towards freedom, love and a sacred hope.

When you are aligned with your trusting self, when you accept rather than attack yourself, when you let go of conflict, your self fades into the background of your life, and you flow. Happiness, in many ways, is a state of selflessness.

HAPPINESS AND SELFLESSNESS

Happiness is a condition in your life in which you don't view your world in relation to what you have gained or lost. There is no balance sheet or self-assessment. In fact, when you flow with life your self fades into the background. You are in the present. You are not even evaluating your happiness or how you are happy: you are functioning on a different level.

It's how you give yourself to life, how you give your life to your family, job, activity or experience. When one is deeply happy one gives one's life away with a generous and open heart, expecting nothing in return. There is a full participation, a full handing over to the life that you have at that time. This, in essence, is heroic. It's heroic to forget your self and to forget security, status and safety. In this quiet alignment with life, one doesn't lose oneself—paradoxically, one gains oneself: the single mother who cheerfully gives her life to her child, without hesitation; the nurse on the ward who hardly notices the hours go by as she gives herself in service to those she cares for. Here is the ordinary happiness of everyday life. A happiness without balloons, fireworks or shallow fun; participation without measuring profit or loss, winning or losing, getting or giving.

To enjoy a rich happiness we must travel into a very distant country—even out of ourselves. When you are in this zone and can look at your world with a poetic eye you know what I mean when I say that you can look at a child and see with its eyes, at a lake and feel its coldness, at a bird and fly with its wings.

> When the splash of sunlight
> on the distant hills faded,
> I returned to my self.

When we connect with the infinite immensity around us we naturally personify our world with that sense of universal self.

> The stars gaze at their reflection in the quiet sea.

You know what I mean when I try to describe the aching beauty of life by saying:

> The daylight moon looks down in awe across
> the green and ochre landscape
> at the fox sitting at the crest of a hill,
> the gannets plunging into a willing sea.

This is the experience of the artist who enters fully into the life of that which is painted or sculpted. When painting an old, rotting boat, marooned on its side in a little seaside harbour, my father fell into its world, its memory, its grief, its loss and its death, and in doing so he brought out from beneath its paint-cracked wood its unspeakable beauty. When you gaze at the ordinary thing with a generous heart the extraordinary spills out. A plastic bag dancing in the wind, a pair of shoes by the fireside, an old coat left behind by your deceased mother.

When we reach this gateway we assume the qualities of Creation. We, for these moments, are not ourselves, our names, our roles or our responsibilities. In these moments we are selfless and are in harmony with the infinite. Happiness rises up in us not because we have achieved anything but because we have come home to ourselves; we have let go of all worry and preoccupation and have stopped thinking about problems. We have been *feeling our life.*

We have emptied ourselves of our self and entered into our Self. We feel at home, at one with things—not in a grandiose religious sense but in an uncomplicated pleasure in being part of this enchanting world.

However, while this often does just happen it must also become a practice and a discipline. In discipline you turn towards the sun—you enter into activities that open your body and heart in these ways. These activities evoke compassion for life and for others. The virtue of service to others is part of this.

Now, you may read this and think this is airy-fairy stuff. You may conclude that this sounds good but that it's not scientific, hard fact or attainable. But let me suggest that this experience of selfless oneness with life, nature and one's world is so universal to all cultures, religions, artists and creative peoples that this deeper connection with all of life is a universal virtue. It is called transcendence. This is real and can be practised as a discipline. I would go so far as to suggest that you are obliged to open this inner eye, to be evoked in this way, to spend time in the world of the arts, and to keep that connection with the eternal awake.

Three times a day you need to connect with this reality. Three times a day you need to remember who you are. Every cup of coffee you have should be prefaced and closed with an inner genuflection towards the universe that holds you.

SELF-WORTH AND HAPPINESS

> *Our deepest distress is not that we are unhappy. Our deepest distress is that we are profoundly and naturally happy. It is our hidden joy and not our despair that most frightens us. We wonder to ourselves, Who am I to be thrilled, blissful and content in a life that is so precarious. How can I be worthy of a happy and joyful life? But the question is: Who are you not to be happy? You are worthy of the great blessings and possibilities that life has laid before you. You are worth everything. Do not be afraid or ashamed of the joy that has been with you since your dramatic birth.* (My rewriting of a speech by Nelson Mandela).

One of the greatest impediments to our achieving well-being is our feeling that perhaps we are not worthy of happiness. This may seem like a strange thing to say, but you are familiar with the inner doubt that you have about yourself. You are aware of this inner insecurity that you have carried with you all of your life, this lack of inner certainty.

Deep within most of us there is a feeling of not being worthy. A part of you doesn't feel that you are good enough just as you are. You may be plagued by guilt. You may have a feeling of having done something wrong but are not sure what, and you wait for someone to catch you out. You may have this vague feeling of being bad in some indescribable way. Or you may feel a disquieting self-conscious shame not about anything you have done but about your very existence. These are common human experiences that haunt the inner dreams of most people to greater or lesser degrees. 'I am not quite good enough; I am not worthy of real happiness.' This may not be a clear thought, but it can be an unequivocal sensation. The origin of this is not always in childhood, as you might think. No, there is a universal human feeling of self-doubt. Strangely, we all have traces of natural guilt.

For now, though, notice this in the ways you try to prove or exaggerate yourself to compensate for some inner inadequacy. You may engage in excessive self-control, self-monitoring, self-rejection, self-doubt or self-neglect. Your sense of self-worth is always precarious. To be resolved it must be befriended and coaxed into the light, where these anxieties can be soothed and joy can recover. Your uncertainty about your very worthiness guards the prison within which your joy lies waiting for its release. Joy is your captive. If we feel unworthy we subconsciously limit our capacity for happiness. We will trivialise, undermine and sabotage our right to it. We will diminish it.

Take a look at ourselves: we choose lives that don't fulfil us; we hang around with people who are bad for us; we maintain habits that are destructive for us; we keep lifestyles that don't fulfil us; we stay in relationships that abuse us; and we work long hours for people who don't appreciate us.

Or we diminish the good things we have in life: we have loving partners and families who we complain about; we have good jobs that we turn into drudgery; we whinge and complain about a life that is so good to us. We have countless ways of poking at the embers of disgruntlement and begrudgery. We find reasons to be unhappy. Even the healthiest and most rational of us find ways to keep it alive.

We have so many different ways of barricading ourselves in and turning happiness away at the gates to our life. We let it pass by, fearful of not being deserving enough to welcome it. We feel like a phoney. You say, How can I be happy? How can I act happy when I have this inner world of chaos and self-doubt?

The cynic in you might add, 'No, I must turn away from joy, for it will discover me to be flawed. It may see my disfigurement. Not only that, I don't trust its innocence'.

Security

We inhibit happiness in favour of security. We become afraid of losing the little bit of security we have, so we choose a limited life over the possibility of a rich and fulfilling one. 'Oh, I couldn't take that path,' you respond, when life opens up a clearing into its meadows. When we don't feel worthy we can't feel deserving of the good things in our lives. And when we don't feel that we actually deserve the good things in our life we anticipate their loss, we prepare for their loss, and we make it happen. We cling to relationships, jobs and lifestyles, believing that nothing else will come our way. This fear creates behaviour that is a self-fulfilling prophecy. We protect ourselves by having nothing to lose! We fear the worst and deprive ourselves of the best.

In order to pursue happiness we must consider ourselves worthy of it at the outset! We must appreciate our core self and believe that we are worthy by virtue of our existence. When we don't accept this we undermine our talents, accomplishments, potential and joy. We live life according to the 'Yes, but . . .' attitude. We say, 'Yes, I have good things in life, but . . .' However, there are experiences and epiphanies in life when the gates to this part of yourself are open, when self-doubt and guilt forget themselves and when you are shocked into the delight of natural joy.

Positive trauma

It sometimes takes positive trauma to awaken us from our hypnotic selves. Positive trauma is the experience of being overwhelmed in a positive way by our close proximity to life or death. Positive trauma confronts us with new life against the background of mortality. It can be the birth of a baby or of a dream. It can be an awakening as a result of bereavement or illness. When we brush shoulders with our ever-present vulnerability we are awakened to what gifts we really have. We are shocked out of self-doubt and hesitancy.

Out of character

When it comes to your well-being and happiness you have to be fearless in your confrontation with these elements within you. To make some significant improvements in your well-being, you will likely have to engage in out-of-character change. That is, you will have to persistently do a number of things that are typically out of character for you. This is because your dominant personality style helps you to survive but not to thrive as you might.

THE BENEFITS OF HAPPINESS

Is fearr an tsláinte ná na táinte.
Health is better than wealth.

There is actually nothing worth developing more than your own well-being. Nothing. Your wellness, your happiness, your contentment and your sense of living a meaningful and purposeful life are, in the end, all that matters. However, as I have pointed out, we have no model for how to do this, we have no permission to do it and we have no values to guide it.

If you ask any parent what they want most for their children they will say, 'For them to be happy.' For a couple on their wedding day, what is it that everyone wishes for them? Yes, to be happy. When you think of the rest of your own life, what you want for yourself is simply happiness.

Universally, what people want from life is to be happy. Aristotle suggested thousands of years ago that what humans seek above all else is happiness. He suggested that happiness represented humanity's greatest good. He believed that every action we take is aimed at bringing greater happiness and the alleviation of suffering. Happiness, very simply, is the aim of all our actions.

However, we are ambivalent about how to pursue it and how to achieve it. We are confused about what will cause and sustain it. We usually get locked into the five Ss of success, security, significance, status and safety. We tend to assume that they protect the little bit of happiness we appear to have secured for ourselves.

The general benefits

Deep happiness and well-being have a host of essential and necessary benefits. Deep happiness has a powerful purpose. Forget for the moment the feeling of happiness. Forget the nice reassurance of happy feelings—just consider happiness as a reading of your mental health. Consider the benefits to your system when this reading is high.

When we are happy we function much better. We engage better with other people, we form better relationships, we solve problems more effectively and we are more creative. We are more kind, effective, efficient, healthy and loving. Being happy is not just about feeling happy inside: it's 'doing' happy in ways that dramatically improve our interaction and effectiveness at home, at work and in our community. Happy people are significantly more effective, industrious, social and creative. For all these reasons it's vital to recognise the benefits of happiness for life in general and for you in particular.

Happiness helps us to solve problems. They are easier to solve when you are happy, and they look easier when you are happy. When you are emotionally well you have an inner confidence and belief that problems are soluble. Your motivation is inspired by your positive mood.

Twenty-two reasons why being happy is critical to your health

1. When you feel good you are more active, positive, social and energetic.
2. *Your inner confidence, relationships and personal development are accumulated* during phases in your life when you are happy.
3. Happiness *enables social intelligence and engagement with others.* Happy doctors make *better diagnoses.*
4. Happiness *gets you to play,* which has been shown to be essential to mental health and human development.
5. The display of inner happiness through outward expression is socially powerful.
6. Positive emotions dissolve and *put into perspective the negative emotions* associated with stress, anxiety and depression.
7. *Problems seem solvable when you are happy.* Feeling good inspires and motivates you to take a positive attitude to problems and to persevere in your attempts to solve them.
8. Your *objective assessment of the difficulty of a task* is influenced by even slight elevations in your mood.
9. Your happiness is one of the most important *indicators of your physical health.*
10. Happier people *feel healthier* than unhappy people, even with the same diagnosis.
11. Happier people are *much less likely to get infections* than unhappier people.
12. Positive moods *improve all kinds of health* and improve longevity.
13. Unhappy people have lower pain tolerance and therefore feel worse and go to the doctor more often.
14. Unhappy people have more *bad habits and a worse lifestyle.*
15. The *immune system* of happy people is more effective than that of depressed people.
16. Depressed people are several times more likely to get *heart attacks and hypertension,* as are people suffering from stress and those in bad relationships.

17. High stress levels elevate the heart rate and make sufferers more likely to experience *cardiac problems.*
18. Organisms, including humans, *recover much more slowly* from injury when under stress.
19. The rate of ageing may be related to stress at the level of cell replication and replacement: there is less capacity to replace worn-out cells. *Stress makes us age.*
21. *Social supports*, such as loving parents and a good marriage, are related to better health. Giving support to others is more important to longevity than receiving support!
22. Happy people are *kinder* people.

Two amusing pieces of research have shown that when people are climbing steep hills the incline seems much flatter if the climbers are listening to uplifting Mozart music on their portable music players! Our objective assessment of the difficulty of a task is influenced by elevations in our mood. When you are walking with a friend, as opposed to walking alone, your estimation of distance is much shorter—something that shows that that little elevations in your happiness result in a reduction in your perception of the difficulty of a problem.

You will doubtless have had many similar experiences in your life in which you noticed that, because of your good mood, problems and difficulties were so much easier to resolve. Your happiness is so important to your everyday ability to navigate through life. It enhances your problem-solving skills, social intelligence, and reasonableness! When you are stressed or depressed you make poor judgements, misinterpret the importance of things, and respond in disproportionate ways.

Happiness inhibits SAD (stress, anxiety, depression)

We are all familiar with the 'Three Amigos' of stress, anxiety and depression. They have an awful habit of supporting each other, and they create long cycles from which it's hard to escape. When we experience long periods of SAD we develop bad mental habits. We learn to doubt ourselves, neglect ourselves and put ourselves down.

Practising the disciplines of well-being eventually reverses this pattern of SAD.

When happiness breaks through, problem-solving improves. A sense of perspective is gained, and the despair of anxiety and stress can dissolve, leaving the sufferer often wondering, 'What was I so distressed about in the first place? I see now that it was all a thing of nothing.' In this way, happiness activates the imagination in ways that are optimistic and good-humoured. It inhibits self-ruminations and obsessiveness. Positive feelings dissolve the negative feelings.

Happiness is essential to your morbidity and longevity

Deep happiness has dramatic positive consequences for morbidity and for longevity.

Your morbidity is a measure of whether or not you develop or contract a specific illness. Happy people, believe it or not, are much less likely to contract specific illnesses than SAD people. Ed Diener and Robert Biswas-Diener report that longitudinal studies found that *positive moods improved morbidity for virtually every class of illness*. The conclusions also remained the same when one took into account other influencing factors, such as age, sex, class and education. This is really quite amazing, when you think of it. It proves the mind-body connection beyond reasonable doubt. Happy people have fewer heart attacks than depressed people. When you are happy you have a better lifestyle and better habits, and this helps guard against infectious illnesses. Diener and Biswas-Diener conclude that there is an emerging body of research that suggests that knowing someone's happiness is one of the most important predictors of health and longevity. However, few GPs and consultants actually assess it.

When it comes to your longevity, that is, how long you live, it appears that happy people live longer than SAD people. This is very interesting, as it also suggests that happiness assists people in ways that benefit them an awful lot more than just feeling good.

Happiness is an investment in your life

It's a fuel that lasts into your future. Happiness *now* helps you to survive the ordeals of the future, because you carry it with you. Happy children learn that bad times are not permanent and that problems can be overcome. When you know deep happiness you develop an inner certainty that it can be found again. It's a well from which you can draw sustenance during emotionally lean times.

Most happy people can identify this inner well. It's an inner resource built up during periods of deep happiness. Therefore, happiness is an investment in the future as much as in the present. You need to build, invest in and deepen happiness not because it's nice to enjoy the growth of spring and the heat of summer but because it sustains you through the inevitable ordeals of autumn and winter.

YOUR INEVITABLE JOY

When you consider the stress, anxiety and depression that is in your own life you are in danger of concluding that joy and natural happiness are gone from you—that stress, anxiety, fear and relationship entanglements have taken its place. But a sensitivity to our life can enable us to see joy's fingerprints in everything we do.

Joy and happiness is ultimately a story about love. Life pulsates with love. If you trace the origins of human love back to its original evolutionary genesis you will understand how the pure force of life is love itself. Joy and love course through our veins ceaselessly. However, the expression of joy and the courage to stay in love with life awaken our terror of mortality, for the simple reason that the passionate love of life is just so because it is so painfully brief. Joy, in a strange way, exposes the nerve of our ever-present vulnerability and helplessness in the face of an awesome mystery.

Life is therefore inherently romantic. Love and grief are reverse sides of the same coin. When the veil between the essentials of life and our everyday obsessions is lifted we are pierced with a wondrous love of the world. Yet it is the great ache in our hearts, because it's a love that will die.

Soul-work and love

In my work with couples I see every day that people in anguish are driven by the paradoxical frustration of joy, the grief at the loss of joy or the anger at unrequited joy. Much anger, negativity, neediness and coldness is a fragile joy that is unable to acknowledge itself as such. The conflicts, which beset your heart, are not caused by the absence of joy but by a frustrated joy that loses its way under the guidance of fear. So much of your stress, anxiety and depressiveness is caused by a deep longing and joy that has been turned in on itself. The desire for happiness and the energy for happiness is constant in you. That love, that wanting a better life, is the trapped energy of joy within you.

If one holds open a simple heart, if one refuses to become mired in the complexities of human psychology, and if one refuses cynicism and distrust, one sees that joy and love are at the centre of the creative life. You can see that each of us wears a mask that conceals the simple and joyful face of humanity. It's the thesis of this book that it takes courage, discipline, imagination and hope to keep joy awake. We are under the influence of joy. Uncomplicated nature is, we might say, animated by joy and is immersed in the pleasure of being alive.

We are a mixed blessing

As most philosophers have remarked, the gift of self-consciousness and awareness is a mixed blessing. It's divine in that it awakens our senses and our heart to the mystery, miracle and wonder of life. It is troubled when we are conscious of our mortal fate and helplessness to overcome it.

Our joy and happiness are disturbed by this conflict. We try to be happy, yet in our terror we flee anxiously towards false securities and false idols. Our simple happiness in being alive is countered by our anxiety. We are bound in the anguish of opposites yet are straining for some kind of release.

In a smiling face of false optimism we want life but not death. We want joy without suffering, security without risk, love without vulnerability and life without helplessness. To choose life without death is actually to live in a world of illusion that, as I have discussed earlier, fosters a retreat from life by using the strategies of self-control and other control.

Let me use intimacy as an example of how we engage with life. The unpalatable truth is that we can't evade the signs of our imperfect mortality, such as the imperfections of our partners, their impatience and moodiness, their difference and selfishness and their irritability and incompetence. We just want their perfect and permanent qualities, such as their beauty and tenderness, their laughter and love, their kindness and compassion, their uniqueness and reliability and their sexuality and affection. The deathly in life is unpalatable, yet it actually causes passion and love. Therefore, to love your partner as they really are means that you are obliged to love the total reality, to accept those unsavoury traits that reveal their mortal imperfection. I can't repeat it often enough: when we reject the imperfections of our beloved we are, in reality, running from mortal life itself.

Every sacrifice you make, every kindness you show, every effort you make that asks something of you and every gesture of love is in fact an acknowledgement of the transience of life and the inherent loss involved in loving. To deplete oneself for another is a kind of death, yet it's the only truly courageous and honest response to life: to be—secretly—grateful and joyful with whatever life offers.

Deep happiness only thrives at the centre of the cruciform, at the point of tension between helplessness and control, between vulnerability and security, between inadequacy and competence and between humility and arrogance. It's at this point that joy and love spark into being.

In this way, joyful love of one's life is an essential transcendent function. It's the impulse that rises above the physical anxiety and mortality of death. Joyful love of one's life is conceived in the conflict of these opposites; yet, once it happens, it lifts the heart above the terrors and anxieties of life, and in those moments one is in touch with the infinite—with the sublime.

Once the soul connects with the infinite, the concerns of the personal ego dissipate, and the mystery and deeper meaning of life are not analysed but experienced. In the surrender to joyful life one has the experience of *being alive*, and in such experiences one's heart lifts above the conflict of life and touches the eternal. Listening to the rain beating against the window on a windswept night with the warmth of one's lover at one's side reveals for a moment the wonder of living.

In times of trauma and distress one forgets oneself while supporting those one loves, and in those moments the divine appears. Whatever the epiphany, the beautiful and the mysterious are revealed, and one rises above and beyond the anxiety of life.

Somewhere in everyone's heart there is an intuitive knowledge of the truth of these things. I know from experience and from working with thousands of clients that deep in everyone's heart there is the music of innocent joy, of happiness broken and betrayed, of its abuse and degradation, and of the horrors of those who seek to flee from the tragic brokenness of life. I work with paedophiles and abusers, with anti-socials and addicts, with hateful, controlling people and masochists; yet there is no awful, sadistic mind behind which there is not the echo of a broken and betrayed heart.

Most people have a boarded door into an inner room that knows the sound of joyful love, that aches for its simple affirmation and that longs for the soothing rhythm of its heart. The contents of such rooms are denied and repressed because of the terror of death, which it symbolises. The 'batterer' who, as a child, was abused has been taught to betray himself; and when the tender footsteps of longing arise in his heart he stands up to defeat it, because somewhere in his history those were the footsteps of his father, who, instead of soothing him to sleep, beat upon his door like a monster. The awful terror of simple joy or love has taken a foothold in his heart. Yet not for a moment can we surrender to such psychic terrorism. We must face it with bravery and work to free the hostage that is innocent joy.

For exercises related to this chapter please check out the book web site at

www.couragetobehappy.ie

Chapter 4

The 'why' of happiness

Your theology of life

HAPPINESS AND YOUR EXPERIENTIAL THEOLOGY

Have you not on occasion found yourself weeping when you witness something beautiful? Have you not found yourself deeply moved by the majesty of nature or by the magnificence of something small, such as the beauty of a small stone, a wild flower or a winter tree standing against the skyline? In the quieter moments of your life have you not felt touched by a sensitivity to the wonder of your life? And, at the same time, have you not found yourself chilled and unnerved by death? Has not bereavement changed you irrevocably?

These kinds of experience are like small revelations of a deeper reality. They are soulful, because they open your heart to the mysteries of life.

As I emphasised earlier, to understand your happiness and well-being you must look not only to psychology but also to the spirituality of human life. We draw our wisdom here not from scientific research but from art, literature, poetry, music, drama, prayer, spirituality, philosophy and religion. These are the places we look to get a *feeling for* who we are. These are the sources we draw on when we are confronted with the tragedies of life. When we need to be inspired or encouraged during life's dark and difficult times none of us go to science or research to find solace. We turn to sources that speak the language of the heart and soul. Equally, at times of joy, exuberance and celebration we don't turn to books, television, politics or academia to give these occasions meaning. We find means and vehicles of expression that have nothing to do with what is rational or reasonable. We ritualise, drink, sing, eat and celebrate. So, to find happiness our methods must be symbolic.

Your happiness and well-being is attained as a consequence not only of your genes and behaviour but also of your existential attitude to purpose and meaning. The inspiration for action arises because of the particular meaning we give to our lives.

Experiential theology

I don't use the word 'theology' in reference to any religion, institution or church. I use it in the context of the everyday struggles we all have to find meaning. I use it to refer to the consistent search for direction and meaning in life and to how we reach *beyond* the confines of our thinking brain in so doing. To some that beyond may be God; to others it may be Creation; to others still it may be the willingness to lean into a mystery that is larger than the self.

Our spirituality is our imaginative ability to overcome our mortal and physical anxiety, panic and terror. It's also our imaginative ability to create hope, faith, love and compassion out of the raw materials of life. Our theology is what we create from this. It's the inner map we develop to make sense of life, to find emotional confidence in life and to establish a living direction for life.

I use the term 'experiential theology' to refer to this. By that I mean that you find answers to the big questions in life through your lived experience and not in books or thinking. The purpose and joy of life are discovered more through experience than by reason. I know that if I were to ask you to write out an intelligent and well-reasoned outline of the meaning of your life you would struggle to articulate it. The meaning you draw on is condensed into an emotional, cellular and symbolic language. This is your experiential theology. You live it—you don't think it.

You develop your theology in response to the circumstances of your life—particularly to your puzzling, disarming and secretly terrifying transience. From the moment of birth the infant is in a struggle against mortality, and that struggle doesn't end until old age and death. Every fibre of the infant's being is working to survive. This is the passion of evolutionary life. You have evolved into a being that will at all costs wade upriver against the current of mortality that threatens to sweep you away.

The child cries, groans, kicks, screams, cuddles, coos, talks, clings, seeks, wakes and crawls in its efforts to stay alive, to survive and thrive. The infant's primary impulses are what ensure its survival. The reason it has to survive is that it knows, physically, that it will die if it doesn't. It will, from the moment of its first breath, scream for food and attention. That is its life. And it's yours too. Everything you do in life is a reaction to this terrifying and glorious adventure. How we live this adventure is our theology.

When Alice, aged seventy-two, a simple, uneducated woman, finds joy in reminiscing about her life, tending to her little garden, minding her cat, taking care of her even more elderly neighbour, visiting her church, tending to her late husband's grave and laughing with her friends over Tuesday night bingo, she has found an experiential theology that is rich beyond measure. It's not an intellectual theology and never should be. If you asked her the meaning of life in theological terms she would, quite rightly, respond with gracious humility by saying, 'Sure what would I know about those kinds of things?' But her physical spirituality is rich.

Spirituality

The attitude with which you approach life is essentially a spiritual one. It's spiritual because it can be no other. It's spiritual because life presents you with an insoluble mystery, places you in a situation over which you have no control, places you in Creation with no information about its purpose and leaves it to you to make whatever sense you can out of it. You have no real control over life. You had little say in the conditions of your life, and you have absolutely no control over your ultimate fate. Life has happened to you. How you respond to it is influenced and determined by genes, circumstances and learning. However, you have been blessed with the freedom to imagine your life in many different ways. The dilemma presented to you is to figure out how you want to respond to this life that has been given to you. It's left entirely up to you to give it purpose and feeling. This endeavour is not a mental exercise: it's an experiential one; it's an existential one; it's a transcendent one; it's a spiritual one.

UNAVOIDABLE UNHAPPINESS AND INEVITABLE JOY

We must continue with our fearless inventory of life and living. Regretfully, we must, as the psychotherapist Irvin Yalom put it, look towards the sun and contemplate the way in which every single action we take is shaped by mortality. Our dread of our mortality and everything to do with it keeps some of the truths about our existence at the periphery of consciousness. Our desire to promote our individual sense of status, significance, power and influence is a counter-phobic consequence of our powerlessness over our fate and future. Yet hardly a day goes by in which our denial is not confronted by some news, accident, tragedy, illness or death that jolts us out of dreamlike invincibility and innocence and reminds us that we are vulnerable and mortal.

Without saying why, parents watch carefully over their growing child because of the everyday spectre of death: 'Mind your step,' 'Look when you cross the road,' 'Don't forget to put on your scarf,' 'Wait there until Mam gets back,' 'Don't move.' Every news bulletin you hear has three simple message that never change: 'People die,' 'Dangerous things happen' and 'You are not safe.' It's never announced directly, only metaphorically. (When you notice this you can't stop hearing it!)

However, if you mention death and mortality directly you will be accused of being 'morbid'! To mention the possibility of one's getting sick is seen as tempting fate. We have a host of still-active superstitions that steer us away from looking fearlessly at life. This is okay, but we must not be naïve about our happiness, believing that it derives from avoiding, denying and ignoring our deepest vulnerable humanity.

> We must realise that feelings of fear, inadequacy, insignificance, helplessness and vulnerability are not indicators that there is something wrong with us, nor are they indicators that we are weak. They are simply the symptoms of mortality and life.

To feel these things is not to be unhappy—but you may mistake them for such. No! This is not unhappiness. This is life.

The tension of life

There are nine basic life conflicts that can generate inner unhappiness and distress. These represent the inner tension of life and have been common to all people since the dawn of humanity. They are already uploaded onto your emotional system from the moment of birth. They are in your DNA.

We don't quite know how to be happy, because we have to struggle with the following nine basic inner conflicts. Each of these conflicts is deeply human and captures a unique part of our human experience.

1. We are both afraid and brave.
2. We are both insignificant and important.
3. We are both inadequate and capable.
4. We are both helpless and in control.
5. We are both separate and connected.
6. We are both vulnerable and resilient.
7. We are both broken and healed.
8. We are both lost and found.
9. We are both shipwrecked and saved.

Everyone knows these inner tensions. We all feel anxious, insignificant, inadequate, helpless, isolated, vulnerable, flawed and lost. These are the symptoms of life itself. To summarise these inner natural tensions felt by all living things: *we are stuck with our mortality while we strive for a transcendent life; we are terrified of death yet hunger for more of the life that guarantees it!*

The conflicts of life

These core issues relate to the great enlivening and disquieting mysteries of life. Religions, cultures and mythologies have all sought to help societies resolve these unsettling conflicts. All the great religions seek to address and solve the problems created by our passionate mortality. All rituals and practices have addressed the problem of human happiness in the context of these essentials. The inspiring quality of human nature is that we find joy and happiness in life while inhabiting our human suffering. This is the heroic courage of life.

Therefore, our exploration of human happiness begins with, and returns to, these truths. Instead of starting off with attempts to stick smiley faces on our lapels and tell ourselves to cheer up and think positively, we need to look fearlessly at, and get a real feel for, who we are. From this point we will get a feel for the origins of our love of life, our natural joy and our human potential. Let us take a look at some of these inner conflicts.

Your constant anxiety

You are an anxious and stressed creature striving for a happier and safer life.

In the morning, flocks of starlings often come to feed for worms in my garden. Watching them is fascinating. While they search, listen and peck for worms they are constantly vigilant against any threat. Their heads lift up every couple of seconds and dart in different directions as they check for danger. All I need to do is to wave my hand from the window for them to take to wing in a whoosh of panic. It doesn't really matter that a cat has never succeeded in killing one of them: they watch out for the attack that never comes. In this ever-present fear of something bad happening they are just like you and me, because this is how we are in life. As Samuel Beckett so humorously illustrated in *Waiting for Godot*, humanity expends great energy in anxiously waiting for something to happen that never quite does.

We are constantly anxious. Evolutionary psychology has shown that the physical brain has not changed much in a hundred thousand years. We respond to life in ways that are not very different from those of early humans as they walked the plains of Africa.

Our evolution from comfortable animal ignorance into acute consciousness of our mortal vulnerability had one great consequence for all of us: it infected us with unavoidable dread and anxiety. If we were just apes we wouldn't be plagued by a small fraction of the human anxiety and stress we suffer from!

Like that of other organisms, our essential function is to defeat death for as long as we are able. This is the will to live, to endure, to sustain oneself. Anxiety enables us to do that. Any creature that doesn't experience fear and anxiety is quickly obliterated. This is the legacy of evolution and the survival of our species. From the moment of birth we are afraid. Therefore you are an anxious person, and, like everyone else, you are watchful and careful.

When you worry about your children, your relationship, your security in life, what people think of you, your everyday problems, your bank balance, your difficulties at work, your health or your marriage, the energy source that drives these worries is your physical anxiousness to ensure safety and avoid death. The unfortunate thing for most of us is that, like the starlings, so much of this anxiety is wasted.

It's hard to get a full grip on this fact, because in your mind your worries are deserving of such anxious attention. They feel entirely logical. But this is not so. Essentially, you have many units of anxiety in your system, and you have to use them up on something. Your experiences of psychological worry and distress are, at their very core, existential—if not religious—in origin and nature. Our basic fear is of an unknown and dangerous future over which we have little control and that may threaten our happiness and security.

Our conscious fear is of symbolic death, that is, of losing our attachments, such as money, family, status, security, love and approval. Because we are so vigilant about our safety and security, anxiety is our constant companion. We are always afraid of the future. So billions of people all over the planet are worrying about making their little worlds safer. So don't fret about the fact that you feel insecure in yourself: you can't help it!

Your vulnerability

We always feel at risk—at risk not only of death but of all its derivatives, which are no less terrifying for us: abandonment, attack, rejection, isolation, failure, ridicule, humiliation, abuse, neglect and embarrassment. These experiences are terrifying for us, because they expose us to negative forces that threaten to annihilate the sense of security, safety and confidence we strive to establish. We are genetically coded to be forever vigilant. Danger lurks everywhere.

Even when your life is going really well a part of you remains restless. A sudden noise in the middle of the night, a bad dream, a cold shoulder from a colleague, an insult from your partner or a bit of bad news can send your emotional system into a momentary spiral. We have an inherent and unavoidable vulnerability to distress that, if not managed well, can unravel into emotional unhappiness.

Anxiety has a twin sister called desire. While anxiety makes you fearful, desire makes you courageous. While your anxiety is an experience of your fear of bad things happening to you, your desire is your expectation that good things will happen. You fear death and you desire life. Just as you have inherited the 'anxiety software' that runs through your system, you have also inherited the 'desire software' that makes you want more life, love and happiness. Your desire for life is the universal expression of love, of wanting, of moving outward into the universe. When your anxiety is soothed your natural joy and happiness begin to flower.

Your felt insignificance

Everyone can identify with a feeling of insignificance. Everyone can look up at the stars at night and get a genuine feeling of how small they are in relation to all Creation. Humanity has always known this feeling. Your life can feel as brief and unremarkable as that of an insect that lives and dies in some distant forest. Your place in life can feel infinitesimally small.

One of the consequences of this awareness is a compulsive and obsessive drive and desire to prove this wrong, to prove one's significance and status. We can make a life project out of proving to others that we are important. Just look around and you can see so many people urgently committed to securing their sense of importance and significance in life purely because deep down they doubt it. However, when that anxiety to prove oneself eases we awaken to a peaceful bliss within ourselves.

To admit that you are just one of 7 billion people on earth desperately trying to prove themselves while at the same time being destined to die an unremarkable death can and does—to put it very mildly—puncture your balloon. 'Surely I am more important than that,' you ask. It can seem like a an absurd joke that you have this wonderful life that is destined to fade away. Shakespeare put it so well when he said that life was 'full of sound and fury, signifying nothing.' Not only does your mortality seem to evoke your sense of insignificance, so also does your life. At its worst moments it seems to mock you.

Not only does death awaken your abject vulnerability and trembling soul, so too does life's majestic and miraculous beauty. When you experience the enormous majesty of Creation, the stunning universe or the miracle of the tiniest of natural creations—such as the beauty of a single leaf—you also inevitably feel small and somewhat insignificant. Against the majesty of the world and its indifference to individual life you can't but feel small. 'Lord, I am not worthy to receive you,' says the Catholic prayer.

But you can also experience the opposite of this—your significance in the world: you can experience deep gratitude for being blessed with the gift of life. You can experience the wonderful uniqueness of your own life. You can experience a profound significance and meaning because of the special people in your life. Rather than being overwhelmed with a feeling of unimportance and insignificance, or being compelled by a need to prove your self-importance, you can lean back into a Creation that supports you. You can, in an exquisite way, get a sense of how your life is sacred, special and wonderful. You also see this in those you love. You become aware of each person's unique integrity and feel reverence, respect and awe. You experience the divine in the ordinary. When you look up at the wonderful stars at night, or when you watch your children growing up, you can feel a resonant belonging and purpose that connects you with the significance of all life. When this channel to Creation is open you can feel profoundly at peace. But your bubble can be burst by the intrusions of self-doubt and anxiety.

The philosopher Pierre Teilhard de Chardin suggested that you don't look up at the stars to feel how insignificant you are but to realise how significant you are and that you have a vital role to play in the evolution of life; that your unique singularity of being is profound; and that you have a unique glimpse of the universe that no-one else has. And, because of this unique and sacred place, you must contribute to life.

Your physical limitation and your ache for transcendence

You are a somewhat helpless and mildly happy mortal striving for a transcendent and spiritual life. A considerable amount of your life is defined more by effort than by happiness. Life, in many ways, is an ordeal. Yet it's strangely and deeply satisfying for that.

We have an imagination that can transcend everyday life and float out into the universe while we are trapped in a body that decays and dies. We are simultaneously confined animals and free spirits. We remain both animal and angel.

You bump up against this inherent conflict every day. At its most mundane it's evident in the way you are constantly struggling with the fact that life is never the way you want it or imagine it to be. Every day you are irritated by little things that don't go your way, by people who don't do what you hoped they would or by things that don't work out as you had planned. Every day in every way you struggle with the tension that there is life as you imagine it should be and life as it is. Your obsessive attachment to life 'as it should be' puts you in conflict with life as it is. Your daily frustration with things comes from this deeper conflict.

You are always being pulled in two different directions at the same time. You are both an awkward creature and a self-conscious being.

You are forever trying to climb out of the limitations of your animal nature, but you can't quite do it. It's as if you are forever straining against your very self—always striving to be better than you are. You have this subconscious fear that, without your effort, you might sink into the quicksand. So you strive to be a good person, to achieve something, to develop and to be happier.

Your body is a shell that is alien to you in many ways; the strangest and most disquieting thing is that it has a life of its own. The conflict that arises in your life as a consequence of this reality spreads like a dye through the liquid of your life. Each and every one of us thinks great thoughts about our lives and ourselves but is awoken from our slumber when we realise that we are ill and growing old.

If you were either a simple animal or a transcendent angel you would be happy. But you are neither! You are caught between both, one drawing you into the earth, another drawing you to the stars. So you are stuck with yourself, always striving to be happier and trying to rise up from the earth in which you are set. You are straining to pull your roots out of a soil that inhibits you, wanting always to fly.

You can dream and fall in love and yet die for the most trivial of reasons. Floods, tsunamis, earthquakes, hurricanes, famines and droughts can all obliterate the endless strivings of million of people with careless and cruel disregard for any individual man, woman or child. The relentless indifference of death doesn't spare you. When we allow ourselves to dwell on our condition—on the fate that awaits us and those we love—it's at times the most chilling and unforgiving of realities.

However, you have a mind that soars, an imagination that helps you rise above your condition. You have the wings of an angel. You can give your life a special meaning that brings you up and out of yourself. You imagine your life in so many wonderful ways. It's what makes you most human and what allows you to experience something beyond the confines of your very self.

Imagination, spirituality, love, hope and faith: by means of these we transcend our limitations and inadequacies. These are humanity's solutions and responses to the facts of mortality, suffering and ageing. It's a wonderful solution, and through this faculty we have created great art, music and literature. Through it we sing, daydream, hope, celebrate, delight in and imagine so many things. This is your everyday spirituality: rising above your condition and giving your life a meaning; imagining your life as it could be; and celebrating your life as it is.

To blend in or to be different

One of the beautiful things about humanity—about all of life—is our inner yearning to be good—our inner sensitivity to the way things ought to be. Ernest Becker writes that this is one of 'the sublime mysteries of creation—this self-feeling at the heart of nature, at the heart of living organisms.' He continues: 'All organisms like to feel good about themselves.' The heart of nature is flowing in its own joyful self-expansion. We have this tremendous urge to grow and to feel right about ourselves—to be happy.

However, nature has arranged for it to be difficult for you to feel happy in any obvious way, because we have urges that point us in opposite directions. You search for happiness by blending into life, and you search for happiness by trying to stand out from life. You want to be the same as everyone else, and you want to be different from everyone else.

You have a powerful drive to merge with life and to lose yourself in something bigger than yourself. This is usually in family, work, social relationships, projects and so on. Being part of something bigger makes you feel at peace and connected. This is natural co-operation. Only by living for something outside of one's own ego is one able to live at all. This is a natural urge to join in and participate in life. Without this participation you would be left isolated, facing the anxiety of life alone. So you try to live in some larger, more expansive meaning. This reaching out—this inner longing for a meaning bigger than oneself—is one life's urges and one of the great sources of well-being and happiness. However, it's not that simple, is it?

You also search for happiness in an opposite way. You also want to be unique. You want to be important and somewhat special. You are understandably not happy to be invisible and unimportant. You have always wanted to stand out as someone with some special qualities, no matter how modest they are. You have an urge to emerge and to shine in some way. It's your need to have an effect, to have influence over things, to matter, to be seen as special and to be noticed for some personal quality. In your own heart you know that you are unique, and you strive to grow and blossom in a way that is true to you. You don't want to merely blend into life anonymously: you want to give and engage in a way that confirms your significance. You thrived as a child when this was seen in you, when your mother affirmed your specialness and when your father approved your uniqueness.

Your wounded vulnerability

Your human woundedness is experienced in countless moments. There have been moments when you have been moved by beauty or broken by grief. There have been moments when you have had a deep awareness of the breakable vulnerability of life. At times it seems so tragically beautiful.

Your vulnerability is the emotional experience of how precarious your happiness in life is. You are therefore vigilant and seek to ward off all reminders of your vulnerability. Experiences such as rejection can cause you terrible distress. Although you don't *think* about your human vulnerability you constantly *feel* it.

It is felt at a physical level. Your body reacts to the threat of mortality, your mind reacts to the symbols of it and your emotions react to the derivatives of it. This may be the cold shoulder of your lover, the harsh rejecting word that makes you feel unsafe, the dark shadow of a diagnosed illness or the grief of a break-up. Each situation touches the exposed nerve of your precarious vulnerability.

When you can take this into account you begin to realise that mortality is not something that simply awaits you: it's present for you now and defines the nature of the intimacies of your domestic life.

You are reminded of this in form and symbol. Your partner forgets you, dismisses you, leaves you, insults you and, in doing this, exposes you to the elements of life from which you seek shelter. This is the climate of everyday life. When you are open to this truth you open yourself to the first possibility of happiness.

Your helplessness

Part of our unhappiness derives from the fact of our powerlessness and helplessness. You actually have quite limited control over your life. Everyone knows the distressing experience of helplessness. It exposes our inadequacy. We strive to control a life over which we have no ultimate control: we are powerless, seeking to be powerful; we are helpless, seeking to be in control; we are vulnerable, seeking invulnerability; we are inadequate, seeking competence; we are peasants seeking to be a kings; we are cowards seeking to be heroes; we are insignificant, seeking to be important; and we are afraid, seeking to be courageous.

You can't escape from your ultimate powerlessness. Though there is a lot that you can do to manage and control the elements of your life, there is a larger context that you have to accept and that you can't influence. This is the source of your fear and helplessness. There is only so much you can do.

It's no coincidence that Alcoholic's Anonymous have as their first step 'to admit that you are powerless.' This is such sound thinking, because it's based on a fundamental spiritual truth about life. All great spirituality demands surrender, a surrender of the ego and of our desire for control and power. You will realise, on reflection, that one of your greatest psychological enemies is your desire to control. You will know the incessant anxiety associated with your daily realisation that life doesn't co-operate fully with your efforts to control it or yourself.

THE DECLARATIONS OF EXISTENCE

Existential and insoluble conflicts rumble beneath our everyday beliefs and attitudes. We come to subconscious conclusions about ourselves that can make us happy or unhappy. The good news is that our life instinct has been winning; and, in truth, it proves itself stronger. The bad news is that you can't escape the consequences of mortality. Your life instinct can win out by ensuring that you believe in living and that you endure; but your death instinct can drag you down into the grey world of fear and unhappiness. You survive, but you pay an emotional price. Your body lives, but you spend a lot of your time anxious and afraid. You endure, but you carry the inner bruising.

But this is not good enough. You want and need to thrive. Your imaginative and eternal self needs to give expression to its pure and uncomplicated joy and bliss. And this is most definitely possible for you. In fact, it's your obligation to set this captive free.

The deep-rooted tensions I have identified become reduced to very basic beliefs that you have about yourself. You can genuinely influence the choice you make about which side of the conflicts you choose: the life-generating side or the death-defying side. It takes self-awareness and self-discipline to make these choices. It takes discipline to keep the window open to your abundant and joyful self—a self that often lies buried under the layers of self-doubt.

I have therefore distilled the unavoidable conflicts of life into what I am calling 'The Declarations of existence'. These are the declarations we need to make to ourselves in order to ensure that we continually tilt the balance of inner tensions toward the light, toward life and toward joy. Without committing to these kinds of declaration, or versions of them, we passively let life happen to us rather than mobilising the courage to declare who we are, or who we want to be.

Declarations that awaken your natural joy

Anxiety
There is no need to be afraid.
Everything you are afraid of has already happened.
You have nothing to lose except the symbols of your mortality.
Your eternal self is untouchable.

Adequacy
You are divinely perfect.
You have nothing to prove.

Significance
You are worthy of great joy.
You are a unique and sacred person.

Belonging
You have a special place in the universe. You belong.
You have been chosen and blessed with life.

Helplessness
Helplessness is inevitable.
You can let go control.
You are free.

Isolation
You are not alone.
Invisible hands support you.
You can lay down so many of your burdens.

Vulnerability
You are safe.
Nothing can harm your abundant self.
The source of your being is joyful.

Woundedness
You are perfectly beautiful.
The wound of life is your brokenness.
Behind the veil of your self-doubt you blossom effortlessly.

Setting your captive free

To the degree that your mortal condition makes you anxious and afraid, the bliss, abundance and beauty of life offers you peace and comfort. To the degree that your inability to control life makes you feel inadequate and impotent, your innate love and desire for more life allows you to feel capable and blissfully perfect in your imperfections. To the degree that death ensures that you are powerless and helpless over your ultimate and more immediate fate, life blesses you with a courage and determination that is heroic and transformative. To the degree that you feel trapped or imprisoned in life, you can set yourself free when you inhabit it fully. To the degree that the conditions of life leave you vulnerable and wounded, life reminds you that in your brokenness and compassion you find love and belonging. To the degree that life or death leaves you feeling ugly, deformed or disfigured, life itself urges you to dance in celebration of your unseen perfection. To the degree that death and loss highlight the terror of your isolation, life itself calls you into connection with natural and human creation.

Imprisoning your self

However, to the degree that you seek to conquer and banish your innate anxiety you become a bully. To the degree that you reject your innate inadequacy you become an over-achiever to prove life wrong. To the degree that you are uncomfortable with your insignificance you compensate through righteousness, self-importance and status-seeking. To the degree that you are unable to tolerate human helplessness you seek out power and control to ward it off. To the degree that you are unable to inhabit your vulnerability and woundedness you will seek exaggeration, falsity and pretence. To the degree that you can't tolerate your innate isolation and loneliness you will seek to dominate another or to submit to them to quell your fears. Finally, to the degree that you can't abide your self-responsibility you will seek to attack and blame others and life itself.

Your inherited joy

1. Every being has a natural resting state of simple pleasure and joy in being alive.
2. Every human being has been provided with a brain that, of itself, seeks faith, hope and love.
3. Every human being experiences happiness and joy in secure and loving attachment.
4. Every human being is inclined towards compassion and kindness.
5. Every human being is inclined towards happiness.
6. Every human being has a sense of their uniqueness.
7. Every human being has the resources to overcome adversity and obstacles.
8. Every human being has the momentum to experience confidence in themselves.
9. Every human being has a heroic purpose.
10. Every human being is able to influence their world.
11. Every human being experiences grace and gratitude.
12. Every human being has a lightness of heart.
13. Every human being delights in their own existence.
14. Every human being is beautiful.
15. Every human being has a sense of the sacred in life.
16. Every human being is passionate.
17. Every human being is in tension.
18. Every human being is urgent.
19. Every human being has inherited the often frozen gift of joy.

By virtue of your life, of 13 billion years of evolution, of thousands of generations of genes and struggle, you exist today. You would not exist if you were not, in so many ways, perfect. When you were born you were perfect, when you were four years old you were perfect, when you were twelve years old you were perfect, and today you still are!

Today, you are perfect, but you have forgotten this. Today, as you read this, you are adequate and worthy and capable beyond measure. You are, today, as worthy and significant as a king or queen. Love pulsates through your veins, joy remains repressed in the back-rooms of your emotional life; but, despite this, you are a person who has much to give to the world. You are special because you are entirely unique. There is no-one quite like you. What you have to celebrate within yourself is your unique magnificence in all Creation. You are beautiful. There is an innate and invisible strength and confidence in you because you are you. You belong. You were meant to be. You have a destiny and purpose that is accessible to you. All the burdens that you carry—you can lay many of them down. You are free. Don't be afraid.

All these things are accessible to you, and all these things are your birthright. And all these things are the upbeat of life. The downbeat, as I have outlined, is your tragic condition. The vitality for your life is a consequence of Creation's unwillingness to make you permanent—or to make anything permanent, for that matter. Everything changes. Everything is broken.

HAPPINESS, GRATITUDE AND ACCEPTANCE

From this point, I am hoping that you will get a feel for the origins of your love of life, of your natural joy and of your human potential.

This is heavy stuff, but once it's felt and appreciated there can be a lightness of being: a realisation that fighting against life or trying to control life works against the self. Rather, then, we see the natural spirituality of Buddhism and mindfulness: the realisation that a grateful acceptance of life's contradictions, tensions and ironies is the path of the easy mind. So let us feel our way into the soft happiness that is grateful acceptance.

Grateful acceptance

Your well-being and happiness is a state of grateful acceptance of your inner and outer life, of your limitations and the limitations of your particular life circumstances.

Whatever the state of your relationships, self-confidence or life, when you are spiritually alive you always feel some sense of gratitude. This is an experience of life in which you are not feeling thankful when things go your way. Rather, you are aware that you have no disposable days in your life to be disgruntled about. You feel, like George Bailey did in the film *It's a Wonderful Life*, that every ordinary thing is its own unique blessing. Now, that may sound a bit too much to expect; but, even in the darkest of moments, the poetic and spiritual eye can somehow see cracks of light breaking through. And, even in that, the irony and paradox of life must also not escape you: the cruel joke that playfully dismantles all our illusions of control and power.

Therefore, from the position of well-being you see your life in the round. You take in not just the 5-degree arc of delight but also the 360-

degree sweep of seasons, time and erosion. First comes the seed, then the shoot, then the blade of grass, then the petals and then, finally, the falling away. When you see yourself in the round you have a reverence for the climates and seasons of your own life—the ups and downs, good times and bad—and you roll with them in acceptance. The bad humour of your partner or the tedium of certain aspects of your job may irritate you, but they don't destabilise you. You can keep that alignment with life that makes all these irritants inevitable, in yourself and others. The shortcomings of others are accepted by you because they mirror your own imperfections, and they mirror the beautiful imperfections of all of life.

When Jesus pointed out the lilies of the field and the birds in the air, when poets write of the fallen leaves of winter and when Dante wrote of the inferno, you get a real sense of the inevitabilities of life. False self-help books that promise you five easy steps to happiness are nothing more than disguised magic. These promises twist time and all the unavoidable storms, dark nights and deluges of life into a promise of *relief*. The relief is a false promise to help you to escape from life and all its inevitabilities.

Science essential to spirit

That is why, in this book, it's critical that we also look very closely at what science and research tell us, to prevent us from escaping into some lovely sounding fantasy-land of promises. When we look at the research on happiness and well-being we can remain grounded in reality and not lose the run of ourselves. So many therapies and therapists are like those old travelling salesmen in the Wild West who sold magic tonics in a bottle that cured the lame and the diseased, that cured impotence and strokes, that offered an escape from life. And who among us doesn't from time to time want this escape? Are there not times when we would willingly buy these emotional tonics?

But our psychological relief and our pursuit of a new hypnosis don't open a window into what life is: they don't teach us what life is. They don't show us a more abundant life. It's for this reason that this book emphasises the critical importance of one's spiritual reflex, one's poetic nature, one's artistic sensitivity and one's religious longing. It's the function of these human qualities to enable us to hear the music of life and to see into the nature of things.

This is poetry. And our imagination points us towards this realm. Prayer and poetry, art and music, religion and spirituality: all these open the window into the immensity of Creation and answer Jung's question 'Are we part of an enchanted universe, or not?' Poetry, art and imagination break open the harsh shell of mechanical escapism: they warm our science and give it heart. The poetic in life dismantles the cold, sterile truth that we erect around ourselves, and it jump-starts our scientific research. It converts it, if you will, into the currency of the human heart.

A word about perfection

We are each and every one of us in the process of growing, desiring and becoming. You still want more information, more security, more wealth and more love. Because you 'want' you therefore feel somewhat unfulfilled. You can fall into the illusion that when you get everything you want you will be happy. You feel imperfect. However, when you are fully aligned within yourself you realise that you are already perfect. Let me challenge you with a simple example.

Think of one of your children when they were five years old. If you can imagine a child of that age you will remember the natural delight they have in just being alive. You will love their innocent passion for life. You will see that they *have* nothing and still have to achieve and *get* everything. Now let me ask you this: When children are five years of age, would you describe them as perfect or imperfect? As complete in themselves or as needing a lot of work? You will, hopefully, see in them a glorious perfection. In fact, a perfection that makes you ache, knowing that it will pass quickly. Well, let me put it to you that, right now, as you sit there reading these lines, you are as perfect as that five-year-old child. Right now, at this moment in your life, you can't be more perfect. Like that child, accumulating or getting anything else not only distracts you from what and who you are now but also creates the false feeling of inadequacy. You are perfect in your becoming. The entire universe—all life, all Creation, all happiness, all life's sweet sorrow—is available and is with you right now.

These are not just idle words. They are the words of the wise and the saintly. They are the truths that inspire us. They come not from my head but from the inspiration we find in things that have one foot planted in the world of the poetic.

When I was a small boy, like every other child I used to play wonderful games in my imagination. Whether in rugby, soccer or golf, I played out wonderful stories in which I was heroic in my victories. My little daughter Ciara, at six years of age, plays out the same kinds of games with her dolls, with princes and princesses. This child-like imagination is a step towards the poetic and creative world. Therefore, as Plato said, don't become preoccupied with the trivial affairs of your life. Don't get distracted by the golden glint of status: keep your eye focused on life's fixed stars, the stars that wise men follow, and on the principles of life.

The leaves from your garden trees fall. They lie where they fall. To be able to see life in the round and to hold it with a calm and peaceful acceptance: that is the enlightenment of Buddha, the peace of St Francis.

I find now, at 51, that I think often of death and of how it confronts all the manifestations of myself. And in some strange ways the prayers that arise from my fragile heart are meditations on life: on the exquisiteness of our mortal life; on the piercing beauty of my beloved; on the ageing hands of a mother that buttered a thousand loving sandwiches. With regard to dipping your toes into the immense joy of all Creation, sit content knowing that at any time you can slip easily into this life-affirming river.

Peaceful death

'Well, Colm,' my dying father half joked with me, 'we must all arrive here at some point, must we not. There is no other way to the Glory of God.'

'I suppose we must, Dad,' I agreed.

'Sure we would put the funeral homes out of business if we didn't oblige. Look at your man over there,' he nodded at the consultant leaning over another patient in the hospice: 'He's just trying to keep your man alive long enough to pay his bill!'

We laughed. Then my father, the red flowers on his bedside locker, and I sat in gentle silence, until he fell asleep.

The openness to happiness must include the welcoming of joyful sorrow. To avoid them is to miss the point of a rich and fulfilling life. This is where we must embrace our destiny. To know our destiny is to accept something deep in ourselves that so many others cannot. It's this that gives a person character. To use an old, simple phrase it means to be at peace with the world.

So, whatever your situation, status, security or significance, to have the window of your heart opened onto the vast landscape of Creation is to know that—whether you are rich or poor, king or peasant, at home or abroad—you are handed the same conditions in life. You have the potential, with grateful acceptance of life's conditions, to reveal the glory of Creation.

The nursery rhyme of life

I love children's nursery rhymes because they don't dwell on any explanations or offer theories about why things are they way they are. They are like simple prayers: if things are the way they are, it doesn't matter why. The spirituality of incident is sweet.

> Humpty Dumpty sat on a wall,
> Humpty Dumpty had a great fall.
> All the king's horses and all the king's men
> Couldn't put Humpty together again.

That is all there is and all there is supposed to be. 'I grow old, I grow old. I should wear the bottoms of my trousers rolled.'

Life loves to just happen. Children love the happening incidents of life. 'Little Bo Peep has lost her sheep!' is all there is and all there needs to be. Your lovely imperfect little life is full of incident, and you can let it unfold both anxiously and joyfully. In this gratitude there is happiness. You are born, you blossom, you fade and you die. That's the nursery rhyme of your life. Delightful, is it not? All your lovely theories, escape hatches and shortcuts bring you back onto the same road. Yet this is where life's desire, well-being and electricity begin.

The science

There isn't a scientist, an economist, a physicist, a hard-nosed statistician or a mathematician who doesn't, after a hard day's work, go home and listen to Mozart, enjoy the passion of a football match, visit the grave of their beloved, prepare Christmas presents for their daughter or dance in their kitchen at 4 a.m. This is because even the harshest cynic lives life as a poet. Therefore, this book is about stepping back from oneself and looking at the science and then stepping into oneself to experience oneself as a passionate being. So happiness in life is a two-step dance, is it not? You go through the motions of your daily life, sometimes with boredom and sometimes with patience, and at the same time you have moments of prayerful delight, or abundant and simple joy.

Let go of profit and loss

In my early twenties, like a lot of students I fell in love with Buddhism and Zen. My interest faded as my intellectual and incident-filled life poured in on me. But I have never lost that sensation of life's happening, that longing to be able to say, like Goethe:

Never refuse to give anything,
Never refuse to take anything,
For it is all God offers.

Whatever it is, take it or give it. It's all there is. I love the spirit of that awareness and sentiment. Here we find the root of the spiritual disciplines. The Buddhist teaching encourages us to sink into the natural joy and happiness of life when you silence your evaluating mind—a mind that is forever thinking 'this is bad' or 'that is good.' You find happiness in life when you can simply live without this kind of evaluative thinking and have a heart that opens to all of life's little joys and irritants—when you accept and know that *all of it is good*.

So don't be angry at the slow traffic, your reluctant teenager, your crying child or your imperfect spouse. You have to—I mean *have to*—love it all! You can't cherry pick life itself, because you must accept your destiny (your cosmic fate over which you have no control) and all the derivatives of that destiny (your daily fate). However, you do have full control over how you wish to participate. And how you participate in life is the crux of the matter. It's here that spiritual sensitivity, religious longing and artistic creation have such profound meaning.

To participate in life you turn your hand to the disciplines of an awakened life. The feeling of gratitude is an immense response in life. It touches you when you see it and feel it. It marks the difference between the self-absorbed and the life-awakened person.

Gratitude

> When you are grateful for the little things in life it's poetic; when you are grateful for all things in life it's religious; when you are grateful for the little things because they are no different from the big things it's spiritual.

This illustrates that the mastery of the little disciplines and actions of happiness is a mastery of the larger mystery of life. You see, then, in your beloved the sacred presence of the infinite. Your children and those close to you are portals to the infinite universe that cares for you. You can only fall into gratitude and acceptance. God and all Creation are funnelled into the figure of your little child laughing at the water's edge. Your little heart applauds. The moon that shines upon you as you sleep glows in your heart when you wake; the sun that shines its light upon you also lives within you; and when the leaves fall from the trees you feel grief land on the soil of your heart.

The world in which you live, which was there when you were born into your parents' arms, and which will be there after you pass away, is not there for you or for any one person. It never promised you an easy life. But the world in which you live has shone such a generous light on you, electrified you, breathed you, 'heartbeated' you through an extraordinary Creation. It has given you life and has forced you to inhabit yourself. In these ways it has given you the extraordinary gift of your physical happiness.

For exercises related to this chapter please check out the book web site at

www.couragetobehappy.ie

Chapter 5

The 'what' of happiness

The research

MYTHS AND CORE FINDINGS

The myths about happiness

The myths examined in this chapter may create difficulty for you. You will find yourself resisting the truth because it will, in some instances, seem counter-intuitive. But I urge you to go with them because they move towards a constellation of new beliefs and attitudes that can inspire you to see yourself differently.

You believe a lot of things that prevent you from being happy. I believed quite a few of them myself until I began to let the scientific research dissolve some of my assumptions. In many instances I was shocked by what I discovered, in most instances I was pleasantly surprised, and in some I was quietly relieved. Hopefully some of the same will happen for you.

These myths and findings are the things you will need to understand in order to prepare for self-improvement. They represent some of the essential cognitive tools that will enable you to find purchase as you climb up to higher ground and will help you rid yourself of the excess baggage of false beliefs! Some of these myths are quite exciting in their implications. They will challenge you to move closer to the self-belief necessary for achieving fulfilment and for being the best person you can be.

Do you believe that you will be happier when things in your life are different? That you will be better when the relationships in your life are sorted out, when your financial pressures are alleviated, when you achieve the goal you are working towards, when a specific family problem is alleviated, when you recover from an illness or when someone close to you changes? I will show, as we progress through this book, that this general analysis of your life is seriously flawed. You will discover what you need to change, and you can begin to claim back the authorship of your life. It begins now. What this chapter will show is that when it comes to being happier:

Don't try to get good things to happen.
Don't pursue happiness.
Don't try to think yourself happy with happy thoughts.
Don't try to avoid unhappiness.
Don't try to change your character or personality.
Don't try to be consistent or normal.
Don't blame your childhood.

FIRST MYTH: THAT GOOD THINGS MAKE YOU HAPPY

The myth

This myth states that good things make you happy. It's a universal belief that good circumstances, good fortune, good luck, good wealth, good health and success cause happiness. It appears to be common sense, because everyone, you and I included, spends their life trying to improve their life circumstances, in the seemingly obvious belief that happiness is dependent on it. In other words, you believe that if you change some of the big things in your life—for example your job, your house, your income, your health, your marital status or your country of residence—you would feel significantly better. Also, you tend to believe the same thing about some of the smaller things in life, such as your car, your hairstyle, your clothes, your holiday destinations or your home decor. Why else would you do it? Why else would I do it? It's hard not to agree with this myth, because it's at the very heart of what you do every day. You are always trying to make things right, to change circumstances, to improve things.

It has been quite shocking to me, as I hope it will be to you too, to discover that this myth—that good things or events will make us happy—is seriously flawed! The evidence that refutes this myth is consistent, compelling and irrefutable. Contrary to what you want to believe, the circumstances of your life have only a very small effect on your well-being and happiness.

Research that refutes this myth

There are a number of significant and well-researched psychological reasons why your life circumstances have only a small effect on your happiness. They can be summarised as follows:

- We adapt very quickly to both positive and negative situations, so the effect of things is only temporary.
- We are notoriously bad at estimating the impact of events on us and therefore overestimate how happy things will make us.
- Our brain manufactures happiness out of every situation, so whether we are in prison or in paradise we can find contentment.
- We focus on the wrong things when trying to estimate what is good for us.
- Life circumstances only account for about a tenth of our happiness.
- We mistakenly think that security and status bring happiness.
- Human anxiety forces us to obsess about improving external circumstances.

We will look briefly at each of these compelling evidence-based principles in the hope that you will gradually begin to break down some of your beliefs and to make room for some new ones.

It has been shown that people—with occasional ups and downs, which are part of normal life—maintain a fairly stable level of happiness. Yes, unpleasant events bring us down and joyful events bring us up; but—and this is the point—we adapt to almost everything. What this means is that if you believe that your happiness will be affected in any significant way by attempting to change your life circumstances you are misguided. For example, research in this area has shown that wealthy people are no happier than ordinary people; that married people are no happier than single people; that attractive people are no happier than less attractive people; and that lottery winners are not much happier than ordinary people. It has found the same to be true for physical illnesses. For example, blind people are no less happy than seeing people. Smaller, less important things also seem to have little effect: cosmetic enhancement makes no difference to well-being, moving house has only a temporary effect on happiness and living in a place with good weather has no effect!

When you let the truth and implications of this in you will find it to be increasingly disquieting. Your brain will want to reject it, because you will be searching for exceptions; but the list of references supporting it is formidable.

People consistently overestimate the impact of things such as romantic relationships, job promotions, exam results, medical results, sporting events, being insulted, being cheated on, losing money, gaining or losing weight and moving home.

Though they are linked, the effects of money on happiness are small, with modest differences. Rich people who overspend can feel insecure; poor people who manage their budget are secure! The traditional Maasai of Africa are very satisfied with their lives despite having no income! Materialistic people are generally less satisfied with their lives than people who value friendship, parenting and love.

The conclusion that psychologists and researchers reach is this:

> You look in the wrong places for your happiness.
> You believe the wrong things will make you happy.

Six reasons why good events and circumstances have such little effect

(1) *The principle of adaptation*

The reason for good things having little power to lastingly affect our level of happiness and fulfilment is what psychologists have termed the adaptation principle. The principle is a simple one: we adapt very quickly to both positive and negative events. We do this to such an extent that, except for a short initial period, changes in life circumstances have very little effect on our lasting happiness and well-being!

Whether you are in prison or free, in hospital or at home, in the Arctic Circle or California, disabled or able-bodied, you have an astonishing ability to adapt quickly to your situation. Neurologists know that adaptation is a property of neurons: they habituate, firing less in response to stimuli that they have become used to. It's change that contains vital information of interest, not steady states. In other words, we react to novelty and new situations, but we adapt quickly to them. You may love an ice-cream cone occasionally, but not every day.

Your initial response may be, Well, if that's the case, what's the point of anything? Why try to change anything in my life?

What this book shows is that there is every reason to change—*but you have to change the right things*. The research shows us that you think you need to change your life circumstances but that, though it may give a temporary high, its effect fades quickly. If only ten per cent of your happiness can be attributed to your life circumstances, the other ninety per cent is still unexplained. We will get to that, because there is actually so much that can be done.

So, in the meantime, follow the ancient wisdom that says:

> Get rid of the mind that thinks
> 'This is good, that is bad';
> Simply live without such thoughts,
> And that life is good to live in.

(2) *The impact bias*

The second reason for us being incorrect about what makes us happy is that we are notoriously bad at estimating the effect that good and bad events have on us. Studies show that people tend to anticipate that getting more money will bring a lot of happiness for a long time, when, in fact, it brings some happiness and only for a little while. People keep making these kinds of forecasting errors. You and I are no different. Psychologists refer to this error in our ability to forecast how things will affect our happiness as the impact bias. It consists of two things: you consistently overestimate the positive effects that good events will have on you; and you consistently overestimate the negative effects that bad events will have on you.

An example of the first type of overestimation is that of winning the lottery. Studies show that, soon after winning the lottery, the winners return to their previous level of well-being. Conversely, with many life traumas, studies report that, after a few months of adjustment, people tend to return to their normal level of happiness. It really is quite startling to discover that our predictions are so poor.

(3) *The principle of poor forecasting*
Daniel Gilbert presents research that shows that we frequently make very poor decisions regarding estimations of the value of something we will do in the future. Economists, pension providers, mortgage financiers, banks, supermarkets, spin doctors, newspapers, political lobbyists and the entire retail industry have realised that the way in which we make decisions and evaluate things is crude, simplistic and unreliable. Psychologists and retail professionals have realised that we tend to use very simple rules when it comes to evaluating something.

Observe your own behaviour in the supermarket: you will buy something not because you value it but because its price has been reduced. We resist the notion that we are naïve and simplistic in how we evaluate things. We feel affronted when we have been caught out by a sales gimmick, and we will even rationalise it by saying 'Well, I knew I needed that.'

We are equally poor at evaluating things that are good for us. This relates to wearing seat-belts, communicating with our loved ones, seeking help, going to the GP, monitoring our cholesterol and so on.

Research shows that people are bad not only at predicting what they will feel but also at estimating how unpleasant an experience might be for someone else. For example, if I were to ask you the amount of time you would spend in a bad mood if I took away your car, or if you were much older and in bad health, your estimates of your unhappiness would be double what they are in reality!

> When it comes to bad things, you think things will be worse than they are.

I bet you, as a reader, this very day, are worried about a whole host of things that, even if they come to pass, will not make much difference. In the meantime, your desperately poor evaluation cripples you with unnecessary worry.

(4) *The principle of creative happiness*
Gilbert has shown that

> Well-being and happiness are created spontaneously and gradually out of adversity.

This is because of the remarkable psychological immune system we all have. Gilbert showed that our immune and recovery system is an unconscious system of cognitive processes that helps us change our views of the world so that we can feel better about the situations in which we find ourselves. This is an exceptional and quite extraordinary ability that we all have. The interesting thing is that, though you have this internal programme running all the time, you seem not to know it. You seem to grossly underestimate your response to adversity or good fortune.

Gilbert's studies show how our brain spontaneously begins to manufacture happiness as a response to the situation in which we find ourselves. Our happiness chemicals soon begin to kick in, regardless of our situation. Of course, there are limits to this; but the general point applies to most of us, most of the time. So happiness is not really a consequence of getting what we want. People can find almost as much happiness when they don't get what they want! You see this in people who have dealt positively with serious adversity. You may even look with pity on their positive attitude, as if it was a somewhat artificial yet noble denial of some awful situation. The research shows us, however, that the happiness we manufacture and develop in bad circumstances is as durable and as real as so-called obvious happiness.

(5) *The principle of the 'focusing illusion'*

Daniel Kahneman, a psychologist at Princeton University, in New Jersey, received the Nobel Prize in economics in 2002 for showing that our decision-making is not rational, and that, as a result, economic models, which assume rationality, are inherently flawed. Economists thought that if we know what people want or like we know what they will do. The belief of economists, that we assess things rationally, turns out to be quite false.

Kahneman introduced the term the 'focusing illusion' to refer to the process of exaggerating the effects of various circumstances on well-being by focusing on the wrong things.

What he also shows is that the amount of time we focus on something determines the degree to which it affects us. What people focus on when they think of their life is interesting. Kahneman's half-humorous conclusion, after many years of research, is that

> Nothing in life matters quite as much as you think when you are thinking about it.

In other words, merely thinking about something causes you to exaggerate its importance. There is considerable evidence that this is the case. So when it comes to your happiness and to what things in your life will make a difference, be very careful about what your mind leads you to believe.

(6) *The principle of evolution*
The principle of evolution is that we are hard-wired to behave in ways that ensure the survival of the species more than the well-being of the individual. Evolution and your 100,000-year-old brain want and need us to be far more concerned about security and survival than happiness and well-being! We are hard-wired to respond to impulses that make us do things that don't necessarily make us happy. For example, our sexual impulses, hoarding impulses, anxiety impulses, safety-seeking impulses and self-absorption impulses all prompt us to behave in ways that may be good for the survival of the species but that are not good for the individual. We interpret and react to our world in ways that ensure our survival more than our happiness.

The implications and consequences of the myth of circumstance
I can't overstate how radical these findings are. These are revolutionary findings that have not filtered down into common awareness. They go against everything you tend to believe about your own well-being and happiness. If you allow yourself to accept their meaning it would change your life in dramatic ways. We come to a startling possibility: we are stuck on our goal-hungry treadmill, running after things but staying in the same place, like hamsters on a wheel. The truth *seems* now to tell us that

> What happens to us doesn't matter half as much as we imagine.

So, trying to be happy by changing the circumstances of your life unfortunately doesn't work, because of how rapidly you adapt to the new situation. The consequences of the truth are:

1. *You can no longer blame your circumstances.*
2. *Your daily thinking will have to be revised*, because it's peppered with plans to change your life circumstances under the illusion that it will make you happier.

3. *Your goal-setting will have to be re-examined*, because you devote yourself to the pursuit of goals that won't make you happier.
4. *Money is not that important.* Our daily, yearly and lifelong obsession with money and the symbolic power and security it appears to offer is a false god.
5. *You waste time.* You may be spending enormous time and energy on things that you imagine will yield significant results for of your well-being, when, in fact, it may yield little or none!
6. *You can find happiness in a range of circumstances.*

And I have been like you too: always wanting to get things right, believing that one day soon everything is going to fall into place. Day after day, week after week, month after month, year after year, we postpone our bliss and happiness in our wishful, childish and somewhat innocent expectation that *soon everything is going to be all right*, not realising that it already is.

SECOND MYTH: THAT YOU SHOULD PURSUE HAPPINESS

This myth states in effect that happiness is something 'out there' to be pursued and found. It suggests that happiness is a goal that must be sought.

I imagine you are like me, going through life searching for something that will unlock some dormant potential within you. Like most people, you hope that you will find this magical something some time in the future. You convince yourself that certain impediments in your present life prevent you from finding it now, but you believe that it's there to be found. You might imagine that it will be a situation, an event, a relationship or an experience that will unlock this potential. In many ways, your life has always been like that: planning for the future and looking forward to times when everything would come together. You have gone through life with this mild rejection of the present in favour of something in the future; but, like the greyhound chasing the hare, that which you seek runs ahead of you as fast as you pursue it.

This myth of pursuit believes that happiness is a consequence of achieving your goals, of 'getting what you want' or of 'making your dreams come true.' It implies that, though it may not be experienced in the present, your true happiness will be achieved when you 'go after' and get what you want from life.

A great deal of research and ancient wisdom actually tells us that life is somewhat different. Real happiness is something we experience as we work towards a goal, not just when we achieve it. The emphasis on happiness being really about process rather than goal-achievement is emphasised throughout the extraordinary work of Ed Diener, who has been described as the 'Indiana Jones of happiness research.' What he concluded, after a lifetime of research on well-being and happiness throughout the world, is:

> *Happiness is a process, not a place. For ages people have assumed that happiness is an end goal. It is more of a process than an emotional destination. Happiness comes more from doing than from having or achieving. If you enjoy the pursuit of a goal more than the achievement of a goal your life is infinitely richer.*

If happiness is not our main goal we associate it with other goals. When we see happiness as a consequence of goals achieved we overlook the process and working side of happiness. We set off in pursuit of the good life, not realising that it's in the pursuit that happiness must really be experienced. The paradox is that the achievement of much well-being is in the honest and open endeavour to seek it. The hokey advice that we must 'stop and smell the roses' is not as superficial as it sounds.

Happiness comes more from active and rigorous effort than from the satisfaction of success.

If you are honest you will see that ninety-five per cent of your life involves good-humoured 'efforting' and striving. The achievement of goals represents an infinitesimal portion of your life. In truth, working *towards* the things you value is what brings authentic happiness. The happiness that comes from the achievement of goals is actually short-lived. The illusion that goal-achievement brings permanent fulfilment and well-being is seriously flawed.

Ordinary heroism

Well-being is a consequence not of having all your dreams come true but of being able to wring joy and happiness from the fate that you have been handed. 'Love your fate,' wrote Nietzsche.

I am deeply moved by people who heroically adjust themselves to the adversities of life and find joy in what appear to be abject situations. I am not so affected by those who make their dreams come true, make a million euros, become famous or win gold medals. I think particularly of family carers, people caring for seriously ill family members, people caught in poverty traps and still passionately loving the little life they have and people having small and modest goals and finding the greatest of pleasure in achieving them.

Well-being is not a consequence of crossing the line, winning the gold medal, being offered the job, becoming pregnant, getting married, getting a good pension or whatever other goals punctuate a life. Rather, happiness is what we experience along the way. The journey is far more important than the destination, the training far more relevant than the race, the climbing far more invigorating than reaching the summit. Shakespeare said that once you have achieved a goal it's finished: 'Joy's soul is in the doing.' The kingdom of Heaven in within you.

I recall a radio interview recently in which John Treacy, an Olympic silver medallist, was asked to describe how he felt when he had achieved his dream. His response, without hesitation, was 'Relief!' He described how his love was for the running and the training. Once he had achieved his goal he was free to move on to something else. Our true happiness is more in the practice than in the performance. I have to remind myself, even as I am sitting writing this, that the deepest satisfaction is in the 'efforting' and striving.

THIRD MYTH: THAT YOU CAN THINK YOURSELF HAPPY

This myth is that we are primarily rational and thinking people and that it's by reason and rationality that we change ourselves. It suggests that the path towards greater happiness is to be achieved more by positive and proper thinking than by anything else. It suggests that we will, once we realise what is right and reasonable, do what is necessary to address our well-being.

The dominant belief in a lot of popular psychology books—that positive thinking will make you happy—is an extension of this assumption. You believe that the way to overcome unhappiness is to think positively. Another variant of this myth is that if you know what you need to do to increase your happiness you will take steps to do those things. This seems logical and reasonable. Amazingly, these things are not true.

Despite our best intentions, we do not do what we know is good for our well-being

Seventy per cent of people who have lung cancer as a result of smoking continue to smoke! Ninety per cent of people who suffer from obesity continue to eat too much. Most us know what to do to improve all sorts of things in our lives, but we don't do it. Such simple things as losing weight, staying fit, saving money, working on relationships, studying for exams and eating healthily are all examples of areas in which, despite knowing what is good for us, we don't improve. We convince ourselves that we will act according to the correct information. But hardly a day goes by that you don't find yourself doing things despite yourself.

When it comes to your well-being, knowing what the problem is doesn't make a whit of difference, because the problem is not related to a lack of knowledge. You will surely recognise this in yourself: that the reason you continue to act in ways that are not really in your best interest has nothing whatsoever to do with lack of information. The truth is that you and I are emotional, symbolic, fearful and insecure in so many ways.

Extensive research in social psychology suggests that we are far from being reasonable and unbiased. To mention just a few (and, remember, all of these apply to you):

1. You have limited capacity to process information and are a cognitive miser who takes all sorts of shortcuts when evaluating things.
2. Your assessment of a person is not objective: you go with what you hear or see first.
3. You are biased towards negativity: once you form a negative opinion you will hold on to it tighter than to positive information.
4. Your thinking about why people are the way they are is resistant to change.
5. You judge people by how they look.
6. You stereotype people. You have enormous difficulty incorporating stereotype-inconsistent behaviour and traits.

7. You will readily make polarised judgements with exaggerated confidence about someone deemed judgeable.

Despite any claims you make to being unbiased in how you view people, to being flexible in how you see people and to using fair means of assessing people, you are influenced by many deeply set attitudes and convictions that are neither rational nor reasonable. We deal in, and relate to, symbols. We are deeply affected by our imagination, our aesthetics, our moral sensitivity, our spirituality, our unconscious motives, our emotions, our moods and our psychological needs for security, safety and significance. We bring all of this to bear on our happiness also. We don't think straight!

The principle of positive thinking

One of the dominant beliefs related to this myth of rationality is that you can think yourself happy, or that positive thinking will make you happy. It's this belief that triggered much of what is contained in this book. I realised that most of the advice given in books, newspaper articles and popular versions of psychotherapeutic methods was basically little more than—if you excuse my *trivialisation—just think happy thoughts and you will be happy.* Or *just do any of the things on this list and all will be well.* Without doubt, one's attitudes and thoughts about oneself and one's life are critical, but the reduction of well-being to problems of thinking is seriously flawed.

This idea causes more problems than it solves. It assumes that happiness is caused by thinking, and, as a result, that it's improved by thinking. The real problem with this is that it sets so many people up for failure. In fact, it's extremely shaming and demoralising for people to be told in effect to look on the bright side, to cheer up, to think positive thoughts, when they have been trying this for years. Just as many couples can't talk their way out of problems in relationships, individuals can't just think their way out of unhappiness.

What's wrong with me that I don't follow rational advice?

I'm sure you have seen article after article in magazines and newspapers offering the top ten tips for improving happiness or overcoming depression. They seem eminently sensible. You read it and think, That's so obvious. And there is a pause, followed by: But what is wrong with me that I can't follow simple advice like this? However, advice like this often leaves you feeling worse. Not only do you feel unhappy but you also now feel inadequate, because you seem unable to do what is rational and reasonable. Not only do you now feel inadequate and unhappy but you also feel stupid, because you are not thinking positively or following rational suggestions. So you feel unhappy, inadequate and stupid. To make things worse, you now feel helpless about what to do or say. You may even feel angry at those giving the advice for seeming to miss the point.

As I have mentioned, the unconscious and subconscious motives that affect our daily life, thinking and choices are huge. We superimpose reason on a great deal of our behaviour to try to make sense of it. We find it hard to make sense of our own behaviour because of the degree to which it's driven by powerful motives, emotions, values and preferences that are unconscious. So, from this viewpoint, telling someone to think themselves happy is trivialising and flippant.

FOURTH MYTH: THAT YOU CAN CHANGE YOUR PERSONALITY

Your set-range

Up to fifty per cent of your happiness is genetically determined.

All the leading researchers in genetics and psychology have shown that our enduring level of happiness is influenced significantly by our genes. The research suggests that our genes give us a set range within which our happiness falls; it also shows that it's difficult to change it and that 40–50 per cent of our felt happiness is attributable to our genes.

Your level of happiness tends to stay the same over a range of experiences. There are temporary fluctuations over time and temporary dips in happiness following distressing experiences, but you have a recovery system that keeps returning you, more or less, to your own water level of happiness. Therefore, because of this set-range, *regardless of whether things are right or not, your happiness and well-being levels don't change too much because of circumstances.*

Therefore, your happiness is highly hereditable—as are your anger, depression, anxiety and optimism, for example. What you feel today has been shaped to a large extent by your parents' genes! So the answer to the question whether you can become a happier person is 'Yes, but within some limits.'

The research sources

Research suggests that our set-point is very stable and that our happiness returns to the same level consistently. Follow-up studies suggest that people at the age of 35 have more or less the same level of happiness at 45, regardless of their life situation.

Studies in the 1980s on identical twins have become classics in the field of psychology and psychiatry, and they show conclusively that the psychology of identical twins is very similar. Studies on identical twins who have been separated at birth and brought up in different places have shown that the influence of the biological parents on their temperament is greater than that of the adoptive parents. All the studies have shown that between forty and fifty per cent of almost every personality trait is determined by genes.

We can inherit a gene for depression or unhappiness that lies dormant within us until we experience a certain level of stress, which can activate the depressive gene.

The discovery that we have a set-range within which we function is supported by some research that has shown that even dramatic experiences don't permanently change our set-point! In other words, our happiness level is resilient to even the most extreme good and bad events.

This is not surprising, when you think of it. If you think of families you have known you will be aware of the similarities between family members.

You often recognise family members by things as simple as the way they walk, the way they stand, a quality in their voice, their physical stature or the sound of their laugh. I have been mistaken for my father because of the tone of my voice on the phone. I have been in company when people have said, 'You must be Joe's brother!' If you think about the physical features and mannerisms common to family members it's not a big leap of logic to realise that a person's emotional temperament, disposition and mood are also influenced substantially by the same genes.

This is common sense to people who grew up in villages and towns in Ireland, because families were known to each other over the generations. The fact of genetic influences in families was unmistakable. It's far less visible in modern urban life, in which you haven't got small communities growing up together for generations. The genetic influence is much less visible.

It's a dramatic thought that, despite your life circumstances being totally different, what you feel in your life now may be almost identical to what your father or mother felt at the same stage in their life.

Caveats

It's important to realise that our genes define a set-range more than a specific stable point: what you have inherited is a range of happiness. You can influence where you are within that range. Within that range you have the potential to be happier.

There is also what is called 'the error of the average.' Not everyone stays at the average, and the average number includes people who are outside the average range. In other words, there are a lot of exceptions to the rule, and you may be one!

If you exaggerate this discovery and conclude that all of one's emotional well-being is genetically determined you miss the point entirely. We have no control over our genes, but we do have control over our activities and practices. We also have control over our attitude to our genes by means of self-acceptance and self-compassion, which promote well-being. There is an awful lot you can do to change the other sixty to seventy per cent of your well-being.

Following on from the classic research carried out by Caspi and Moffitt in King's College, London that showed that dormant depressive genes can be triggered into action late in life, it's equally possible that there is a happy gene dormant within you that could be activated by an extreme situation. It's possible that—in theory, at least—you have the potential to be exquisitely happy if you could only find the right kind of trigger to set it off!

Exciting and disappointing

The role of genes is both an exciting and a disappointing discovery. Why is it exciting? For a number of reasons. You don't have to give yourself such a hard time for being the way you are. You can't help at least half of it! When your partner complains that you are always irritable you can respond by saying that you are not responsible for at least half of your crankiness! More seriously, if you have a real sense of your inherited nature you can befriend yourself more and get off the treadmill of self-rejection. You can be more tolerant of yourself and others.

It's a little disappointing, I suppose, because it puts a limit on what you can change. It says that you can't fully change your nature. This is okay if your nature is more or less good and untroubled. However, if you suffer from serious emotional difficulties like your parents or grandparents it may not feel like good news. But the important thing to realise is that it only claims a small part of you. You are mostly free! However, there are real limits on what psychology and psychiatry can achieve.

Regrettably, these professions are very coy about their limitations, and this discovery forces we practitioners to face up to them. Certainly, in writing this book and studying these discoveries, I have found that what I say to parents has changed. For example, I talk a lot to parents about the temperament of their children and the limits of parental influence.

FIFTH MYTH: THAT HAPPINESS JUST HAPPENS TO YOU

Your happiness is determined mostly by your attitudes and activities and not by your life circumstances or childhood.

About forty per cent of our happiness is determined by our activities and attitudes. Our happiness is determined more by what we do and think than by our life situations—in fact, four times more. This is a radical finding. Happiness is something you do with your body and brain and is less to do with what happens or has happened to you!

Though your genetic set-range is something you inherit, the rest of it is up to you. You have to 'do' happiness. What the research suggests is that people who are happy with their life tend to make things happen, they remain curious and interested in life, they try new things, they stretch themselves and they manage their thoughts and emotions. Acting with intent, focus and purpose has a powerful effect on well-being. It's the thesis of this book that you can learn the disciplines of happiness once you know what you need to do.

From this viewpoint your emotional health and psychological wealth is shaped by what you do, how you think and what your goals are. Happiness is a verb. It's measured by the actions you take and your self-discipline in pursuing what is good for you.

Your childhood

Martin Seligman suggests that one of psychology's best-kept secrets is that the effect that your childhood has on your lasting well-being is limited, and that it's not half as significant as people think. There is often a tendency to over-psychologise one's past and to assume that everything one feels and thinks has been learnt. Well, experts are long past accepting that conclusion, given the findings regarding the influence of genes on personality. Your genes have a greater effect on your emotional life than your upbringing has.

Now, that doesn't mean that your upbringing has no effect. But, aside from traumatic abuse in childhood, the influence of your past is important but not defining. For example, I have learnt many significant things growing up, and a number of my traits have been shaped by past experiences; but, according to researchers, that influence represents a maximum of about ten per cent of my personality.

If we know our personalities and our inherited temperament, and if we are willing to work with what we have, we can, by means of good thinking, actions, feelings, virtue and right meaning, find the essentials of happiness in our own unique way.

SIXTH MYTH: THAT FINDING HAPPINESS SHOULD BE EASY

Happiness is not just about pleasant feelings—it's about work and toil.

Work is intimately related to happiness. Unfortunately, we tend to carry a prejudice against work and underestimate how critical it is to our overall well-being and deep happiness. The prejudice against it is expressed at different levels: socially, culturally and institutionally. At an early age children begin to draw a distinction between the freedom of play and the obligations and tedium of work. We grow up often equating hard work with punishment. People used to be sentenced to hard labour!

In appreciating the sources of rich happiness we must include work as foundational. We have examined the pleasures of life, but they are all meaningless without their counterparts: toil and work. We tend to prefer our comforts, our pleasures, our savouring, our loving relationships, our play, our joy and our purpose. However, as the research has shown, we tend to experience more flow when we are working. We seem to function at our best more when we are working towards some goal than when we are relaxing at home or 'chilling out.' Our peak experiences tend to be when we are at work, applying ourselves to a goal that engages us fully.

It is very important for us to allow ourselves to experience that reality fully. We often find ourselves complaining about work in a prejudicial way, and we are shy about admitting to the intense flow experiences we have when working. Inner prejudice can make a person come home from work complaining about, rather than praising, their day's toil. Similarly, when considering the work of home-making and child-rearing, a parent can downgrade the toil in such a way as to trivialise the flow that is experienced when working hard.

In understanding your happiness and well-being it's very important to resist the inner discrimination against your working self and to realise that it's a real source of contentment and well-being in your life. It's not until times of recession that one begins to appreciate the real personal, family and social value of work. We realise the necessity of work as a fundamental right, as a human need and as a source of deep satisfaction.

Unemployment is not just about money: it's about self-significance and self-status. Work is a psychological necessity, because it's an essential function of the human person to be working. Happiness, then, is not about nice feelings, pleasantness and cheerfulness: it's about good and meaningful work.

Various psychological research studies have shown that we can only tolerate doing nothing and relaxing for short periods. The human brain cries out for challenges, obstacles and learning. We need to be engaged fully in activities that are not about pleasure, comfort or pleasantness but that are about ordeal and challenge. As cows graze, birds nest and the tides ebb and flow, so we must work.

Effort, struggle, adversity, repetition and discipline are intrinsic to deep life satisfaction. Work, therefore, has this enormous potential for giving us purpose, meaning and deep happiness. If we try to design a life for ourselves that is void of work, effort, struggle and challenge we create a blueprint not for a happy life but for an easy one. And you don't grow, develop, find confidence and emerge from yourself in an easy life.

If people are encouraged in their jobs to value the intrinsic meaning and worth of what they do, they develop more pride and happiness in their work. If people are encouraged to see their work only in relation to what they get, or to how they are working for someone else's gain, they become depressed and cynical at their work. Pride in one's work, no matter how trivial the work may seem, enhances well-being in dramatic ways.

SEVENTH MYTH: THAT WE KNOW WHAT MAKES US HAPPY

> We are cognitive misers when it comes to happiness.
> We are not good at figuring out what makes us happy.

The social psychology of happiness

I will summarise and adapt some of the findings of social psychology, specifically in relation to our human understanding of emotional well-being, and I will present some arresting findings, which I hope will at least motivate you to think more critically about your happiness.

Everyone is an amateur social psychologist. Everyone is what social psychologists call a naïve scientist. In your attempts to understand other people's happiness you will, in naïve ways, look for motives, personality traits and external causes. You evaluate the cause of your own and other people's happiness in crude ways, in order to plan your actions. Research has concluded that we are all cognitive misers: that we are mentally lazy and use shortcuts in our logic in order to come to quick conclusions about what causes human happiness and well-being. In nine out of ten cases the following unpalatable facts can be attributed to you.

There is something social psychologists call the actor-observer effect, which means that, though you will blame others for their own unhappiness, you will tend to blame outside factors for your own. So if you are unhappy at home you will blame your partner. However, when your partner is unhappy you will blame them! When they are unhappy it's their fault; when you are unhappy it's their fault too! This is frighteningly common.

You are also likely to use what is called the false consensus effect, that is, you will see your own unhappiness as reasonable, normal and typical of people, while you will, more often, see your partner's unhappiness as abnormal, unreasonable and dysfunctional. You will often believe this quite passionately!

You also will tend to have what is called a self-serving bias: if you are happy you will tend to credit yourself; if you are unhappy you will tend to blame the outside world.

These are just some examples of the errors of our everyday social thinking about happiness and well-being. The explanations we come up with for why we are happy can have a profound effect on our emotions, self-concept and relationships with others. The fact is that your reasoning about this whole issue is poor. You are actually biased in many different ways. The most significant one is the fundamental error of attributing others people's unhappiness to their personality and your own to outside factors. What all these findings encourage us to do is to foster the virtue of humility.

EIGHTH MYTH: THAT HAPPINESS IS NOT A DISCIPLINE

The science of self-discipline and happiness

Throughout your day you have to exercise self-discipline or will-power in some way or other. You have somehow to resolve the tension between taking the easy or the harder path. Self-discipline is that ability to resist taking easier options and to maintain a commitment you have made to persist with some challenging task in pursuit of a goal.

What researchers have found is that will-power is like a muscle that needs to be exercised and trained. Roy Baumeister, at Florida State University, has studied self-esteem for decades and found that, when it comes to success in life, self-discipline is much more important than self-esteem.

The ability in children to exercise self-discipline and modest restraint has been shown to be predictive of success in later life. Amazingly, children who were able to resist eating some easily accessible marshmallows, which were set up in a controlled experiment, were better able to resist temptation as teenagers, to focus on their studies and to control themselves.

However, it appears that our energy for self-discipline is limited. Self-regulation depletes our mental energy. We can only exercise a limited amount of self-control at any one time. Although will-power is one of those 'invisible' concepts, it still has limits. When you have to control yourself in one area of life there is less will-power available to you in others.

Research also suggests that self-discipline can be improved and strengthened by practice on small tasks. A little bit of self-regulatory exercise seems to strengthen the will-power muscle. Other studies show that simple things, such as getting better sleep or boosting positive emotions, reduce the drain on will-power.

Learning self-control and self-discipline has a wide range of positive results: children do better at school and adults do better at work. Most people who succeed in life—be it in sports, music, business or study—will feel that their achievement has been a consequence of practising a few basic disciplines regularly.

There are positive consequences for every disciplined effort towards a worthy goal. When it comes to the disciplined care of one's physical health, psychological well-being and general happiness, there is a myriad of positive results. In fact, self-control and self-discipline are factors in virtually every major category of well-being.

Research has also shown that calling positive memories to mind can enhance self-control. Kathleen Vohs, at the University of Minnesota, has found that self-control is boosted when people conjure up powerful memories of the things they value in life. Laughter and positive thoughts also help people to perform better at self-control tasks.

Finally, some research suggests that people struggling with self-control should start small. A few studies show that people who were instructed for two weeks to make small changes, such as brushing their teeth with their other hand, improved their scores on laboratory tests of self-control.

A vow to do one of the activities described in the next section once every day may be a way to strengthen your self-control. This, apparently, gives you more will-power for bigger challenges in other areas of life. A fascinating study about these phenomena by Baumeister found that students who practised walking with a book on their head to fix their posture ended up eating better, studying harder and sleeping more. Without even noticing, they were making those changes.

One has a lot to gain from doing little things that require practice, repetition and success. Things that require discipline, such as painting, sewing, collecting, spring-cleaning, weeding, gardening and exercising, will have knock-on effects. And through the practice of small disciplines one moves to another discipline, because, gradually, it rewards itself. Self-discipline snowballs. Learning to bring your behaviour under control builds character. It makes you better able to achieve the things you want to achieve in life.

For exercises related to this chapter please check out
the book web site at

www.couragetobehappy.ie

Chapter 6

The 'how' of happiness

The twenty-one things to do

Disciplines of the mind

(1) Developing good thinking patterns
(2) Learning and practising optimism
(3) Avoiding obsessive thinking
(4) Focusing on the right things
(5) Learning and adventure

Disciplines of the body

(6) Having goals
(7) Engaging in 'flow'
(8) Savouring experiences
(9) Managing time
(10) Appreciating work

Disciplines of the heart

(11) Experiencing gratitude
(12) Valuing relationships
(13) Being kind
(14) Forgiving oneself
(15) Being of service
(16) Creating something new

Disciplines of the soul

(17) Being spiritual
(18) Participating in something larger than the self
(19) Overcoming adversity
(20) Cultivating meaning
(21) Using your character strengths

WHAT THE RESEARCH SAYS ENHANCES HAPPINESS AND WELL-BEING

I trust that you will find this section of the book as interesting as I found it when I began to look at the research about what makes a difference to your well-being. The activities presented here have been examined in robust ways and represent a fairly good summary of what has been found. These, of course, are not the only things that are influential, but they do represent a good guide for what you need to consider doing with the time available to you in life.

This is not my research: it's a compilation of what has been presented by Martin Seligman, Sonja Lyubomirsky, Jonathan Haidt, Daniel Gilbert, Russ Harris, P. Alex Linley and Stephen Joseph, Todd Kashdan and others. I wish to salute each of these authors, particularly the summaries of Lyubomirsky, Seligman and Gilbert. I have pulled much of this material together, summarised it in a particular way and added to it with other research.

Having a menu of things to do doesn't give you motivation or inspiration. You will recall that one of the limitations of many books on these subjects is that they present prescriptions for change without considering the essential missing ingredients of motivation, inspiration, will-power, existential purpose and discipline. You must have your own theology and inspiration that can motivate you to consider the maintenance of your emotional well-being and discipline. The 'doing' is not so difficult if we derive influence from these separate sources.

The most important discovery for me in all of this has been that the activities we engage in have symbolic importance and meaning. In this way, one operates at the highest psychological level and lives with integrity and passion. This is made possible by living the symbolic life, in which the small, ordinary activities in our lives are imbued with particular meaning. In this way, your job can be vocational, caring for a family member who is ill may be sacramental, being a parent can be sacred, personal development can be redemptive, life change can be a form of atonement, gratitude can be a thanksgiving, and daily rituals, such as physical exercise, can be a form of prayer. What I mean by these examples is that one's life can have a theological meaning that is passionate, inspirational and peaceful.

Activities can have elements that are of the mind, the body, the heart and the soul. In truth, all human activity serves a symbolic purpose. Each activity serves a transcendent function, as well as a literal, physical one. What we do has a meaning at a larger level.

THE 'DIAMOND OF ACTIVITIES' AND EXISTENTIAL SOLUTIONS

Mind, body, heart and soul

I examined most of the specific activities described by research as positively affecting happiness and realised that they could be meaningfully clustered under four headings: mind, body, heart and soul. These distinctions are important, because there are different gateways to well-being. Activities for the mind relate to any activities that produce a change in thinking style or thoughts, such as optimism or obsessiveness. Activities for the body have more to do with doing than thinking, and they include such things as setting goals and managing time. Activities for the heart relate to one's emotional attitudes, such as gratitude and kindness. Finally, activities for the soul relate to larger issues, such as meaning, suffering and purpose.

These four sections present the findings of research on what improves happiness in the areas of the mind, body, heart and soul. These activities are by no means exhaustive, but they have been widely researched by scientists in the field.

The 'disciplines of happiness' is the integration of the 'twenty-one things to do' and an experiential and theological framework that gives those isolated activities a location and meaning.

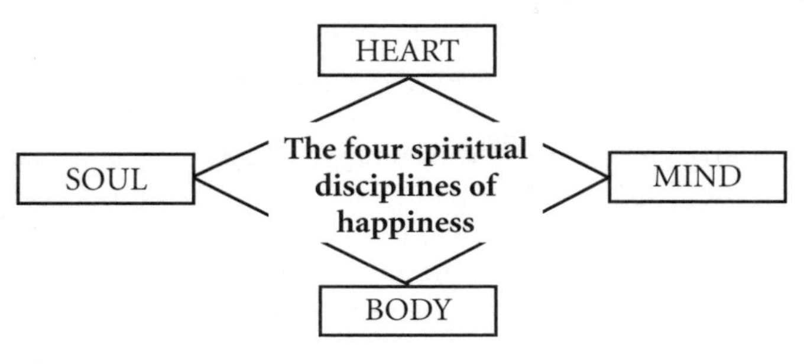

The following list summarises the content of this section.

- The section on the activities of the mind refers to how we develop well-being through clear thinking, learning and expansion. The evidence-based activities that produce happiness include thinking patterns, optimism, under-thinking, focusing, learning and adventure.
- The section on the activities of the body refers to the development of well-being through work, vocation and skill development. The evidence-based activities that produce happiness in this sector include goals, flow, savouring, time management, work and the practice of a craft.
- The section on the activities of the heart refers to the development of well-being through relationships and feeling. The evidence-based activities that produce happiness in this area include gratitude, relationships, kindness, self-forgiveness, service and creativity.
- The section on the activities of the soul refers to the development of well-being through transcendence, meaning, purpose and symbolism. The research-based activities that produce happiness in this area include spirituality and religion, participation, overcoming adversity and finding meaning.

Existential solutions

I have also included in each section the main activities by means of which humanity has sought happiness in life. These activities are the solutions that people have used throughout history to engage fully in the enterprise that is life. These solutions are the way we have resolved the tensions and conflicts of existence in order to meet our biological and psychological goals and to be happy. Humanity has developed its own ways of being in the world. These have been the basic ways that people have lived, coped and got the best out of life.

The nine broad solutions included in this section are: nurturing our spirituality, living a life of service, seeking love and attachment, being artistic and creative, giving ourselves to work, developing craft and skill, learning, giving symbolic meaning to everyday life and engaging in adventure. These are life commitments that strive for integrity and happiness. They provide symbolic meaning and avenues of self-expression. They are consistent with research and are a logical extension of our experiential analysis in earlier chapters. Therefore, each section on the research includes these ancient human solutions that support the research.

Our life satisfaction relates to how we cope, consciously and subconsciously, with our experiences of helplessness, vulnerability, anxiety, inadequacy, hopelessness, insignificance and isolation. Our solutions create our influence, safety, courage, hope, competence, worthiness, significance and belonging.

We are at our best when we can accept and endure the times of loss, terror, anxiety and uncertainty with patience, self-acceptance and a deep understanding of how life is. We are at our best when we appreciate that these experiences are just one aspect of life and that they are not permanent. We are at our best when we understand that our anxiety and vulnerability are not signs of weaknesses or of something from which we should take flight. We are at our best when we sense that our anxiety is the heartbeat of life and not the heartbeat of weakness.

We blossom when we have a very real sense of our ability to influence and shape our lives, when we feel safe and secure in the world, when we are fearless and courageous in how we live, when we overcome dread and have a real sense of optimism about our future, when we feel competent, capable and confident in our skin and when our sense of self-worth, importance and significance is strong and deeply felt. We find this not by trying to eliminate the effects of psychic seasons, emotional climates and harsh weather systems that batter the coast of our well-being: we find it by remembering the other seasons—by remembering who we are.

SECTION 1: DISCIPLINES OF THE MIND

Developing well-being through clear thinking, learning and expansion

This section presents five activities of the mind that have been shown to enhance happiness and well-being.

Research finding 1: Habitual thinking patterns determine well-being

Our thoughts are involved in almost every aspect of our happiness. They influence our emotions and our experience of things. A situation may evoke pleasure or distress, depending on how we think about it. Our happiness and well-being is determined in large part by our habitual thinking patterns.

Research suggests strongly that the cause of many of our emotional difficulties is our thinking. Cognitive behavioural therapy, one of the best-researched schools in psychotherapy, shows how negative thinking causes negative emotions and behaviour.

The fascinating thing about thinking patterns is that a lot of it is unconscious. Often we are not aware of the mental assessments that underlie our feelings of happiness and unhappiness. We have patterns of thinking that we imagine are logical but that are really habitual. We often fail to realise how arbitrarily we interpret the way things are. Our thoughts are often triggered automatically.

Your patterns of thinking can become predictable in the way that they evoke the same feelings over and over again. These feelings can then reinforce the same thinking. Therefore, your thinking and feeling get into a self-reinforcing loop that is very hard to break. For this reason you tend to come to the same conclusions about things and end up feeling the same way about life.

Therefore, research has revealed how happiness is related to our thinking, and it has found that we are not unhappy because of what happens to us, by and large, but because of how we attend, interpret and recall what happens to us! Happier people tend to recall more positive memories. They tend to look for, and attend to, positives and often think of neutral events as being positive. In difficult situations happy people tend to interpret their situations in the best possible way, finding some positives in even the most trying of circumstances.

Implications for your happiness

Your level of happiness will be influenced in large part by how you think and the importance you place on those thoughts. What you have to realise is that your thoughts are not objective facts but mental creations. One of the hardest things to counteract is our blind faith in, and reliance on, our thoughts. Our thoughts and conclusions about emotional things feel very certain but are often one-quarter reality and three-quarters creation.

These conclusions are not new. To different people the world can be a place of distress or a place of joy. 'To different minds, the same world is a hell or heaven,' wrote the American philosopher Ralph Waldo Emerson. The Roman emperor Marcus Aurelius wrote in the year 170 that 'the whole universe is change, and life itself is what you deem it.' Boethius, a philosopher in the sixth century, wrote that 'there is nothing good or bad, but thinking makes it so.' In ancient times, people realised that each individual perceived the world in a unique way.

The way you think about life and happiness is entirely unique to you. Your conclusions are not objective fact! When you get this into your head it can be a little disconcerting. But after a while you can begin to get a feel for the potential you have to think creatively about your life. There are no objective happy life circumstances: what creates happiness is how you perceive and then think about these circumstances. When it comes to happiness we think too much and then rely too much on that thinking.

Evolutionary psychologists have shown how our thinking brain has developed in part to identify threat. Evolution, as natural selection, is based on the survival of the fittest, and the people who survive are those who react quickest to threat. A simple rule that your brain has always followed is to *worry more about a bad thing happening than a good thing happening*. In other words, your brain is vigilant, on the lookout for things that might go wrong. This is called the negativity bias: our bias towards seeing or anticipating negativity. This trait of ours is a bit of a 'pain in the ass,' because it generates more unhappiness than is logically necessary.

Research finding 2: Optimistic thinking boosts happiness

Optimists maintain a high level of well-being and mental health. People who think optimistically cope very well during times of stress. Optimism promotes positive moods, vitality and morale. It boosts happiness, because it's self-fulfilling.

It may seem rather obvious to be stating that optimism is essential for your happiness and well-being. The important point, however, is that research shows that optimism can be learnt as a mental skill. Optimistic thinking, when you break it down a bit, can be practised.

People who come through tragedy or trauma effectively are those who practised optimistic thinking. In whatever difficult situation you find yourself, you can find grounds for hope.

Specific findings

Martin Seligman, following his research on learnt optimism, broke it down into five main characteristics. When a bad thing happens, such as failing at some task, an optimist assumes that it's not permanent and that it only applies to the specific area in which it happens.

Pessimists tend to assume that it is permanent, that it pervades everything and that it applies to everything.

To summarise, the beliefs behind optimistic thinking are that:

1. The cause of your distress won't last.
2. A bad thing only affects one part of your life!
3. You can't be good at everything.
4. When you persist at doing something it tends to succeed.
5. You have to practise having good thoughts to eliminate bad thoughts.

Talking to a group of school children recently, I summarised this research for them in this way:

'You can have big good thoughts and small good thoughts. When you have *big* good thoughts they are about everything, like knowing you're a lovely person, that your family is great and that God loves you. Big good thoughts make you think about tomorrow and next week in a good way, with a smile on your face. You can have small good thoughts like "pain will go away like a cloud," that your sore finger will get better and that you can learn your homework.

'You can't have happy thought clouds over you all the time, because things can sometimes go wrong. That's okay. Sometimes things can hurt. That's okay too. When bad clouds come along you can just wait, because they blow over after a while, and the sun is always there behind them anyway. So don't worry.

'Good thoughts make you happy. Three rules are: good things always happen; the sun stays shining behind grey clouds; and you are good at only some things, because no-one is good at everything. When you have good thoughts you are happier, you have more energy in your body and you are cheerful! Good thoughts are like food for your heart!'

Research finding 3: Obsessive thinking makes you miserable

One big problem we all have is that we think too much! When we think too much we can go round and round in circles trying to figure out how to solve some problem.

You think that, if you feel down, the best thing you can do is to think and think and think, thinking that you can think your way out of the bad situation! This going round in circles in your head is very draining. It's like when you're trying to read some intensely boring book for an exam and can't concentrate, and you end up reading the same sentence or paragraph over and over again: nothing goes in! Obsessive thinking is just like this. It is self-focused and inward. Despite how it might feel to the thinker, no insight is gained by this kind of thinking, and an inner light gets gradually dimmer, until clarity fades.

Obsessive thinking involves the inability to come to straightforward conclusions. There is this endlessly running tape of doubts, uncertainties and unsolved problems. The thinking causes bad feelings, which trigger the need to think more—and round it goes.

For most people bad feelings trigger this need to think, based on the assumption that one can think oneself out of these bad feelings. Very often, more thinking is the last thing that's needed. Instead, one needs a change in emotional state, activity or distraction. Obsessive thinking causes a whole range of negative consequences. The combination of obsessive rumination and bad feelings is lethal.

Rumination is also compelling: it pulls you in. What we have learnt is that, if you are distraught or upset, no insight is gained from more thinking. Rather, it draws on your mental resources.

How do we know that going-round-in-circles thinking is bad? Over-thinking simply makes you unhappy. In the face of even a minor unpleasant situation, such as a negative comment or criticism, your thinking can go haywire! Susan Nolen-Hoeksema, a professor of psychology at Yale University, compiled a great deal of evidence to show that it makes you feel more miserable and hopeless, and that round-in-circles thinking actually makes you less intelligent, less motivated and less alert. Combining such thinking with bad mood is a disaster: it makes you feel utterly miserable!

So, if you are one of these types, you have got to change it somehow, because even the slightest events can make you feel bad about yourself. You have got to sort this out, because it can have a desperate effect on you. Like a snake coiled around a struggling body, your round-in-circles thinking can strangle the life out of you.

The bottom line is that no insight is gained from endless thinking.

Research finding 4: Mental happiness is shaped by what you focus on

It has been found that couples who misremember their time together as being more positive than it was, turn out to be more likely to remain together than those who are completely accurate in their memories.

Sonja Lyubomirsky has shown that, with regard to the memory habits of happy people, there was no difference in the amount of positive and negative events they experienced but that there was a big difference in how they recalled events weeks later! Happy people tended to err on the positive side! Research also shows that, with a little mental effort, recalling good events from the past can boost well-being.

Make-believe is a perfect term to describe what a lot of your thinking is. Philosophers, psychologists and other wise thinkers have repeated that what makes us unhappy in life is not what happens to us, who we are with, the kind of job we have or how much money we have. No. The research supports all this ancient wisdom by showing us that our happiness is shaped by one simple activity: what we focus on and how we interpret it.

We can't focus on everything at one time. The thinking brain has to select what it wants to attend to.

What we focus on has a direct bearing on our feelings of happiness. So, of the thousands of possible things that we could focus on in our lives, unhappy people tend to focus on their own faults, mistakes and misfortunes. Happy people, living exactly the same life, would focus on the things that make them feel happier. It's as simple as that.

There is no objective truth about your life. Your happiness is entirely dependent on what you focus on. So you are not allowed to conclude that your life is unhappy, or that it's stressful, or that it's great, or that it's miserable. Your life really can be almost anything you interpret and imagine it to be! It's wonderful that you have this freedom to see what you want to see. Everything is in the background of your life: good things, bad things, wonderful things, frightening things, sweet things, boring things, interesting things, exciting things. But where are you going to focus the camera of your inner mind? This is the question for you. To where does the camera of your inner mind keep returning? If it's to the negative things, you are going to need to learn how to focus differently. This will require practice, repetition and self-discipline!

Imagination and make-believe

You must get this into your head: it's not possible to have an objective view of yourself or of your life. Your view is always subjective.

Philosophers, physicists and many other clever people have long since let go the ideal of objectivism, that is, the ideal that there is a fixed, rock-like and stable reality that you can understand.

You can achieve partial objectivity about simple concrete events, such as 'I have filled my coffee mug with coffee.' Fact! Simple enough; but the further out your focus has to go from the concrete the more variables there are that determine what is actually fact. For example, what colour is the wall beside you? Whatever answer you give is wrong, because it's dependent on the nature of the light in which it's seen.

Two things in life about which you can't have an objective view are your self and your life. There are so many variables that influence your answer. Your view is always subjective. I know you think you have an objective view. It feels like that because nature wants you to think that.

To conclude: *your mental life is mostly make-believe!* And that's bad? No, it's good, because this brings us to the point of realising the wonderful potential within all of us to imagine the life we need. The role of imagination is central to our emotional and mental life.

Your everyday life shows this to be true, when you look at it. Think of romantic love, for example, and your ability to see in someone what no-one else sees. Love is an act of imagination as much as it is any possible act of objectivity. What makes someone desirable is really a kind of idealisation, an act of imagination that highlights the qualities that make that person unique, special and out of the ordinary.

The reality of your life is open to huge interpretation. *The more depressed you are the more likely it is that your life appraisal is flawed.*

In the same way, positive thinking and optimism are like a subjective sweetening or the sauce of imagination that brings reality to life. Positive thinking makes a black-and-white life colourful, turns a cartoon strip into animation and makes Pinocchio turn into a real boy. Our thinking and how we view the world are what awaken reality.

Naïve and popular views suggest that imagination and fantasy are potential contaminants, because they threaten to obscure our direct perception of how things really are, how others really are and how we really are. However, what research and depth psychology teach us is that we must now think about imagination not as a wish-fulfilling illusion that contaminates objective perception but as a vehicle by means of which the world comes to life for each of us in a personal, vibrant fashion.

Reality-testing is really an experiential test of the openness to our imagination. People who hold pervasive positive thoughts about other people, no matter what they are like, tend to be happier and better liked in life. Nothing is good or bad, but imaginative thinking makes them so.

Research finding 5: Learning and adventure enhance well-being

The simple act of learning produces its own well-being. Nature needs us to be learning and has created us in such a way that when we are learning we are happier. Evolution has ensured that when we are trying new things we are developing and growing. Our mind is engaged in a different way when we are learning. Look at a child's face as they are engaged is some task or trying to master simple skill. It's fascinating to observe how nature gets our entire system to co-ordinate in its efforts to assist in learning. Concentration alone is fulfilling. When we are concentrating fully on anything we are fully operational.

The other life approach associated with happiness is the universal urge to adventure. I don't mean a 'discovering the world' adventure but the small adventures in life in which you push yourself well outside your comfort zone in order to experience the challenge and exhilaration of something new. This could be taking up an adult education course, moving home, deciding to have another child or re-prioritising your life. This is our urge to expand outwards into the world, to learn and discover new things. The adventurer is not satisfied with the five Ss of stability, security, status, safety and significance. Happier people detect their unhappiness and seek wellness beyond the safe frontiers of the self. There is a particular form of well-being that comes from pushing onwards and upwards. Inventors, adventurers and risk-takers live for this kind of life.

At the extreme end, being an 'adventurer' conjures up images of explorers, sailors, mountain-climbers and extreme athletes. However, we are more interested in the everyday versions of this human urge: the part of you that wants to do something different, that doesn't want dull routine and that seeks novelty, surprise and newness. This part of you wants to keep learning, seeing different things and doing things in a different way.

Curiosity is another human trait that takes you through this gateway. In fact, this has been well researched by Todd Kashdan, a psychologist at George Mason University, and his conclusion is that the exercise of one's curiosity muscles is essential to growth, development, happiness and well-being. When curiosity begins to die so too does the imagination. When we lose our curiosity we lose our sense of adventure and our desire to learn, and we lose the greatest source of well-being: learning.

SECTION 2: DISCIPLINES OF THE BODY

Developing well-being through goals, action and the body

Research finding 6: Having goals makes you happier

Find me a person who is happy and I bet you will find them decorating their home, writing letters, pursuing a hobby, educating their child, growing flowers in their garden or painting a picture in the back room. People are at their best when they are pursuing some goal in life. In many ways, a goal or aim in life is really the best future you can find for yourself. Research shows that people who have goals do better in almost every area of life. If you want to be happy, have goals. It's simple and effective. What psychological research proves beyond doubt is that working towards a goal makes you happy and is more important than attaining it.

When you are engaged in meaningful and purposeful activity it casts a warm light over everything. Happiness flows from committing yourself to something of simple value and working towards that goal. It may be tidying up the back garden for the summer or learning how to paint.

Goals are essential to our well-being, because they reveal our ability to overcome obstacles. They show us that overcoming small adversities is actually the excitement of living. A goal funnels all our psychic energy into small achievable things that we can do. They counter our deepest anxieties, which shiver in the shadows of consciousness. A goal is a very simple and unremarkable act of unseen heroism! Why? Because it means that you will—and that you do—persist, endure and thrive!

Goals set you free to enjoy the present, because they eliminate a lot of doubt about what you should be doing. If you don't know where you're going, every fork in the road creates anxiety and hesitation. When you do, decisions are easier. You can say 'No' to people and things that are not aligned with your goal. Therefore, when you have goals, whether large or small, you are able to have a focus in your life.

When you have this you are able to relax in ways that you can't otherwise.

It's not enough to just have any old goals: it's very important that the goals you have are *your own goals*, that is, that they are not goals you have downloaded from society, from your family or from your partner. No, you need goals that are yours.

Psychologists call these 'intrinsic goals'. These are ones that are meaningful and satisfying to you as an individual. They need to be inherently good for you and to enable you to develop as a person. Extrinsic goals are ones you follow for some external reasons, such as social pressure and 'keeping up with the Joneses'. These goals are not all bad, but they are not usually in the service of your well-being. Goals are appropriate if they are somewhat flexible, positive in orientation, achievable, and generate activity rather than thinking.

Your dream board

Here is a simple exercise: create a dream board. That is, get a good-sized cork notice-board with drawing pins. Place the notice-board on a wall where you will see it regularly and stick pictures or key words on it to symbolise your goals or dreams. Put up symbols of the dreams that excite you and that represent the kind of things you would like to do or achieve over the next five years or so. Your dream board will quickly become something you love. It will inspire you. It will change you, because you will be taking the little risk of converting your quiet and maybe unvoiced dreams into concrete pictures that you have to see regularly. Try it.

Finally, goals are self-fulfilling prophecies. Those who are more confident at the outset are more likely to succeed. There is plenty of evidence to show that doing something can change how we feel about any problem. Once you begin to succeed at your goal you will feel positive and bring more success. You will get a sense of the many benefits of having goals for yourself. Here are some of the obvious ones:

1. The process of working towards a goal is fulfilling and enhances well-being.

2. Goals give you a sense of purpose and control.
3. Goals bolster your self-esteem.
4. Goals add structure and meaning to daily life.
5. Goals help you to master your use of time.
6. Goals enable you to overcome crises.
7. Goals liberate you to enjoy the here and now.
8. Goals are self-fulfilling prophecies.
9. The feeling of being trapped is an extraordinarily common experience: goals open the prison door.

Achieving your goals is less important than the commitment to them. They are means as well as ends.

Research finding 7: Engaging in 'flow' activities improves your well-being

Have you ever noticed that there are activities you engage in during which you seem to lose track of time? Have you noticed how you can get so absorbed in certain activities that you lose touch with your everyday reality and get into a 'zone'? Though the activity might require a particular effort and concentration, it's as if that effort is exerted with a certain ease. This experience is aptly described by researchers as 'flow'.

It has proved to be an important phenomenon in relation to personal happiness and well-being, because when we are in flow a number of very important things are happening. We are usually functioning at our best, and at the same time we are replenishing ourselves. Flow does for your waking self what REM sleep does for your sleeping self. It repairs and replenishes your psychological life, because when you are in flow you are rediscovering your inherent adequacy and forgetting your daily stresses. Flow usually involves expanding the limits of your mind, striving to accomplish something challenging or novel, being open to new experiences and learning and discovering rewards in the process.

Not every activity produces flow. Watching television or doing one's accounts, for example, usually doesn't create feelings of flow. Examples of activities that might produce flow include reading a book, baking a cake, helping someone, hill-climbing, cleaning a room, jogging, painting, studying and learning a skill.

The characteristics of flow activities

- They are challenging.
- They grab and hold your attention.
- They draw on your strengths.
- There is a form of total absorption.
- They lead to accomplishment and improvements.
- There is a suspension of consciousness: time passes easily.
- Emotions and sensations tend to move into the background.
- They tend to trigger self-improvement.
- They are an antidote to self-obsessiveness.
- They enhance one's personal strengths and virtues.
- There is a deep satisfaction and happiness when the activity is consonant with some noble purpose.

The benefits of flow

- It is fulfilling.
- It tends to provide a 'natural high'.
- Flow activities are intrinsically rewarding.
- We test ourselves when in flow, which stretches the concept of self.
- We really enjoy the struggle of self-improvement.
- When in flow we are not preoccupied with the goal but with the process.
- When we are 'flowing' we are usually without stress.

Comparing the comfortable life with the satisfying life

Take a look at the following table. The activities in the left-hand column tend to produce a satisfaction that goes beyond the activity itself. The pleasant things in the right-hand column, while essential and necessary, produce pleasure that is transient. Martin Seligman in *Authentic Happiness* discusses this issue in depth and points out that when you engage in activities that are deeply satisfying, that is, that are more than simply pleasurable, it usually involves accomplishing a goal and growing as a person. For example, people who exercise various forms of kindness report longer lasting good feelings than people who engage in self-indulgent pleasures.

The 'satisfactions' produce emotions that are gratifying to the self, accentuate a quiet sense of purpose and relevance, and evoke a contentment that lingers long after the activity has ceased. In relation to flow, there is usually a loss of self-consciousness and a complete absorption that is freeing for the self. For a while, it's as if the thinking brain can go into hibernation and can regenerate itself.

On the other hand, 'pleasant things' produce feelings of pleasure, enjoyment and relaxation that can punctuate a person's day and can make it worth living, if only for the passing moments of delight.

The interesting thing for most of us is that we have a tendency to choose the pleasant things in life more than the satisfactions, despite the real investment in well-being that results from the latter. To choose the activities on the left over the ones on the right is not at all easy. This is of real concern and is, I believe, very relevant to the education of our children.

Satisfactions	**Pleasant things**
Painting a picture	Watching television or a film
Helping a neighbour with something	Having a hot shower
Teaching your child something new	Having a glass of wine
Reading a book	Skimming through a magazine
Going hill-walking	Going shopping
Exercising	Eating a nice meal
Creating something new	Enjoying an ice-cream
Fixing something with your hands	Lying on in the morning
Meditating or praying in the morning	Having a morning coffee
Studying	Surfing the internet
Training for a team sport	Spending time with friends
Making love	Having sex
Learning a musical instrument	Listening to music

Effects of engaging in deeply satisfying activities that produce flow	**Effects of engaging in pleasant activities that produce pleasure**
An experience of growth	Transient pleasure and contentment
A sense of accomplishment	Simple enjoyment and gladness
Quiet contentment	Excitement or thrill
A feeling of improving oneself	Relaxation
Satisfaction from learning	Temporary relief from stress
Long-lasting good feeling	A sense of enjoying the moment
A sense of purpose and relevance	A feeling of being rewarded for effort
Contentment	Fun and good feeling
Self-worth	Light-heartedness
Enhancing of strengths and virtues	Enhancing self-consciousness
Being absorbed in flow	Being absorbed in pleasure
Building up store of a self-confidence for the future	Can become addictive as a form of relief from stress.
Investing in one's future	Consuming for the present
REM sleep	Naps
The 'morning after' is usually good	The 'morning after' is not always good

Teachers and parents are intuitively aware that engaging in the satisfactions and flow-producing activities is essential for personal development and character formation. Children who do these things are happier and more resilient. One problem is that most of the pleasant things are now easily accessible through modern technology and the internet (music, films, social connections and so on), making it more difficult to expose our children to the activities that produce deep satisfaction.

Have you ever noticed a feeling of being down that follows spending a night watching television, a night out drinking or gorging oneself on a high-calorie meal? And have you noticed the sense of well-being that follows going for a walk, completing some long-avoided task or helping a family member? So, while we need our pleasures, nights out and good food, we need the other activities even more.

Anti-depressant

It's very interesting to examine this from the viewpoint of anxiety, depression and stress. Satisfying activities that produce flow are really anti-depressants, because they diminish the self-absorption that is very much part of clinical anxiety and depression. In fact, investments in the satisfactions, if one could be disciplined about them, would be far more powerful than most medications. The loss of self-consciousness and the elimination of self-indulgence and self-absorption make anxiety and depression impossible.

Flow and deep satisfaction

To summarise, there is a world of a difference between the comfortable life and the deeply satisfying life. The former evokes images of someone relaxing in their nice house, with plenty of money and with one's needs catered for. The latter evokes images of someone engaging in something deeply satisfying, such as a community project, travelling or doing something with a loving family. Pleasures and comfort activities come from pleasing the self, while satisfaction comes from overcoming a challenge or developing as a person.

Although we may want the comfortable life, we need the satisfying and rich life; we may want to win the lottery, but we need activities and goals that inspire us; we may want a stress-free life, but we need challenge; we may want more money, but we need more flow.

It's important to understand that there is a deep satisfaction to be found in life that has nothing to do with having fun or being outwardly cheerful. There is a deeper contentment and satisfaction that arises from applying oneself fully to the task at hand with commitment and relish. In a strange way, hard work never causes depression. Working towards a goal can provide a deep-set happiness that flows under the surface of everyday life, particularly when it's applied to something purposeful and engaging. The farmer tilling the field late into the summer nights can be happier than the wealthy man sipping Chardonnay on his yacht in the Mediterranean.

Research on flow shows that peak experience and peak performance go hand in hand! To increase the likelihood of flow we therefore need to engage in activities that are not too easy or too difficult but that are challenging.

Research finding 8: Savouring life's joys and pleasures improves happiness

Life's delicious moments come and go like days, leaving nothing but a regret that they were not appreciated. It's as if God sprinkles gold petals on our day but we only notice them when they are gone.

Savouring is a lovely word. To savour is to focus one's attention on the pleasure of the present experience and to enjoy it consciously. It's a step up from simply enjoying it: it's to bring that enjoyment into consciousness and to appreciate it at another level. It's an ability that we all neglect because it appears self-indulgent. However, when one savours one's experiences with a deep sense of gratitude, the disposition is not indulgent but thankful. It comes from an appreciation rather than an entitlement. When you savour you luxuriate in the pleasure of being alive in the moment: you bask in its light. It's the state of enlightenment when one appreciates the present with an acute sense of its preciousness and transience.

Savouring doesn't come easily, because of our tendency to gorge and rush through pleasant experiences. We rush through things because we are moving to the beat of a stress that plays through our lives. Often it's not until one goes on holidays to get away from it all that one gives oneself permission to do this. But it's very important not to let those moments, experiences and passing delights pass without a savouring appreciation.

Consistent with the theme of this book is the fact that it requires self-discipline to be able to savour the ordinary moments that go unnoticed. It's tragic that it's often only when we are ill, or when someone we love is ill, that we are shocked into the urgency of savouring life. Until then we realise that we have been moving through life as if hypnotised by its fragility. Even minor illnesses can have this effect. When you come down with a stomach flu or a heavy cold you appreciate everything you had taken for granted when healthy. However, the point I want to make is that the reason you are shocked into this realisation is that savouring doesn't come naturally. You have to practise it!

Savouring the past, present and future!
People who do savour the experiences in their life tend to be happier, more confident and more enthusiastic about their lives. In research studies, people who were instructed to savour the events and experiences in their week reported increased happiness and decreased depression. This is also noted in the case of the elderly. Retrospective savouring is extremely important for people. To be able to think back on past moments, to savour them and to retell them is very important for people in later life. It's also important for families and family definition. You may notice how important it is for your own family to gather together and savour past incidents, funny stories and holidays. Such savouring is natural and essential.

Studies have shown that if you reminisce regularly about good events in your past it will increase your happiness. Also, the more intense and visual these recollections are the better you feel. So this kind of thinking is not 'dwelling on the past' or 'resting on your laurels'; it appears to be a charging of batteries for the present, because the body really doesn't distinguish between past, present and future—it just recognises and relishes positive emotions, even if they are artificially created!

Stress
Being able to savour things in life means that you are able to blot out and appropriately compartmentalise the negative, which is a great mental skill. To savour the present you need to be able to close the door on your problems. As we get older, perhaps we regret not having savoured the pleasures of youth?

Research finding 9: Managing your time is essential to your well-being

The manner in which we use time is a very real predictor of our well-being. Daniel Kahneman, an eminent psychologist, has concluded that, of all the things we can do, '*time use may be the determinant of well-being that is most susceptible to improvement.*' Time is probably our most neglected resource. Time affluence, according to research, is a much better predictor of well-being than material affluence.

How we use and appreciate time is therefore critical to our well-being.

Time is a measure of our mortality. Time would be of little interest if we were all immortal beings. It's the symbol of our human condition. The clock and the calendar symbolise human life and its preoccupations. It's our most consistent reference point through our day, our week, our year and our whole lives.

Your time is your greatest commodity, and if you don't care for it like a precious life source you give it away in ways that can cause you great stress. Your time gets handed over to others.

The symbols of the clock and calendar

When we only see time and the clock as measures of the degree to which we have maintained a kind of daily perfection, we are in trouble. We are in trouble because the clock has then become a reminder of our inadequacies, a measure of what is not done and a measure of our control and management of our life. Such phrases as 'I'm late,' 'I haven't got enough time,' 'I wish I had more time' and 'Where has all the time gone?' are ones you use many times a day.

There is a web site called 'Death Clock', which is both funny and alarming. You enter your vital statistics, and the site calculates your estimated time of death and, from that, how many hours you have left to live. It then sets its digital clock to a countdown. As each second ticks by, as it counts down towards zero, you have an alarming awareness of how time is rushing away from you. As you are just sitting there at your computer you get a sense that your invaluable time is ticking away. Try it.

Time pressure

Almost everyone is under some form of stress-creating time pressure. This time pressure inevitably corrodes well-being. Most people have many pressures and demands on their time that create stress. It eats away at happiness. We resent the time we invest in things we don't like, and we feel frustrated that we can't find the time to do the things we do. We often feel that we have to invest bad time (weekdays) in order to gain good time (weekends). We get anxious, stressed and depressed. We are too busy—or so it seems. Daniel Kahneman actually discovered that we don't enjoy our weekends as much as we think and that we enjoy our weekdays more than we realise.

Meaningful time use

You need to have the feeling that you have sufficient time to pursue activities that are meaningful to you. Even if you don't use that time you do need to know that it's accessible to you. It's also important that you know what is meaningful and beneficial to you. Very often you will be wrong about what is good. For example, relaxing and having downtime may, more often than not, be less rejuvenating than you imagine. Though you may imagine that your evening activities are relaxing and good for you, they may be quite the opposite. Eating, watching television, staying up too late, drinking and 'messing around' may actually be more likely to result in mild disease than in rejuvenation.

If you can use your time to do the things that improve your happiness, it will be used well. For example, working on small goals, savouring moments, doing something that creates flow, practising optimistic thinking or creating a 'dream board'. What this section of the book emphasises is that there is so much you should be giving your time to.

Emotions as time-sensitive

Finally, you may never have considered how your emotions are time-sensitive, that is, that their meaning is relative to time. For example, hope, trust, faith and confidence are all future-oriented emotions that prepare us for a positive future. Emotions that are sensitive to the past include regret, satisfaction, pride and fulfilment. These are emotions that refer to how we have been. Emotions that are present-centred include pleasure, joy, calmness, happiness and flow. Emotions about the future tend to be more spiritual, those about the past tend to be more soulful and those in the present tend to be more mindful.

Research finding 10: Appreciating the value of your work is vital to your well-being

This approach or gateway in life is less to do with service than with the innate satisfaction and gratification that comes from work, productivity and investing oneself in a discipline or skill. The deep satisfaction of work provides a non-verbal meaning. It's physically satisfying and is, in many ways, our purpose. There is little choice here for us, because productivity and participation are also socially necessary. Therefore, work is as essential and natural to the human species as grazing is to cows. It's what we are created to do. To the degree that we can invest ourselves in work and skill-development our well-being is considerably enhanced. If that work can be imagined as vocational or as a form of service, all the better.

Work aside, having things in one's life that could be described as a skill or craft is deeply rewarding. We are by nature industrious and hard-working: sitting still is not an option.

It's important, then, that one's life is shaped around one's vocation; if it's not, some changes need to be made. Similarly, learning any new skill is as powerful as counselling or therapy. The concentrated mind is a mind at its best.

SECTION 3: DISCIPLINES OF THE HEART

Research finding 11: Practising gratitude improves happiness

Gratitude is the most generous of virtues. It's the feeling of being blessed to have received the various gifts that life and other people have given you. Gratitude comes from a humble heart that doesn't feel entitled to much and because of that is deeply appreciative of everything. It's a sense of thankfulness and appreciation for life.

Experiencing and expressing gratitude are core ingredients of well-being and happiness. They are an antidote to negativity and disgruntlement. Their opposites are dissatisfaction and resentment: the feeling that one doesn't have enough. Gratitude is more than saying 'thank you': it's letting yourself experience and sense how blessed you are.

One can experience gratitude towards life, towards your God, towards Providence. It can be in a consideration of the essentials of life, such as health, family security and the basics of living. One can experience gratitude for other people and what they give to you, or for many of the small things in life. You can learn to savour these things from a position of gratitude.

All the research shows that those who are consistently grateful are energetic, happier, hopeful, positive, helpful, empathic, spiritual and forgiving. It also suggests that those who experience and express gratitude are less negative, depressed, anxious, lonely, envious and neurotic. It was hard to know if positive traits caused gratitude or if gratitude caused positivity—so they tested it. They found that gratitude actually elevated happiness and health. It works. They even conducted research with patients who had chronic ailments and found that gratitude exercises made a significant difference to happiness.

So how exactly does gratitude boost happiness?
Expressing and experiencing gratitude boosts happiness because it—

- promotes the savouring of life's gifts
- bolsters self-worth, as it counteracts our tendencies to be negative
- helps people cope with stress by reframing life experiences and events
- is a deeply human response to overcoming serious adversity, because these experiences remind us of what we have
- encourages moral behaviour, because when people express gratitude it raises their standards
- helps build social bonds and love and improves relationships
- inhibits comparisons with others
- dissolves negativity, with which it's incompatible
- inhibits 'taking things for granted'.

Paths to gratitude
There are many ways in which you can develop and accentuate this faculty. You can find time to contemplate your life. You can look for the extraordinary in the ordinary and everyday things that make up your life. You can do this with a sense of humour and cheerfulness. You can do what we used to do as children: say night prayers to thank *your* god for all the little things of your day.

Research finding 12: Valuing relationships

Friendship doubles joy and cuts grief in half.

Relationships: The currency of well-being
If you wanted to guess if someone was a happy person or not, and you were only entitled to have one piece of information about that person's life, knowing the status of their social and personal relationships would be the most reliable predictor. If you want to know how happy someone is, see if they have good relationships with family and friends. Relationships, friendships and social connections represent the canals through which happiness flows in the city of your

life. Unhappy people tend to have brittle, unstable relationships; happy people tend to have stable ones. A happy person usually has a circle of friends, a supporting family, an intimate companion and a good pal. Good relationships create happiness, and happy people tend to generate good relationships. There is a reinforcing causality between them. All the research supports these conclusions.

We are social creatures who function at our best in the context of human supports. Though we experience ourselves as solitarily functioning beings, we can often underestimate how social we really are. If alien beings were to examine how we function they would first and foremost describe us as working in families, communities, societies and cultures, with each individual fitting in to the roles and responsibilities of civilisation. I don't mean that in a negative way but as a positive illustration of how embedded we all are in social networks. There is an Irish proverb that says:

I scáth a chéile a mhaireann na daoine.
People live in each other's shadows.

In other words, our lives are lived out in proximity to family, community and friends, and this is an essential quality, gift and, at times, challenge of life. From the moment of conception, right through the stages of life, each person lives and functions in the context of social relationships.

Family

Family is the basic unit of our birth, formation and development. The attachment of infants to parents is intense, and the child doesn't reach maturation and self-sufficiency until their late teenage years. This is quite unlike other animals, whose offspring have to become independent very quickly. We are indeed the most social of beings. In every culture, family has enormous value. The bonds you have with your family are physical more than intellectual. These are the ties that bind people together and that create the vessel within which happiness grows.

Attachment as the basic human need

Attachment theory, as formulated and developed by John Bowlby and his researchers, has shown how attachment to others, particularly our primary care-givers, is the emotional blueprint for how we engage with the world and with life. The infant's need for contact, security, touch and nurturing is more important than its need for food. The bonding is innate and stays with us throughout life; elderly people still long for the reassurances of social touch and connection.

Everyone builds up an internal working model of relationships that guides them through life. The style of attachment you had as an infant is still at work now. If your relationship with your mother was an anxious one it's probable that your relationships in adulthood show the same characteristics.

Happiness and well-being are nurtured in a deep and non-verbal way by good and secure relationships. Finding happiness without taking care of, and spending time on, one's relationships is difficult. An evening out with family or friends does more for your well-being than an evening of watching television.

It's in relationships that we engage with the deepest passions, joys, emotions and dreams in life. All our songs are love songs. It's in relationships that we feel both the most vulnerable and the safest. They are our home, whether we like them or not. And even when we are far away, and have escaped the noise and clutter of relationships, our emotions, dreams and inner language are coloured by how we have related to those we love. We can't really ever leave home.

Research finding 13: Kindness breeds happiness

Compassion is the basis of all morality. (Schopenhauer)

Research shows that when we are kind to others and act in kindly ways we are happier. Research in social psychology has shown repeatedly that being kind and helpful to others changes the attitudes of the helper. Researchers have found that caring for other people does more for the carer's sense of well-being than for that of the recipient. The cliché that it's better to give than to receive holds much water.

Showing kindness has a number of positive effects for you:

(1) It cultivates your sense of gratitude.
(2) It improves your perception of yourself as a person.
(3) It promotes compassion.
(4) It makes you feel connected and liked.
(5) It contributes to meaning and purpose.

Researchers have noted that people going through life tragedies or crises who choose to help others experiencing similar things do better than those who don't. Viktor Frankl noted that some prisoners in Nazi concentration camps, no matter what degradation they were suffering themselves, were still able to show genuine kindness to others by sharing their rations, clothes and food, and by encouraging, supporting and helping other prisoners. Frankl noted that these people were stronger and coped much better during and after their ordeals.

The willingness to act in some kind way, no matter how small, is itself good for your soul and is life-giving in itself. In choosing to act in some deliberate way your inner sense of yourself is elevated.

The type of kindness we are looking at here is more deliberate, novel and out of the ordinary than usual kindness. From the viewpoint of happiness, the research recommends that you do some kind things that are a bit different from what you normally do and that are meaningful in some special way. Being intentionally kind, rather than spontaneously kind, does not diminish its positive effects.

Research finding 14: Self-forgiveness

There are two kinds of self-forgiveness necessary in life: forgiving ourselves for what we have done; and, more importantly, forgiving ourselves for who we are. I have found in my work in counselling that most people need self-forgiveness for what they have *not* done rather than for what they have. Most people carry regrets about choices they didn't make, goals they didn't pursue, dreams they didn't follow and self-discipline they didn't apply. Most of us pull our regrets behind us like weights on a leash. We haul our regrets around as if accepting our inadequacies. We fail to realise that we don't need to carry these things. We need to forgive ourselves and let go of the many past wrongs we imagine we have committed.

Whatever decisions or choices you have made in the past, you made the best decision you could make at that time, given your life experience, your limitations, your situation and your motives. You made the best decisions you could make with the resources you had available to you and with the level of self-confidence that was possible for you. You have made the best decisions possible. That those decisions turned out later to have been unfruitful, or maybe downright bad, doesn't in any way undermine this truth. Your self-forgiveness is achieved in accepting your limitations, your humanity and your best intentions.

When you think differently about your past you feel differently. Okay, you have your regrets; but let them go, because they are based on a false sense of yourself. You are entitled to feel satisfaction, contentment, fulfilment, pride and serenity about even your past failures. Insufficient appreciation and savouring of the good events in your past, and overemphasis on the bad ones, is the culprit that undermines serenity, contentment and satisfaction.

Forgiving ourselves for who we are

Most of us are in conflict with our very humanity. Most of us struggle against some of the very qualities that make us human. Most of us blame ourselves for our broken humanity. Most of us think that there is something wrong with us because we occasionally feel inadequate, vulnerable, helpless, afraid, despairing, isolated, insignificant and flawed. Yet these are the characteristics that you have been handed by Creation. You are wounded and imperfect, and you can at times hate yourself for it.

A form of internal forgiveness is necessary to release you from the burden of trying to be different or perfect. You are absolutely beautiful and perfect. And you need to forgive yourself for your imperfection—to breathe into your humanity and love it. Though you may not believe in a god, imagine a god that speaks the words you need to hear:

> I forgive you for all your inadequacies.
> I forgive you for all your mistakes.
> I forgive you for your weaknesses.
> I do so not because you have been weak or bad
> But because you need to hear from me
> What you don't say to yourself.
>
> In truth, there is nothing for which you need forgiveness
> Except how you reject yourself,
> The child that is you.
>
> Go out and play.
> Be carefree in the fields.
> Dance in the quiet of your heart.
> For soon the sun will set,
> And I will call you home to sleep.

Research finding 15: Being of service to others

The virtue of service is an existential and theological response to life. This is the universally practised and valued virtue of wilfully and joyfully giving to, and caring for, others. Service, in this instance, is not self-surrender, self-sacrifice or self-diminution but the meaningful, uncomplicated pleasure and meaning that a person can achieve in caring for other people. It happens in every kitchen of every house in the world. There is an innate desire in parents to care for their children. There is a similar caring of partners, friends, family and neighbours.

However, service is larger than this, and it's seen in how a mother, for example, will find wellness, happiness and joy in the giving of herself to her family for her entire life, and she will find great joy in that vocation. It's seen in the father who spends his entire life working in a factory in order to care for his family. Their drudgery and toil is taken with some ease—if not joy—because the meaning of the work is to be of service. The purpose of their life becomes the dedication of it to the betterment of those they love. It happens all over the world. Therefore, when you feel down or stressed by family or work, it's often helpful to reframe your feelings in the context of the life of service you have chosen, happily; to realise that the things you complain about are, despite the irritations, the very things that give meaning, purpose and trajectory to your life; and to know that your service—your vocation—is deeply purposeful.

It's the most underrated of human virtues. When it goes unrecognised and unapplauded it's tragic. It's likely that service gives your life meaning and enables you to endure and tolerate much distress. It's seen in the joy that emerges within you when you see those you love blossom, or in the pain you experience when those you love are hurt.

When you believe that your purpose is not just to find your own happiness, or to do what you want, or to follow your own dreams, but is also to enable and foster the dreams of others, your sense of what gives value to your life changes. If you measure your happiness and well-being only by how much time you can invest in pursuing your own goals, all the other aspects of your life are unnecessarily downgraded.

There is such unrecognised heroism in the everyday life of ordinary people. The great and glorious masterpiece of humanity is not the sacrifice of men for the their country's flag but the service of parents for the well-being of each other and their children. Herein is the hidden purpose and passion of life. Here are our unseen heroes. Domestic service gets no medals.

Research finding 16: Being creative

Creativity and art are universally recognised as ways in which humanity leaves evidence of itself on the planet. At a personal level your acts of creation are a powerful way of experiencing significance, potency, influence, and worth. The creative and artistic impulse expresses the deepest things about human nature. When I speak of art I am not speaking of painting or sculpture but about the thousands of unseen artistic impulses and creations of the human artist—you. The little ways in which someone makes a cake, decorates a Christmas tree, arranges flowers, tends to a garden, puts together an outfit, tidies a child's room—these are all artistic reflexes and impulses to make something new, to create something personal and to give expression to some inner desire by means of symbols. These are all forms of art. More refined art, such as writing, painting, sculpture, poetry and film-making, is at the upper, more visible end of what is usually called art. These forms are extremely important to our social and personal psyches. Architecture and ancient historical creations also have huge significance for placing ourselves in time and history.

But what has this to do with well-being? Well, for yourself, it's about appreciating how your own small everyday acts of creativity are important and about how living a creative life is an essential expression of well-being. You might not think of yourself as creative in an artistic sense, but you are—it's just recognising how. Maybe you talk creatively; maybe your sense of humour is imaginative; maybe the way you tidy your house is creative; maybe the way you think and solve problems is creative; maybe your parenting is creative; maybe your cooking is creative. Maybe having children is the ultimate act of your creativity—to create new life and prepare it for the world.

SECTION 4: DISCIPLINES OF THE SOUL

Developing happiness and well-being through transcendence, meaning and purpose

Research finding 17: Being spiritually aware

It has been a revelation to me to find that in all the research on well-being and happiness the acquisition of a spiritual and religious viewpoint on life is consistently shown to enhance well-being. The findings are consistent in showing that this improves one's ability to cope, to deal with adversity, to be well and to be happy. In addition, the evolutionary function and importance of spiritual emotions has been shown to be critical to human development. Neuroscience shows how these positive emotions and sensitivities are of central importance to human evolution. Spirituality has evolved into one of our natural faculties. The sociology of religion, and its role in the formation of society and culture, has been examined in depth by Peter Clarke, in *The Oxford Handbook of the Sociology of Religion*, illustrating the profound significance of religion throughout history.

The conclusions of Ed Diener's research into the influence of religiosity on happiness and psychological wealth are that—

- religious people are on average happier
- the active ingredients that underlie religiosity predict feelings of well-being
- the major religions capture important ideas about living well
- there is something about growing up religiously that aids happiness
- parents strive to give their children a belief system that gives reassurance and meaning to life
- spirituality creates positive emotions that connect us to a world larger than ourselves
- religion helps families cultivate virtues and positive emotions.

Apologetic

It's interesting to find that in virtually all the American texts these facts are presented in a somewhat self-conscious, if not apologetic, way. It's as if there is a reluctance to admit to the fact that we are, at the very least, quasi-religious people. We should not, however, be shy about our human need for cosmic meaning and pretend that it's unscientific. In fact, the evidence for its importance is well established. However, we don't draw our wisdom only from empirical research. The religious-spiritual reflex is central to the discipline of happiness. We must be able to confidently experience that sense of belonging to something bigger than ourselves.

The sacred

The identification of sacredness in human and natural life is a universal phenomenon. All peoples and societies have tried to give expression to this sense of reverence for the life force that sustains them. The expression of this reverence and sense of the sacred has been evident in all forms of human expression throughout history in dance, song, ritual, art and religion. The universal nature of this urge is awesome because of the way in which it defines human nature in a unique and interesting way.

If you consider prayer to be an expression of awe and gratitude, in whatever form it takes, you have to conclude that the act of prayer is a universal one. It defines a beautiful and sublime aspect of humanity. Therefore, we must take the human reflex for some form of religious expression as a given.

The virtues

In Martin Seligman and Christopher Peterson's study of the great human virtues, they discovered that such experiences as awe, transcendence, elevation and love of humanity are deeply human, and that they are considered by societies throughout history to be universally experienced and valued. The things you find uplifting and that make you feel good about life lie outside the basic human emotions.

It is indeed wonderful to reflect on this truth, that all humanity, from before the dawn of civilisation, has had a determined spirituality and an innate desire to give expression to it. Here we see the intrinsic purpose of great art, literature and cinema. The motivational effects of these culturally important expressions are critical to the mental health of our societies. Great creations connect us with our heroic humanity and enable us to inhabit our flawed nature with passion and courage. These things help us to transcend ourselves, to elevate ourselves out of our skin and to see ourselves as if from above. From this position we sense the immensity of life and recognise that our purpose is to participate consciously in our blessed destiny.

The experiences of spirituality are those of being uplifted and connected to Creation in a sublime way. There is a sense of awe, gratitude, sacredness and revelation that is inspiring. It's often deeply moving, because there is a deep human longing to belong. These are experiences in which we get an arresting sense of the vastness of Creation, the majesty of the universe, the miracle of natural life and the extraordinary beauty of even the smallest creations. When we have this awareness we are elevated and can transcend ourselves to get a feeling for the miracle of all Creation. We feel intimately connected to the creative project of nature.

Parenting and religion

It's interesting to note that many parents have a real sense of what a certain amount of religious education can provide for children. The task of parenting is to provide children with internal values, self-belief and an awareness that will allow them to navigate through the world with happiness. The task of parenting is as much spiritual as it is relational and mental. The greatest gift a parent can give to their children is the gift of a spiritual life, a life of character and inner peace. We want our children to develop virtue, character and happiness, because we know that, with these three things, they have everything.

The pragmatics of religion and spirituality

Aside from religious experiences, religious life meets vitally important human needs. Non-religious people do, of course, meet these needs in other ways. Religions provide social and mental structures that assist in this. For example, genuine tolerant and humanistic religious beliefs, as in Buddhism, for example, take us out of ourselves and inhibit depressive self-doubt. It can help us sort out the complexities and confusions of life and makes living somewhat easier to manage. It offers a framework for living a good and meaningful life. It can also place us in a larger community of people, which enhances belonging and purpose.

Research finding 18: Participation in something larger than the self

This is one of the essential methods of ensuring well-being and security in life. For example, people's experiences of the GAA, in families and communities throughout Ireland, give proof that participation in non-work group enterprises with noble goals has an extraordinary ability to bolster self-confidence, belonging, well-being and a sense of self. Other social and supporting organisations do the same thing.

At its best, this represents a form of participation in life in which one loses oneself in a goal that is larger than the self. It's what all children feel when they are part of a team: one discovers an entirely different identity, which is an extraordinary relief and is sometimes a 'religious' experience. At its worst, the person surrenders to an identity that is destructive to the self, such as a violent gang, a dictator or an evil ideology. However, because this capacity has the potential to be either, it illustrates how such activities get to the heart of what it is to be human. That ultimate well-being is not really found in private isolation.

Our greatest experiences are found in this special arena. For this reason, sport plays a vital role in ensuring the well-being of men. People actually live for their teams and clubs. The greatest moments in people's lives are so often related to sporting occasions. 'It was the greatest day of my life,' you hear up and down the country when old men talk about their parish winning a county final or some such event. This sentiment is repeated all over the world for all sorts of events. When you attend an important sporting occasion attended by a large crowd it's quite extraordinary what it does to your psychology, emotions, sense of self and well-being. This can also be found in religion, large family gatherings and national pride. In times of war or of national trauma, individual depression and anxiety disappear.

A prescription for the well-being of any young person is to participate in some team or group enterprise that places them in the context of something larger than themselves. The benefits of this are extraordinary. The meaning of national pride and the love of one's country reveals this same human hunger to participate in something bigger than one's personal ego. Letting go of self-obsessions to serve noble social projects fosters genuine happiness.

One's isolation is cured by participation in a collective belief and practice that brings people together and that places them in at the centre of Creation—a project that is so much bigger than our own self-obsessed private efforts.

Research finding 19: Welcoming and overcoming adversity

'The world breaks everyone, and afterwards some are strong in the broken places,' wrote Ernest Hemingway. He was expressing the fact that when we are wounded by life we grow stronger because of it. Leonard Cohen wrote that 'There is a crack in everything . . . That is how the light gets in,' referring to the fact that our brokenness is indeed our salvation, as it were. Because we are broken, cracked and wounded we are open to life, to others, to light. 'What does not kill me makes me stronger,' wrote Nietzsche to express the same thing again.

Have you not been changed by adversity? Has some form of loss, tragedy or adversity not changed the way you experience, taste and savour life?

Common sense seems to suggest that adversity, trauma and hardship are bad for people. It would suggest that the reason we spend so much of our lives trying to avoid these things is that they are obviously bad for us. Who in their right mind would choose adversity over tranquillity, hardship over comfort or trauma over peace? No-one would, of course. Our universal assumptions about these negative aspects of life have always been that adversity damages us, that traumas, such as family break-ups and serious accidents, cause irrevocable damage, and that children from divorced or troubled families will be scarred for life. However, the research on the effects of adversity, hardship and trauma is not at all as negative as you might imagine.

Researchers have been studying resilience for some time. Resilience refers to the ability to survive traumatic events and to thrive afterwards. Researchers began to notice that at least three out of ten people who suffer some seriously disturbing event seem to come through unscathed. Stories of survival and resilience crop up from the debris of every social disaster, family trauma or hardship.

If you think about it, you will realise that if we didn't have some hardship in life we would be deprived of something important to our development as people. What parent has not pointed out to their teenagers that struggle and hardship is the stuff of life, and that the ability to endure it is what builds good character? You intuitively know that adversity is necessary in the development of resilience. Of course, we know that this is not always the case; we know of the detrimental effects of chronic stress and trauma. However, the issue is more complex than we at first thought.

When we meet adversity head on we rise to life's challenge. And when we rise to that challenge we discover our real potential. Rising to a challenge reveals our hidden abilities, changes our self-concept, strengthens relationships, opens our hearts and changes our priorities. It is indeed you at your best. This doesn't mean that you don't buckle and fall at times; but it does mean that, like the hero, you walk fearlessly towards what awaits you, an unknown and uncertain future.

The necessity of adversity

Jonathan Haidt, psychology professor at the University of Virginia, who has examined this issue in some detail, concludes that not only do we have to face adversity, the startling truth is that we *need* adversity in order to develop as people! This is both a liberating and somewhat disconcerting discovery. But it gives us new possibilities. Rather than saying that the adversity in your life can lead to you developing into a richer person, Haidt concludes that *you need it in order to grow*! And the highest levels of growth may be open only to those who have overcome adversity.

Benefits

What Haidt and others have realised is that when you face adversity in life, when you seek to rise to its challenge, there are four positive effects:

1. You discover abilities and strengths within you that you didn't know you had.
2. Your self-image changes and improves. You appreciate and integrate new inner strength in your self-concept.
3. It alters your relationships with family, friends and colleagues. It allows you to open up more to others, and that allows people to get closer to you.
4. It forces you to change some of your values and priorities for the better.

What you begin to realise is that these life experiences are not all bad or destructive. We all have a need to shake up our value systems, life situations and everyday habits in order to grow, develop and learn new things about ourselves.

Conclusion

This leads us to a very interesting conclusion about the relationship between adversity and personal growth: people who have a fulfilling and meaningful life are very likely those who have endured and thrived after suffering and adversity. In fact, we can conclude that it's a prerequisite of personal growth. You become more deeply human through your ability to endure and develop through suffering.

When you allow the truth of this to sink in you realise that it can have very significant implications for the choices you make in life. It really challenges you to counter your inclination to choose safety and security in life over change and even mild adversity. It challenges you to look differently on some so-called bad events and their effects on you or your children. These conclusions encourage you to be more adventurous, not to overprotect your children and always to seek to grow and develop as a human being. It allows you to see that your growth can only be enhanced by facing challenges and hardships. You can be so much the better for it.

Research finding 20: Finding meaning

Man can find a meaning in any circumstance. (Viktor Frankl)

The least of things with a meaning is worth more than the greatest of things without it. (Carl Jung)

We need a purpose in life more than we need to be happy! When we realise that we need a purpose more than we need to feel good or comfortable or satisfied, our approach to happiness shifts. This is because much of what we have to do to thrive is not all sweetness and light; it's often taxing and uninspiring.

However, as I have emphasised, we sense the real meaning of the challenges and events in our lives. This is our spirituality, if you will: the ability to experience something deeply meaningful in the ordinary obligations of life.

You have an extraordinary ability to electrify the dark and dull with the light of meaning—whether it's washing dishes, walking in the rain or getting the bus home from work. Your meaning can emerge from how you invigorate yourself with the experience of being alive, from how you *imagine* your life to be or from how you give your life some quiet, heroic purpose that inspires you. Spiritual transformation is the transformation of the self in the details of life.

Meaning is not an intellectual exercise; it's firstly a living exercise

What you begin to realise is that having a meaningful purpose is more important than your goals in life. The meaning and purpose that inspires your goals is what is important. There is no point in having a list of goals for your day, week, month, year or life if they are not rooted in a larger purpose and meaning. The interesting thing here is that your life can have great meaning without you knowing what that purpose is. However, it can be exhilarating to peel back the layers of your life to discover what it really is.

Your sense of meaning, purpose and spirituality is a subconscious process rather than a conscious one. If I were to ask a hundred people in the street what the meaning and purpose of their lives was, they would struggle to answer. If I were to ask a hundred people engaged in normal day-to-day activities what the specific purpose and meaning of what they were doing was, most would also struggle to answer. However, this doesn't mean that there is not a deep meaning and purpose there; it's just not a conscious meaning. However, it can be an exhilarating exercise to bring that subconscious meaning to the surface of your conscious life, because you can then see your hidden purpose. From there you can enhance your feelings of well-being, which may not have been there. Remember, nature is more interested in you getting things done than in you feeling good about them.

Meaning and purpose

Spirituality is related to meaning. The meaning we give our lives relates to the deeper purpose behind our actions. Many times in life we find that inner purpose, that substantive direction that sustains and inspires us, through the toil of living. Such meaning is usually found at the level of virtue, purpose, religion and morality.

I believe that we find meaning not at an intellectual level but at a soulful level that brings body, mind and spirit together in a common experienced purpose. Such meaning seems to drift in and out of our lives, but when we are in touch with it we are at our best, we paint our masterpieces and we know joy. We can find meaning in the ordinary and in the extraordinary, in times of great poverty and in times of plenty.

In life we want more than happy feelings: we want meaning and purpose, for which we appear to have an internal compass. It's part of human nature to want to rise above our mortal condition and establish purpose. It's the heroic enterprise in everyone to live their life fully and to pursue what they have not yet found.

When I use the word 'purpose' here I use it to give a sense of the forward thrust of our meaning-making. We both have and seek a purpose that is more than just everyday goals and lists of things to do. No, a purpose is the defining narrative that joins the dots of our life. Everyone has such a purpose that may be unconscious, subconscious and partly conscious. It's never fully conscious, because such a purpose works at a symbolic level. The meaning and purpose of our quest through life is both a mystery and a map. One's purpose may simply be to find peace, to create love or to flourish. However, our purpose is what brings meaning, and through meaning we find purchase and significance. Through significance we rise up against the temptations of mortal despair, insignificance and anxiety.

There is something powerfully and inherently natural about having this spiritual purpose and meaning, because when these things are aligned in our lives we find true happiness, joy and bliss.

Everyday meaning

The wonderful thing about our meaningful purpose is that it doesn't have to be lofty, religious or 'pie in the sky', because its real function is to give meaning and purpose to the ordinary and everyday, to ignite them with a fire that is not accessible on the horizontal level: the fire of a purpose. This is what helps us to cope and to sustain ourselves through hardship, tedium or heavy responsibilities. This opens a gateway through which enjoyment or pleasure can enter. The boring work on the production line can then become a pleasurable and willing sacrifice for one's family.

Pleasure needed

However, we need simple pleasures. Work and toil alone, even with purpose and meaning, is very difficult without some experience of present enjoyment. This is simple pleasure. It may be your morning cup of coffee, your chance to read the newspaper or your chat on the phone with a friend. Our days need to be punctuated with the simple pleasures of life. Without them we can become down and depressed. In fact, depressed people speak about the loss of pleasure (anhedonia) in such everyday activities as play, fun, sex and free time.

Research finding 21: Using your character strengths

This section is a summary of the findings of Martin Seligman in *Authentic Happiness*, in which he shows that our most enduring happiness and life satisfaction occurs when it emerges from the exercise of character strength and virtue. He shows what our parents always tried to teach us: good character makes the person. And he shows what our religious sought to teach us: a life built around the axis of virtue is a good one.

If our life is alienated from the exercise of character strengths and the practice of virtue it feels shallow and meaningless. For this reason, addiction to activities that bring pleasure or status grow tired very quickly.

Simple comforts and delights

It's useful to distinguish between the simple comforts and the deeper life satisfactions. The simple comforts or pleasures are exactly what you might think. They are essential to life and include all the little things you enjoy that punctuate your day: a hot shower, a walk, a piece of music, a cold beer, a game of football, your feet up by the fireplace and the froth in the cappuccino. These passing delights are essential and wonderful—but they are not enough, as you know well!

Deeper satisfactions

You also need activities that provide a deeper satisfaction, such as basic work, helping a family member, finishing a home project, being kind to someone, applying yourself towards a goal, overcoming some personal obstacle, adult education and learning, being absorbed in a hobby, or reading. You see the difference, I am sure. These activities and experiences tend to involve more of an investment of yourself. They involve the use of a personal strength in the pursuit of a goal, the overcoming of an obstacle or the exercise of a simple virtue, such as loving kindness. At their best, these deeper satisfactions involve a complete absorption of the self. Self-consciousness is replaced by action-consciousness. In other words, you forget about yourself for a while and get absorbed in something outside your self.

Signature strengths

Seligman concludes that when happiness comes from engaging our strengths and virtues our lives are made authentic. To understand your happiness, and what makes you satisfied with life, you must understand your ability to rise to a challenge and overcome adversity. Getting a sense of you at your best is important, because then you get a reading of your potential, your strengths and your character. Seligman and Christopher Peterson examined the classic virtues common to every culture and broke these down to the character strengths that represent them. (See the table on page 157). Their main finding was that each person has *unique* character strengths and that they are at their best and happiest when they are using them.

With this as a reference point, Seligman distinguished between the pleasant life, the good life and the meaningful life. The pleasant life is characterised by having personal comforts and pleasures but little need to exercise good character strength and virtue. The good life is characterised by using personal strengths to produce authentic happiness and gratification. The meaningful life is one in which you are living for some virtue that is more than your own personal needs.

Living a life guided by virtue is not easy. However, if we conceive virtues as excellences that are achieved through the practice of their particular strengths we have a good guide. Seligman and others suggest that the exercise of these strengths produces flow and well-being.

Virtue and religion

It's not quite so simple to find meaning and purpose. The traditional braiding of religious with social values made the identification of virtues easy and uncomplicated. However, as societies have become more individually focused than community focused, we have become less driven by religion and more diverse and egalitarian. Religious ideologies have lost their social power, and people have been left more to themselves to articulate their unique values.

The individual has therefore to take the heroic journey to find their own sense of virtue. When it is hard won it creates authenticity and character. The research concludes that cultivating such virtue through discipline will make you happy. There is evidence that altruism, as an example of a virtue, creates happiness. Kind and helpful people are happier people. It is indeed more beneficial to give than to receive.

These are the six universal virtues and their associated qualities, as summarised by Seligman and Peterson. Two or three of the listed qualities under each virtue represent your personal character strengths. Research shows that the more you use these the happier you will be.

(1) *Wisdom*
Curiosity
Love of learning
Judgement
Ingenuity and creativity
Social intelligence
Perspective

(2) *Courage*
Valour
Perseverance
Integrity

(3) *Humanity and love*
Kindness
Loving

(4) *Justice*
Citizenship
Fairness
Leadership

(5) *Temperance*
Self-control
Prudence
Humility

(6) *Transcendence*
Appreciation of beauty
Gratitude
Hope
Spirituality
Forgiveness
Humour
Zest

Conclusions: The role of spirituality and meaning

This gateway to well-being recognises that one's happiness is more authentic and is best achieved by searching for meaning and purpose in life by means of some form of transcendence. I don't mean that in a strange, paranormal way but in a very real way. A common phrase in Ireland used to be 'You just have to offer it up.' It was said at times of difficulty, pain or suffering as an invitation or invocation to help the sufferer to realise that there was no escape or relief except to offer one's suffering upwards, to one's imaginary or real god, or to creation. It was a recognition that some meaning can be drawn from the wreckage of tragedy by giving it back to the gods. This was a gesture of your willingness to endure what life had set before you by being able to show it to one's god. It was uncomplicated, simple and old-fashioned, and it was how my grandparents used to approach life. Some might consider this to be naïve or superstitious. I would rather see such small everyday gestures as being deeply meaningful and heroic. The literal truth about the existence of a god is unimportant. What is important is the transcendent reflex, shared by all humanity, to place one's small life into a bigger meaning.

I love this quality in people, I love its heroism, I love its naïveté, I love its courage and I love its imagination. I love the human desire to place oneself in the bigger picture of Creation and to create symbols (like God) to give expression and create avenues of action and intent that draw the great complexity of life into something meaningful. I have shown how the research has supported the nobility of this reflex. If you can give your life a meaning by placing it in the context of something bigger than yourself you can feel better about yourself. This is why you can love a religious ceremony, a wedding, a funeral or a birthday. In hardly recognisable ways you keep placing yourself at the centre of something bigger—even if you don't know what Creation wants of you. This quality in you is beautiful. It's a gateway to meaning and purpose and joy.

Think about the meaning of a simple birthday celebration: it's much more than it seems. It symbolises so much, for child and adult alike. It's a simple mark of one's specialness and significance in life. It's a simple, joyful and subconscious recognition of mortality. This was its earliest origin: to have survived another milestone. It's an expression of hope and joy; it's a ritual of gratitude; it's a celebration of connection and belonging; it's an invitation to self-celebration.

Much of our daily activities serve deeply meaningful symbolic purposes that invoke joy and generate happiness. We must not become cynical about participation in any social ritual that is not just about us. They define us. They place us in a story that is not our own. They give us meaning. Any time you broaden the context of your own life you broaden its meaning. The largest context and meaning is a spiritual one.

Our task now is to integrate our motivation to take our well-being seriously with knowing exactly what we need to do. This will be achieved by drawing our insights into essential conclusions and by bringing self-discipline to bear on our heartfelt aspirations. The following chapters will seek to do this.

For exercises related to this chapter please check out the book web site at

www.couragetobehappy.ie

Chapter 7

Self-discipline and happiness

The passionate heart of self-discipline

Before I present the psycho-spiritual conclusions that arise from looking at the who, why and what of happiness, it is critical that we take a look at the 'how'. That is, how you are going to go about improving your well-being. This brings us to the somewhat unpleasant issue of self-discipline. The castor oil of well-being!

There is something inspiring about watching someone discipline themselves in pursuit of a noble goal: a young mother walks her child to school in the misty morning; a violinist practises their music in the late evening; an athlete sprints up and down the empty track on their own; a monk rises at dawn to pray; a father prepares the morning fire in the kitchen before he heads out to work. If you want to see a happy person, they are probably building a boat, learning a piece of music, practising a skill or writing a book. We are at our best when we apply ourselves with persistence to tasks that haven't got an immediate reward.

Definition

Self-discipline is the ability to postpone gratification in favour of something better. It's the giving up of immediate satisfaction in the service of a higher goal. If you have this self-discipline it gives you the strength to stick with your decisions, to remain persistent and, therefore, to be able to reach your goals. The origin of the word 'discipline' is the same as that of disciple, meaning a student. To discipline means to train a disciple or student. If you can think of it as *training* for the self, as an apprentice might train with a craftsperson, your view of it may soften.

Discipline and happiness

One of the great paradoxes of life is that those who are able to turn away from passing pleasures and choose a certain level of difficulty in pursuit of a long-term goal turn out to be the happiest of people; while people who take the easy option, who reject hardship and discipline and choose the passing pleasure over the long-term goal, end up being unhappy and lost. This fact is supported by extensive research.

Creatures of habit

As creatures of habit, what we repeatedly do defines who we are. We have no choice but to develop habits; it's our biological and psychological way of being in the world. However, we either actively develop our habits or we passively let them develop us.

Our choice, then, is either to be someone who passively accommodates to life or someone who actively shapes life to fit with their values and virtues: we either *let* life happen or we *make* life happen.

You can, I hope, get a sense that the living of your life is more a psychological challenge than a physical one. In conquering and developing your habitual way of being you are conquering your self.

Mental habits

Habits involve not only observable behaviours but also thinking and feeling. The mental habits of regulating your thoughts and feelings are a critical element of your well-being. I am not talking here about rigid self-control but about self-awareness that helps you influence the direction that your thought and feelings take you. This ability comes from a gentle self-discipline that can soothe an anxious mind and calm a troubled heart.

Meaning, happiness and purpose are found in the disciplining of oneself towards the achievement of a higher purpose or goal. This is the case with any athlete, musician, artist, monk or devoted parent. The achievement of the goal is not what it's about: it's about the commitment to it, even if it's not reached. 'Success' is less important than the sustained application of oneself to the process. Self-discipline is the anvil on which good intentions are forged.

When it comes to our happiness and well-being it's only by working with sustained focus that we can accomplish anything of great worth. Like most things in life, work is the cornerstone of a fully lived life.

Happiness, of course, is not a consequence of self-discipline alone. However, to maximise one's well-being and happiness, self-discipline is essential. I am not arguing here for a puritanical approach to happiness. Rather, I illustrate how critical self-discipline is to personal development, growth and happiness.

Happiness is more of an effect than a cause

When you see happiness as something that requires self-discipline you realise that you don't just do positive things because you are happy; you are also happy because you do positive things. The research shows that at least forty per cent of your happiness is something that you make happen rather than it being something that happens to you. So, to maximise that percentage, self-discipline becomes critical. However, if your approach to happiness is passive you start to make excuses for yourself. 'Well, I can't do this or that, because I'm not happy,' you say.

Happiness is an emotional skill as much as a feeling

When you realise that crucial elements of happiness can be learnt, just like any craft, your attitude and expectations shift. When you view your happiness as being partly a discipline the most obvious implications for you are that you now have to do something about it. You have to engage in practice and repetition, like in any other discipline. In emphasising the *doing* part of your well-being you appreciate that *thinking* is not necessary for happiness and that repetitive practice is as important as any understanding.

Insight is less important than practice and repetition

Most of us assume that understanding what you have to do is half the battle. This is the illusion that, because you get an insight about what you *should do*, you will actually do it. Nothing could be further from the truth. This illusion pervades our lives, imagining that we are changing, only to find ourselves standing still.

If all anyone needed in order to change was an intelligent reason we'd all be fit, thin and well behaved. The small print that remains hidden from most of us when we buy any new book, or attend any new workshop, is the warning 'Needs self-discipline to work.' In other words, *the batteries of self-discipline are not included!* It's the batteries of self-discipline you need, not strategies that promise the world.

SELF-DISCIPLINE CAN ELECTRIFY YOUR LIFE

Most of your efforts to change rely on some form of emotional inspiration and motivation. However, motivation can create the illusion of change and can then fade quickly. The illusion is: because I feel strongly that I want to do something I will obviously do it. We think this strong feeling is seventy-five per cent of the battle, when in fact it's only five per cent.

The difficulty we have is not that we don't know what our problems are. It's our inability to be self-disciplined in applying the solution. It's one thing to understand the six steps to happiness or a stress-free existence; it's another thing entirely to apply these principles in a disciplined way to one's life. There is a wide river of ambivalence between aspirations and action.

We are multi-problem people

Developing discipline and focus is difficult. This is because we are multi-tasking, multi-priority, multi-need and multi-valued people. We are forever seeking to balance a whole range of needs, obligations, goals, expectations and priorities simultaneously. It then becomes almost impossible to introduce a new single-focused priority.

> The reason we can't lose weight, stay fit, remain goal-focused, earn money or stay happy is that we are trying to do too much.

If, despite your best efforts, you can't lose the extra half a stone that you have been carrying around for years, what hope have you of achieving anything, you ask yourself. How can you possibly succeed in a larger issue, such as your mental health? That is where this book tries to help! Firstly, by giving you some idea as to what works; secondly, by emphasising that you need to integrate change in your theology and life-meaning; and, thirdly, by emphasising that your problem may not be your motivation or desire but your self-discipline.

You have probably tried to improve and change yourself in hundreds of ways in the past year. You have tried to improve your punctuality, efficiency, weight, fitness, stress, anxiety, relationships, marriage, work practices, sense of appreciation, sex life, social life, parenting and life-appreciation. And it's probable that, though you may have succeeded in one or two of these areas, your success was temporary and you quickly returned to your old self!

You keep returning to that familiar water level of partial success, partial failure and tolerable inadequacy.

You are walking through life with an endless list of false promises to yourself. This applies to your happiness also. You want to be happy and happier. You want more contentment, peace and simple joy in your life. And, though you will always say that you want it, it's disillusioning to feel that you are ageing, and that things stay the same.

Self-discipline is necessary and natural in life

We tend to associate self-discipline with such activities as weight loss, getting fit, giving up bad habits and addictions, training, learning a musical instrument, mastering a particular task and educating children. However, it's very much part of our natural life and existence.

Throughout your day you are engaged in activities that need self-discipline, such as getting up out of bed, showering and washing, waiting in rush-hour traffic and completing unpleasant work-related tasks. Though you do many of these things semi-automatically, they do take self-discipline to maintain focus. The exercise of self-discipline is a constant activity, because it's essential for functioning as a complex creature in a complex world.

There is a natural necessity for self-discipline. All of nature applies itself to the ordeal and adversities of life. It persistently applies itself to overcoming obstacles. Other creatures in the animal kingdom don't give up as easily as us humans. Watch any of David Attenborough's wildlife documentaries to see countless moving illustrations of small creatures persisting until death in their pursuit of something that their nature tells them they must have. A polar bear swims hundreds of miles in pursuit of food; a fox lies all winter with a broken leg, waiting for it to mend; bison wade seventy miles through four feet of snow, looking for grass; a tree bends to accommodate the westerly gales that sweep in from sea. In nature we see the uncomplicated disciplines of eating, sleeping, hunting and mating. Life, for so many creatures, is an ordeal. The wonder is that life drives to stretch itself and apply itself in such a persistent way.

We see this same application in humans. It's a self-affirming encouragement as well as a muscular endurance. Endurance is a particularly noble quality of the human spirit. At the Special Olympics a whole stadium of spectators stand in tearful applause for the young athlete who struggles towards the finishing line. To endure, to survive and never to give up is an inspirational call.

Self-discipline is a universal and natural way of being well

We have evolved as a species because generations before us have applied themselves to survival and learning. Survival, since the dawn of humankind, has meant coping with adversity and triumphing over it. The 'kill or be killed' environment of much of the animal kingdom means that animal species have a natural, persistent and unflinching urge to repeatedly strive to overcome. This takes an extraordinary commitment. In one of David Attenborough's documentaries he showed the extraordinary application of mudfish in taking care of their eggs. The mudfish spent days digging a tunnel underneath the mud to lay her eggs and then spent day after day keeping it filled with fresh oxygen by rising to the surface to gulp air and bring it back down to the water in which the eggs were laid. The documentary showed how many species of fish apply themselves in a repeated, courageous and persistent way to care for their home and young. Nature is filled with extraordinary displays of unconscious discipline.

It's unconscious in that the creatures are not choosing to apply themselves. However, it's no less impressive. In the same TV series, Attenborough showed how tiny goby fish, two inches long, climb up the one hundred foot high cliff face of water falls, by means of small suckers, to reach safe ponds above them. Hundreds of them lose their lives in the process, but the ones that make it to the top can lay eggs in the pools above, which will later get washed back downstream to grow into new fish and later in the year attempt to return to their birthing place to lay their own eggs.

A kind of stern discipline pervades all of nature. To witness the requirement of all social animals to control themselves and to fit in with the needs of the group is indeed fascinating. Higher forms of life require the subordination of self-interest to the interests of the group, be it with the great apes, wolves or dolphins.

Strangely, the striving to be better than we are, to reach up and beyond our very nature, is the thrust of evolution. Our existence is based on our learning, and our learning is based on our ability to try. We try because we must overcome. To try well is to not give up. To face repeated failure until one has mastered and overcome an obstacle—this is all life on earth. This is self-discipline. This is active rather than passive life.

We too have that same survival streak, but it's less visible in our technological age. Watching the survivors of the earthquake in Haiti in January 2010 I saw how the most appalling adversities can bring out the best in people. In many ways, our well-being is inhibited when our lifestyle prevents us from experiencing this physical intensity, this overcoming of adversity. For these reasons, many people seek out challenges in sporting and other arenas. Human nature needs to be facing a challenge. You stagnate in an anxious or boring life, in a life without vigour.

Self-discipline and parenting

Nothing is more beneficial to a child than learning simple disciplines. Through discipline, more than through natural talent, a child discovers their true character and *potential*. The child discovers the exuberance that comes from achieving a goal and from discovering their innate competence, be it in tying a shoelace or managing to feed themselves. (As I write, my six-year-old daughter has just let out a squeal of delight, because, through persistence for the past fifteen minutes, she has managed to get the doll's clothes on to the reluctant doll!)

Through discipline a child discovers that they can do certain things, can achieve certain things and can discover the thrill of growth and learning. As most parents intuitively know, encouraging discipline is good for the child. Lack of discipline can lead to frustration and self-loathing. Paradoxically, self-discipline awakens in us a sense of possibility, potential and control. The self-belief that it ignites never leaves us.

Every parent teaches their small children the little disciplines of life that they don't feel like doing: brushing teeth, tidying up toys, sticking at homework, being nice to their sibling. But the wonderful thing the parent learns is the innate pleasure and satisfaction that is felt by the child who achieves something, who actually *does it* and, after applying themselves to a particular task (like my daughter), shouts out with delight, '*I did it!*' Even playful discipline, such as learning to climb a tree or ride a bike, brings delight and satisfaction. We are innately programmed for learning and practice, for the discipline of the self in the service of a larger goal. In fact, this is how we have evolved, by stretching beyond our limitations.

If parents try to get their children to do things because of the reward or punishment they end up deprived of the natural reward that comes from the successful application of the self towards an unpleasant task! Bribing children to do things, or punishing children for not doing things, is to teach self-interest, not self-discipline. We can train ourselves to do things that seem mentally painful. As they become habitual, the pain fades.

For all these reasons, there is a great benefit in approaching your mental and emotional health and well-being with an active disposition, with a desire to bring some discipline to your priorities and in discovering that informed effort and application will bring their own rewards.

Self-discipline and the experience of being alive

The mythologist Joseph Campbell said that people are not looking for the meaning of life: they are looking for the *experience of being alive*. And how right he was! When we feel most fully alive we are engaged with life; we have let go of our mind and have 'come to our senses'.

You will notice that you are most alive when you are pushing the boundaries of your competence, when you are trying to learn something new or when you are trying to be better than you are. Though you need time to relax in your comfort zone, your sense of accomplishment, satisfaction and exhilaration is attained when you have travelled successfully outside it. When that happens you step back into your comfort zone to appreciate yourself and to prepare for the next journey outwards.

As adults we are still like young children wanting to explore the 'beyond'. The two-year-old, by nature, wants to explore their world.

The child will just not sit in one spot. Curiosity and the innate drive to explore, learn and develop are powerful. This is when we are at our best, when we continue to grow! It's this evolution, this straining to reach a higher shelf, that is our true nature. All this striving requires the 'efforting', the trial and error, the 'not giving up', the 'rising to the occasion', the pushing uphill and the reaching of one's limits, which constitute the experience of being alive. There is joy, because at these times you are *alive*.

You are willing to discipline the self to walk upriver, against the current. You decide to discipline your self to push beyond what feels like your limit. A child does this in trying to learn to climb the stairs; a bear cub will do this in trying to scale a difficult cliff face; an abuse survivor does this when they refuse to let fear impede their growth; a public speaker does this when fighting against their panic; the boxer does this when they push themselves in the gym; the mother does this when she rises early, exhausted, to give her little child time to prepare for school. All of nature is striving to survive, to persevere and to thrive.

In doing this you work against the gravitational pull of complacency, laziness, depressiveness, cynicism and negativity. Each and every day you discipline yourself and come alive.

I love most sport for this reason, for the way warriors engage in the disciplines of their sport in such a passionate way. Sport is theatre, in which the metaphors and struggles of life are played out. In the arena of sport, one does battle with all the symbols of life's hardship, adversity, enemies and gods. The victory and the defeat are equal, because it's the never giving up, the pushing of oneself and the fearlessness that has fans, in all sports, cheering passionately for their team. Above all, there is the discipline required to practise and then to persist on the field of play. It's not only a battle: it's also a stage on which one enacts life and finds bliss and joy in all its richness. One finds deep satisfaction in the struggle, whether in defeat or in victory.

There is a tradition in many team games such as rugby where, regardless of the result, the teams applaud each other off the field. It's noble and proper. Each team recognises, respects and honours the other's application, and they recognise the heroic qualities they share. This is life. Success in everything requires perspiration—including happiness.

PASSIONATE SELF-DISCIPLINE AS YOU AT YOUR BEST

Passionate self-discipline is a human quality that has a unique integrity. The application of the self fosters self-respect and confidence. It's a quality that has honour. There is a compelling integrity to passionate and disciplined commitments, such as Michelangelo sculpting beauty from marble, the prolific painting of van Gogh, a craftsperson's diligent application, an athlete's repeated striving, a mother rising to feed and a musician practising. Honour, integrity and self-respect bring huge satisfaction. It's the soil of happiness. It's wonderful to discover that the application of oneself is the human flesh of happiness and that life creates satisfaction.

The honour of self-discipline is strongly observed in sporting activities, and it was seen in ancient warrior codes. In these contexts we see the honour in the disciplines of courtesy. There is honour between combatants who respect the disciplines of their sport. Games and sports have rules and codes of conduct that express core disciplines. Children at play have the same sense of the honour and value of rules and of the self-disciplined commitment to them.

The integrity of self-discipline is tested by how well it's sustained in times of weakness. Its true character is shown in being able to rise above one's conditions and stay loyal to a principle or commitment. Self-discipline is also like a code of practice for the self, within which one can blossom and flower.

There is pain and discomfort in all discipline. However, as you doubtless know, as people move into their later years there is hardly anyone who doesn't carry some regret at choosing the easy option over the more difficult one. The pain of self-discipline in the present is small compared with the pain of regret in later life.

> The person who lives without discipline dies without honour. Champions aren't made in the gyms. They are made from what they have deep inside them: a dream, a particular purpose and the courage to pursue it.

With passionate self-discipline comes *self-respect*. You have a deep positive regard for yourself when you realise that you have the strength to say No. What you say No to is the other part of you that wants relief from the challenge of life.

There is this deep sense of self-respect and self-regard you feel when you can discipline your powers of focus, attention and persistence in the pursuit of a valued goal. It's part of your very nature to do this and to revel in it.

In your acts of discipline you are competing against yourself. While engaged in this inner battle you are at the front line of what it is to be deeply human. It's to be aware that you have conflicting needs and desires but that you find a solution and break through. Your inner tensions and uncertainties are then, temporarily at least, resolved.

There is no greater contentment than that which results from the application of oneself in a disciplined way towards the achievement of some small goal. This is the case whether you are four or forty-four! A two-year-old climbing the stairs, a six-year-old tying a lace, a forty-year-old getting fit or a sixty-year-old working on simple DIY—these produce their own satisfaction. So whether you are clearing out the attic, painting a spare room, tidying and dusting the house or repairing a broken object, you discover that these unremarkable achievements punctuate life and represent it at its most ordinary and, often, at its best.

Through discipline we defeat, for short periods, the spectre of death. We do not become powerless in the face of the majesty of life. We do not yield! In overcoming some small obstacles with self-discipline our most insignificant deeds can have the most significant meanings.

All our heroes have these qualities: the willingness to strive in the face of adversity, to fall down, to lift themselves up again and to succeed.

So you must always be about the business of self-discipline. It's critical for your joy, exhilaration, exuberance, freedom and happiness. It may seem paradoxical, but the joy that arises from the worker, even from slaves who sang, arises from the unavoidable bliss that arises out of the channelling of the body in a repetitive way towards an achievement.

Passionate self-discipline and freedom

In a paradoxical way, self-discipline moves inexorably towards freedom and its inherent well-being. Many would complain that their freedom is compromised by having to be disciplined. They want to be free to do what they want, and they convince themselves that self-discipline 'confines' them. Nothing could be further from the truth.

Every skilled musician who flows freely and spontaneously on their instrument achieves this through disciplined practice. For the artist, musician, scholar, researcher, writer, homemaker or tradesperson, disciplined practice is what enables them to flow and to soar, to lose themselves in creative acts and to be fully alive and present. Discipline and freedom are entwined.

Self-discipline is a form of freedom. One is freed from sloth and wastefulness, from uncertainty and self-doubt, from weakness and fear. It allows the athlete, artist or writer to find their individuality, their inner strengths and their talents, and to become a master of their thoughts.

There is an intensity and *vigour* that arises from being able to apply one's energy in a disciplined way to a small area. The channelling of life energy creates a particular intensity. A river moves more powerfully when it's narrow. Energy, when it's applied in a focused way, produces dramatic forces and effects. Steam, petrol and gas create energy when they are confined. Your life doesn't evolve and take flight until it's focused, dedicated and disciplined. If you seek relief from the difficulty of self-discipline, if you seek to eliminate the small adversities of life, you will never be the person that you can be. In truth, you will never be free.

Self-discipline is joyful

One of the consequences of achieving self-discipline in different areas of one's life is, surprisingly, exhilaration and joy. You will surely identify with the physical pleasure and well-being that comes with completing a task or programme that has required your self-discipline and persistence. It may have been from completing a piece of art or writing, the successful mastery of a musical piece, the finishing of a mini-marathon, the writing of an essay for school or the completion of a good day's work. They bring a deep satisfaction that is different from pleasure or comfort.

I played rugby for years at school and university, and our team would spend countless nights in the mud and rain running, sprinting and slogging through drills and exercises that, as most sportspeople will testify, bring surprising satisfaction and fulfilment. The disciplined application of oneself, and the self-discipline required in pushing oneself harder and harder, while physically exhausting, was always strangely exhilarating.

The same applies to mental and emotional challenges. You will know the simple pleasure of applying yourself in completing your to-do lists successfully or getting those difficult household maintenance tasks done. All the little obstacles that can only be overcome with focus, application, discipline and persistence bring emotional pleasure that orients one's mood towards the positive. Strangely, your psychological mood can improve dramatically simply by completing a challenging task. Very often our emotional need is not for therapy, emotional support or counselling but for the experience of completing something successfully, particularly when that something challenges the self somewhat. Doing a crossword or jigsaw can at times do more for the psychological self than five hours of psychoanalysis!

The student of Zen, asking the master how to achieve enlightenment, is told to clean out their rice bowl! The richness of a full life is not found in the airy-fairy world of self-reflection but in the concrete world of physical application and mental focus. Cleaning out the attic over the course of a weekend can do more for your broken heart than writing in your journal, meditation or days of personal development.

Because self-discipline brings its own satisfaction it's physically right and good that you should sit down at the end of your day with a feeling of accomplishment, however trivial it may seem.

So, every time you strive against your limitations, and overcome them, in small ways you experience a deep satisfaction, if not great delight. We are meant to be disciplined in how we live. When you observe the energetic humanity that fills any busy city street you see how civilisation is built on this ability to master the self in the service of personal development. It's quite wonderful. The person without discipline is dysfunctional and wasteful. They only exhibit depression, physical indifference and intolerance.

You must kneel by your bed every night. You must purchase a piece of art. You must do something every day that you don't want to do. You must strike the meditation gong. You must change your posture. You must fast. You must exercise. You must keep a plant alive. You must do a jigsaw. You must wear a ring. You must practise the art of living. You must stretch yourself over life.

Self-discipline, hardship and adversity

When you approach happiness as something requiring self-discipline you are genuflecting towards the unavoidable ordeals of life. Any programme of self-improvement that doesn't recognise that life is hard is naïve. Programmes of false optimism, such as changing your life in seven days, avoid the essence of life.

The hardship and unpredictability of life are around us for all to see. We must embrace all this life. We must realise, in recognising the hardship and adversity, and fully accept that finding inner joy, peace and contentment requires work.

If you are truly honest about life you will not be able to avoid the conclusion that to live it fully, to find pockets of joy and periods of happiness, and the strength of character to deal with its adversity, you need passionate self-discipline. It gives you the courage to face up to and defeat life's dragons, after which you step into the clearing and the meadows of life's exquisite bliss.

When you apply self-discipline to doing what is difficult or challenging, or to what pushes you beyond your limits, you discover something special that is denied to those who don't push themselves. The willingness to face small obstacles and adversities, to do what is difficult, is like passing through a gateway to personal strength and confidence. Applying oneself and working hard produces results in the form of character and in the form of success in life. There is no other way. The false promise of many self-help books is usually a sales pitch for something fast and easy. But the harder you can work, the higher you are willing to climb, the more the wonders of the world open up.

Mental toughness arises from the willingness to make sacrifices and to deny the self easy options. It comes from a disciplined will that refuses to give in. It is character in action. *It is life itself.* My son, practising the same guitar riff over and over in his bedroom until he has 'got it', is living life fully.

Every day you should do three things you don't like. The successful person has the habit of doing the things that 'failures' don't like to do. The successful people don't like doing them either, but their 'disliking' is subordinated to the strength of their purpose. Make the phone calls you have been avoiding. Do that house chore that you have been postponing. Say to your loved one what you have been afraid of saying.

For exercises related to this chapter please check out the book web site at

www.couragetobehappy.ie

Chapter 8

Conclusions

The standing stones of happiness

INTEGRATION AND FIFTEEN CONCLUSIONS

Before I lay out a simple methodology for how to bring the right feeling and practice to your happiness, it is important that we pull together the essential conclusions that underpin how we can change.

These have emerged from the confluence of the who, the why, the what and the how of happiness presented in the previous chapters. These conclusions bring a real sense of possibility and integration to one's life. These conclusions are:

1. We are symbolic people.
2. We must do ordinary things with extraordinary feeling.
3. Your human condition demands a heroic response.
4. You must practise the discipline of 'looking to the sky'.
5. Your imagination is central to your happiness and well-being.
6. We have learnt to repress joy.
7. We must not be passive about life.
8. You must find your lost voice.
9. There are eight anxieties, compulsions and joys.
10. You must remember who you are.
11. There are four solutions to happiness and twenty-one things to do.

12. You need focus to counteract the diffusion of life.
13. What you have to do will feel counter-intuitive.
14. You must not use the 'I have no will-power' excuse.
15. You must be a guardian of the whole of your life.

Standing stone 1: We are symbolic people

We are symbolic people who establish our worth and meaning through the currency of symbols. We have an insatiable existential and religious urge to experience ourselves as symbolically worthy and purposeful.

You are given a life, but you are not given the rulebook for how to live it. Neither do you get the godly power to know what to do. You are born into a great mysterious existence. Armed with your genetic inheritance and provided with parents who mind you, you are set on a unique journey of discovery. You set out somewhat lost, and you spend your life searching. You are thrown into life and driven by a force that is not yours. The passion of life is in how you cope with, and make sense of, this wonderful, mystifying and passionate existence that is both ordeal and adventure.

The struggle to get a foothold in life and to find a worthy purpose is an unavoidably spiritual struggle. You have no choice but to search for experiences in your life that give it meaning and purpose; to fight against the conditions of your life; to try to cope with experiences you can't control or understand; to seek out experiences that sustain and inspire you; to grow, develop and mature. When I say that life is a spiritual challenge I mean that you have a relatively constant *desire to attain a happiness that is not given to you on a plate*. Your worth, purpose and meaning—these are not given to you: you have to find them yourself. That search is always psycho-spiritual.

Your need to feel good about yourself is an existential need and not just a psychological one. In other words, your very existence demands it. You don't only want to have your needs met—you want a psycho-spiritual purpose. The way we achieve this is unique in the animal kingdom: we achieve it symbolically. We feel good about ourselves by doing things that symbolise our worth and value. All the little things you do every day are important to your self-feeling. They are vital to your ability to feel good about yourself. Every little success in your day makes you feel that you are a person of worth. You need to feel significant, because you accumulate experiences and symbols that thwart the threat of insignificance: death.

The trivialities of your day have a symbolic meaning. The hundreds of little actions you make every day are about much more than keeping you alive. Everything you do has a meaning that is far beyond the act itself. This meaning is actually profoundly existential, religious or symbolic. Symbolic status is important in overcoming the consequences of our mortal life and in giving special meaning to our ability to transcend it. If someone were to abuse and destroy the things you had secured in life, you could rise up in a murderous rage. In fact, most human violence is a quasi-religious or existential reaction against a feeling that someone has deprived you of what symbolises your life's meaning. People's possessions and achievements are sacred symbols of a person's inner life. To trivialise these things is to insult and injure a person.

For example, to discredit your spouse's argument may seem to you to be just a matter of logic, yet they may fill with tears or react with anger at your comment. Why? Because what you dismiss is not the logic of their argument but an argument that has symbolic meaning to them. 'Tread softly because you tread on my dreams.'

Therefore, because we are symbolically oriented, everyday life is filled with rituals, repetitions, magic and even superstitions. Our attachment to the symbols of the significance of our life means that the most trivial actions can represent the most important meanings. This is where we enter the world of the magical, because little things seem to have magical powers. Little things can evoke all sorts of reactions and meanings. Behind the garments of normality and social roles, we secretly cast spells over each other. We are unconsciously superstitious. We practise rituals and look for omens. Our inner life is much richer, more imaginative and more colourful than we dare to imagine.

If we went behind the scenes of your life we would find the rich and colourful inner coherence that only you really know. It's impossible to describe it, because it's bound together with your unique emotion and feeling. The meaning can be passionate, uplifting or inspiring. Or it may be terrifying, despairing and filled with dread. For this reason, people are shocked to hear that someone they know has taken their own life, because they had no inkling of the inner meaning of all the little things that punctuated their life. Equally, you can be in awe of the joy and happiness experienced by someone living in the most deprived of circumstances.

Therefore, you must be willing to do small, ordinary and apparently mundane things in developing your happiness. These ordinary and seemingly trite things can take on a quite profound meaning if done with the right intent. Which leads to the next conclusion.

Standing stone 2: We must do ordinary things with extraordinary feeling

What fosters deep happiness is engaging in very ordinary activities with extraordinary meaning, purpose and passion.

The book has been working towards the specific. This is the realisation that one plays out one's life, resolves one's relationships and lives one's spirituality in the ordinary world of the everyday. We find our passion and meaning not in books, churches, institutions or the words of leaders and gurus but around the kitchen table of everyday life. It's in our encounter with ordinariness and with the specifics of our everyday lives that we actually resolve the larger existential themes that haunt our dreams. Our rich, multidimensional feeling, imagination, desire, longing, fear, terror and dread are funnelled into the ordinary obligations of life, and we resolve them there.

Love is played out around the dishwashers and televisions in family homes; your loftiest dreams find purchase at the untidy desk of your office; your spiritual longings are experienced while taxiing children back and forth; and passionate life is witnessed in the simplicity of gardening or in painting the gable end of the house. We have inspirational thoughts while sitting on the toilet, we solve problems when tossing and turning in our beds, and our love for our children is revealed in hundreds of lovingly made sandwiches. Life, evolution and your body will not tolerate abstraction, loftiness, intellectualisation or ivory-towered spiritualism. It demands that you live a specific life, discipline yourself and work.

You find the universe in a garden weed; love is traded in the most ordinary of currencies; you see God in the smallest of gestures; and you find freedom because you participate cheerfully in your unavoidable confinement. However, your bliss, your delight and your deep joy are only found when this work and service is transformed from the ordinary into the extraordinary. This begins to happen when its meaning is revealed or rediscovered. There is a deep purpose, virtue and imagination behind everything you do. The trouble is that you can forget so easily what this is. When that happens, life becomes dull and empty.

The spiritual challenge is to love all your imperfection, to find well-being in your imperfect and stressful life, in your half-achieved goals and in your less than ideal relationships. This is life in its beautiful imperfection: the inherent integrity that is honest effort. It's in the most modest of goals, and in our passionate investment in them, that we find the satisfying life.

> Let your goals be ordinary and specific
> and not in fanciful dreams,
> not in making a million,
> not in changing the world,
> but in painting the spare room,
> cleaning out the garden shed,
> helping your child
> across the stepping-stones of life.
> The deep satisfaction in life
> comes from doing the ordinary
> with extraordinary feeling.

The many meanings that underscore our life don't need to be grand or larger than life. When I talk about having a meaning in life I am not talking about knowing the *meaning of life* or of having a biblical kind of purpose. No, I am talking about how we can, for example, find and give meaning to the smallest of activities and infuse them with a purpose that lifts them out of the ordinary, into something meaningful. I am talking about how we can see our basic responsibilities in life to love, care for our families, sustain our friendships and follow our dreams as vocations, as callings to live our life with a special meaning. Everyday housework, for a homemaker, becomes tedious and tiring if it's not approached regularly as a choice that is a consequence of having a virtue-based purpose, as a calling to a life of service, as the small everyday acts of love that require sacrifice.

It's the same with work. It's helpful to rewind your responsibilities and actions to their first principles. You can discover that the reason you tolerate a boring job is your deep love for your children; that the reason you tolerate a sometimes irritating partner is that you actually love them; and that the reason you are not pursuing a particular dream is that other less sexy dreams have to be given priority.

A catchphrase used by celebrities who have fame for a short time is that they are 'living the dream.' If I could do a television slot for the average person it would be one of a homemaker vacuuming the landing floor on a schoolday morning, of the person providing a taxi service for teenage children or serving up a dinner to a noisy family kitchen table; the background music would be 'Hero', and the voice-over would say, 'Remember, you are living the dream,' and the scene would be redeemed by those exquisite moments of joy, love, celebration, birth and, yes, death that, behind the drudgeries of everyday life, give it its real purpose and passion. The challenge is to be able to draw up that meaning and intention when we lose touch with it, as you inevitably do when you ask yourself, 'Why am I doing this anyway?' 'Why am I putting up with all of this?' And then you remember: there is a purpose that gives your life great worth.

When you have this meaning and purpose you have a 'why'. When you have this 'why' you are able to discover 'how'. When you have this 'how' obstacles are easily overcome, because you have a sense of your destiny. When you forget who you are and feel that you have no destiny, life's obstacles seem insurmountable.

You will notice that in almost every film or novel that inspires you the story is usually the same: someone who has a noble purpose that enables them to overcome life's adversities in an inspiring way. We love these heroic stories because they inspire us to be similar—to find our noble purpose and to live in accordance with it. When we have a purpose we also have meaning. Which brings us to the next conclusion.

Standing stone 3: The human condition is a heroic one

The human condition is a heroic one, and deep happiness is a consequence of how well we embrace that challenge.

I work often with people whose dreams have been shattered by life circumstances and, at times, by cruel fate. What is heroic about them is not that they are compulsive in pursuit of goals and dreams but that they transform their life in the face of broken dreams. They live not by striving for a goal that is beyond them but by living and experiencing the life that they have in a way that is gloriously courageous. Instead of trying to make a million euros they strive to be loving parents. Instead of following the five steps to success they are devoted to giving a life of dignity to their handicapped child. Instead of changing her life in seven days the single mother with no income is devoted to her baby. As I write, the World Athletics Championship is on television, and only one athlete can receive the gold medal. But this doesn't stop the hundreds of others from giving their best and rejoicing in their efforts.

You and I must be the same. We must have a feeling for the heroic purpose of life. I emphasise this again, because we have to come to terms with the fact that our terror of helplessness makes us try to compulsively control and manage our lives. This extends even to controlling the people we seek to love.

Unless we find the courage to inhabit life in the round, and to welcome the derivatives of our mortality, we get caught in cycles of trying to control every aspect of our lives. However, when we can let go control (which is driven by fear, death, the evil dragon) it falls to the small sword of courage. The dreaded Wizard of Oz emerges as a frail old man. The terrifying giant turns out to have a soft heart. The hero who dares to look fate in the eye finds not a hurricane of unforgiving rage but the soft breeze of compassionate and vulnerable love. In mythological terms, the dragon, the evil one that needs to be confronted, is not 'out there' but actually resides within us all. The heroic victory is never over 'the world' or 'life' or 'the other'; it's over oneself and one's dread of facing one's fear, smallness and vulnerability. In so doing, we, as mythology tells us, find a true strength.

You don't solve problems in life by looking more and more closely at them but by looking more expansively at yourself.

Our fear of existence can be complemented by existential joy. Existence, in this instance, refers to our place in a majestic universe as transient, helpless beings. We are blessed with the gift of awareness. We are a small part of an unfathomable project that has little to do with us. We are part of a Creation project that is infinite. Yet, in the midst of this extraordinary infinity, we have an awareness of Creation seeing itself. We see as if with the eyes of God. We love living. We love participating. We are at home. Though we know there is no need to be afraid, that the universe cares for us, we are still afraid. We cling to those we love and the things we have—to our life raft.

The check-out operators and existence

Now, you may say that the person at the check-out doesn't think about these things, that your ailing grandparent never mentions them and that your little eight-year-old doesn't give them a passing thought. You may suggest that people just get on with their normal lives and don't give such things any consideration. On the contrary, each of these people has a heightened awareness of all these things, at both a physical and imaginative level. When I talk to ordinary uncomplicated people, it doesn't take very much work to pull back the thin veil that covers everyday roles to find a person of deeply sensitive humanity. Don't let roles and responsibilities allow you to forget the tender, sensitive heart that resides behind them. Tears flow easily when a hand reaches in to touch the forgotten inner self. Each one of us has a lost voice, a forgotten joy and a sweet longing. If you tenderly stroke their face and remind them of their inner beauty, they will cry. If you insult or take from them their dignity, they will rise up in protest.

When your little child dreams, when the person at the check-out falls in love, and when your ailing grandparent tears up when you say goodbye, it's because of this profound emotional sensitivity. Every cell in my six-year-old's body knows that she is on borrowed time and that her existence is geared towards fighting against it, as long as she can. It's astonishingly beautiful, miraculous and terrifying.

All the activities that make us happy are symbolic ways of experiencing life, meaning and purpose. It has been thrilling for me to discover this. This was not exactly what I was looking for, but it emerged as clear as day.

You must love the ordeal of developing your happiness

Without the ordeal of change there is no change. Without the ordeal of transformation there is nothing heroic or inspirational. You must love the ordeal! Your goal must be to experience the ordeal without being impatient or intolerant. You then begin to reframe, transform and understand why it's essential to exhilaration. I am talking here about the ordeal of getting up early to exercise, turning away from the fridge when hungry, talking to your partner when you don't want to, acting positive when you feel depressed and, basically, doing the little things you don't want to do. You have to love the ordeal and see that achieving any of your goals must be changed into setting a *new* goal: the goal is to climb, not to get to the top; to practise, not to succeed; to persist without any reward; to identify the tedium and choose it; to be focused on the pleasure of overcoming the preparatory ordeal rather than the long-term objective itself.

Unlike most popular psychology books based on business models of personal change, which prescribe the 'seven easy steps to fulfilment' or the 'five easy steps to happiness', most of the great religions and philosophies describe the necessity of having to go through some form of ordeal to achieve one's goals. The hero's journey, as described by Joseph Campbell, Carl Jung, Otto Rank and others, always involves a confrontation with the inner dragon, the defeat of which opens the path to success and freedom.

There are many symbols and myths that describe this confrontation with oneself. When this is undertaken with courage and persistence our world myths tell us that the hero is born. The hero faces their dragons, confronts the enemy within—fear—and succeeds. St John of the Cross called this the 'dark night of the soul.' There is hardly a reader among you who doesn't intuitively know that the transformation is a consequence of this battle. The adversary we must forever do battle with is our anxious and self-doubting self. Facing life with optimism and hope is itself a courageous act, because it forces us to step forward into the unknown with a willingness to endure suffering in order to grow and change. I have little doubt that you are reading this book because of the adversities you have experienced in your life as much as because of the fact that you have touched the garments of Creation.

Standing stone 4: We must practise the discipline of 'looking to the sky'

We need to develop and practise the spiritual discipline of looking upwards and of looking more expansively at ourselves to counteract our inclination to look obsessively at our difficulties. Psycho-spiritual disciplines break the hypnotic trance of everyday anxiety and worry.

We find happiness in being able to attend to the specifics of life in a spiritual way that connects the big questions of existence with the everyday obligations of life. Our spirituality is then lived out in the everyday, ordinary world, but it's quickened and enlightened by our spiritual sensitivity and existential awareness. We realise that to keep this connection alive, to remain awake to the beauty and wonder of life, requires practice and discipline. We realise that, through discipline, we can pull the drapes of anxiety and grief aside and keep the window to wonder and happiness open.

Of this we can be certain: we have an urgent responsibility to discipline ourselves to look upwards, to look towards the sky and to keep remembering our origins, our place and our mortal destiny. We have a responsibility to experience life fully, to look towards the sky, under which we live, and to inhale the stunning magnificence of the universe we inhabit. Because we so readily anaesthetise ourselves in dull routine we need to look up and beyond ourselves with gratitude. We have a responsibility to discipline ourselves to look towards the sky and to remember the sacredness and uniqueness of each person in our lives. Unless we have some spiritual discipline it's hard to crash through the shutters that hide us from our extraordinary magnificence and beauty.

We must emerge, by means of the twenty-one things to do, from the hypnotic trance of our everyday life. To open up a new path that fosters happiness and well-being involves wakeful mindfulness.

We all develop self-amnesia. We forget where we came from. We forget where we are going. We forget our origins. (As one little four-year-old child put it: 'I am beginning to forget where I came from!') We distract ourselves with the trivial or anaesthetise ourselves with the banal. We make unimportant things our priorities. We worry about things out of habit. We get into a kind of emotional trance and just go through the motions. We wait for things to put themselves right rather than putting ourselves right.

Therefore, to develop right happiness and right well-being we must overcome our forgetfulness. At our most elemental level we must awaken to our mortality and to our duty to embrace life in the round. Self-amnesia is the mind's way of distracting us from our human condition and focusing our energies, like any good little ant, on the survival of the species! As I have mentioned, you are programmed to do what is good for the human race but not necessarily for what is good for your individual soul.

We must remind ourselves regularly why we are choosing to live the way we do. In most cases we are doing what we want to do, but we forget that we want it. We become habituated to our spouses, children, careers and lifestyles, and, in that habituation, we lose touch with what inspires us. Alas, it's often only at times of serious illness or death that we suddenly remember what is important. When the clouds part, and when new light shines into the darkened valleys of our hearts, we remember things that we know.

However, our stressful, anxious, over-responsible life dulls our existential and spiritual sensitivities and causes us to disengage from the immediacy of our lives. We get temporarily awakened to this when we are touched by something as simple as a scene in a film, a moment of pleasure or an everyday epiphany. We are most often awakened to this by nature—by the beauty, majesty, immensity and sacredness of the natural world.

The hypnosis of everyday life draws you into the stupor of self-amnesia and under the emotional anaesthetic of going through the motions of your day in a waking sleep. To overcome this amnesia and forgetfulness you need to invigorate your life with simple, uncomplicated spiritual-type disciplines that awaken you to simple courage-enhancing truths. (I will explore this possibility in the final chapters).

In this context we sense that our life is of service. Though our disposition is invariably somewhat anxious, we need to be gloriously thankful. It behoves us to lift our eyes from the obsessive puzzles of our small lives to see the sky as a symbol of the broader context within which our little lives are set. This is the discipline of remembering who we are and of choosing our lives again every day.

We need psycho-spiritual discipline

Psycho-spiritual disciplines are essential to well-being. This is the practice of doing psychological things with spiritual meaning. It is the practice of doing what is helpful, according to research, but with the realisation that it's a symbolic act rather than a literal one.

What I discovered about the science of happiness was that none of the twenty-one activities identified is in any way remarkable or surprising. They are ordinary, simple, easy-to-do things that have positive effects on our emotions. I realised at the same time that they could be easily grouped into activities that fell within the four areas of mind, body, heart and soul. I also realised that the research findings were congruent with existential solutions to life. I had therefore a simple and elegant framework for understanding them. Each activity is a core activity that can be organically integrated in a spiritual discipline of personal development.

Standing stone 5: Your imagination is central to your happiness and well-being

We imagine our life. We find self-worth and life-worth through the medium of our imagination.

Life is an exploration of the potential of the world to be a screen onto which our fantasy and imaginative life can shine. Happiness *comes from seeing life for what you imagine it to be.* Your outer life is the soil in which your imagination can be made real; when your imagination takes root your potential can grow.

The objective world of objects and people that we normally consider to be reality is useful for many daily activities, such as loading dishwashers, balancing bank accounts and arranging schedules. However, it's a pale shadow of a fuller experience that is possible when this real world is brought to life through fantasy and imagination.

One's imagination is not fantasy that alienates oneself from the world. Rather, it's fantasy that allows one to experience the world more fully. It takes imagination to develop a vision for what is possible; it takes imagination to extract meaning from the seemingly meaningless; it takes imagination to make something extraordinary out of the ordinary; it takes imagination for love to endure; it takes imagination to feel one's connection with all Creation; it takes imagination to create a god; it takes imagination for a child to feel loved in the dark of night.

Like every other child, you looked up at the ceiling of your bedroom and imagined yourself into life in ways that inspired your everyday existence. Every child plays games of fantasy, role-play and imagination, because they are practising and rehearsing how one lights up one's life with this extraordinary visionary gift. Imagination doesn't create a false world: it brings the otherwise dull and dead world to life.

A Santa Claus brings to life the imagination of a child. He allows a small child to feel loved by 'someone' for no other reason than that they are a child; he enables a child for one day a year to rise above the ordinary and dreary to a world of magic and possibility; he allows a child to connect with an immense love that exists out there in the night sky; he brings a child's heart closer to the magical and miraculous in life; he opens up a child's spiritual sensitivity; and he exercises the virtues of awe, transcendence and wonder.

In all these ways, the imagination of the child awakens their inner world in preparation for life. They are not brought into the world of false fantasy or into a pretend world. Rather, they are awakened. The sparks of wonder, delight, pleasure and awe are kept alive and are turned into the small candlelight of possibility that can stay with them for life. Why do these memories stay with us forever? They don't stay with us because they are false or acts of deception. No, they stay with us because they opened up that window of wonder that opens out into that mystery and magic of Creation and life.

I believe in a poetic god because it opens a window to our innocence. This allows our heart and soul to remain connected to the immensity of life and to our part in it. It allows us to lean towards the good. It encourages us towards delight and happiness. It makes us giggle.

Christmas and birthdays for a child

For these reasons, these special and spiritual experiences can sustain a six-year-old for a full year. Christmas Eve and birthdays punctuate a child's life.

Why is this? What truth about you is revealed on these days? They are special, meaningful and unforgettable because of the conditions of life that are known to every hair on a child's head. However, on these days the spiritual truths about life are revealed, and the child remembers that—

(1) I am special and significant
(2) I am unique
(3) I am worthy of celebration
(4) Somebody loves me for no reason other than because I am me
(5) Out there in the unknown world someone special cares
(6) The world is safe, and I am secure
(7) I am happy.

These events are profoundly spiritual. I remind you of their significance as iconic days in your own life because they reveal truths we carry into adulthood. We forget this at our peril.

Your birthday marks your place in the world. If you are stuck in existential cynicism you see no point in these things. You are clouded by scepticism. However, if you grasp the wonder of life and grasp your life, cynicism is understandable but not tolerated! The cynic sees only a third of the truth.

We need to feel blessed and to bless; we need to sense the sacred and the divine; we need to feel the immensity of which we are a part. How insignificant are our preoccupations and obsessions when we open up the ground of our being, when we turn towards the ocean of life, when we breathe in the landscape that defines who we are.

Standing stone 6: We have learnt to repress joy

We have learnt to repress joy in the service of anxiety.
We learnt to repress joy when we lost our voice. We can find both.

It's a joy to watch all species of little animals, whether lambs, puppies, kittens or little children. It's such a universal pleasure. Almost everyone stops, smiles and enjoys the freedom and playfulness of these young and beautiful creatures. Their playfulness is infectious and their innocence is charming. Their stress-free existence is enviable and their joy is pure and natural. As I write in my little get-away 'poustinia', a puppy is dancing around the feet of its owner at the shore's edge, crouching down on its front legs, teasing its owner and wanting to play. It's simply beautiful, and such simple sights touch us all for spiritual reasons! It awakens something in us about life and its meaning. There is grief at innocence lost, there is joy in life revealed and there is a soothing in remembering what was forgotten.

Most people think, for some good reasons, that as we move through life our childhood innocence dies. You probably believe that once you discover the death of Santa, and once you travel across the cynical self-doubting terrain of adolescence, innocent joy is no more. You believe that the childhood age of innocence has to die in order for you to deal with the harsher realities and responsibilities of life. You suggest that the illusions of childhood innocence must be undone if you are to survive in the world. However, childlike joy doesn't fade away and die. It's denied and repressed.

It's gradually shoved into the back rooms of our psyche. It's always present within us, but it's covered up with heavy layers of responsibilities, insecurities and preoccupations.

It's boxed away like Christmas decorations and put into the attic of our hearts, to be left unused and forgotten. On rare occasions we are caught off guard by joy—dancing in our front room at 4 a.m.!

Why would we repress joy? Why would anyone cover up happiness in favour of stress or worry? Joy is sent into exile in favour of anxiety and stress, because we feel that worry guarantees safety and protection. Joy, on the other hand, can make us feel exposed and vulnerable. We conclude that as we mature we can't afford the luxury of joyful play, because it's then that we are most off guard. If you let innocent joy move in and dance within you, you are off guard and in danger. Innocent joy is the loss of fear. The innocence of the little child unsettles you because of this. However, to you as an adult, danger lurks everywhere—disapproval, forgetfulness, loss of status and insecurity.

At an existential and developmental level we become preoccupied with establishing safety, security, status and significance in our life. We become preoccupied with building up our little immortality projects, that is, all those life projects that we pursue in order to establish our status, significance and security. These include marriages, children, families, jobs, careers, bank balances, athletic prowess, sexual conquests and addictions. The problem is that playful and childlike joy, exuberance and delight in life become incompatible with staking down the fences of our security. We have too much to worry about, we claim.

Therefore, you repress natural, uncomplicated joy, because it shows no respect for all the things your ego has established as important. Innocent joy doesn't act in the service of your need for control.

However, the good news is that if joy is repressed it can also be recovered! We can go back and find this old friend that we let go. We can be determined to hold the door open that welcomes this friend back into our life.

Heroic joy

Therefore, childlike joy is not an innocent illusion that must be gradually eroded by the harsh truths of life and reality. Life is still as wonderful and magical as the child in us once believed and imagined it was. What we experienced as children was not illusion but a glimpse of reality. In fact, what we experience as adults is illusion. *What a laughing two-year-old child is experiencing in life is actually reality and not illusion. What the stressed and unhappy executive in bumper-to-bumper traffic is experiencing as reality is the illusion and the deception.*

In order to survive we create an illusion of safety and security around us. We build up our lives to maximise this. We even choose mild unhappiness as a fact of life. We decorate our life with symbols of safety in a risky world. In truth, we are no safer than we ever were. Many of our adult preoccupations are more like security blankets in an uncertain world.

In later years so many of us realise how illusionary were the causes of our stress, anxiety and depression—how we had deluded ourselves about what was important. We remember our childhood not as fanciful illusion but actually as the heartbeat of life. We remember teenage romance and discovery not as being removed from life but as being the defining passionate moments in life. In other words, innocent joy, childlike happiness and teenage romance were all real. Your safety was an illusion.

After thousands of hours of work with couples in marital therapy I see that this childlike love and happiness is never far from the surface. There is hardly a client of mine whose façade of safety, security and composure doesn't begin to cave in when these feelings are recalled. It's not as if they are repressed, deep in the dungeons of the self. No, they are just there, behind the thin curtains of the self.

I work with violent offenders, sex predators and domestic abusers. They all present veneers of cynicism, aggression, self-loathing, composure and toughness. Yet every one of them has their vulnerable breaking-point. It's the point where all their pretence falls away like cardboard. Behind the façade stands a frightened, vulnerable, humiliated, abused, neglected and angry child. And just behind that child's desperate pain a happy, sleeping child waits and waits and waits to be found—but lies forgotten and unseen.

Your tear-point is a breath away from your composed self-security. Your innocent joy, your naïve longing and your childhood dreams are running, like a silent film, behind your eyes. Your childlike happiness and innocent love of life are a truly spiritual encounter with the conditions of life. It represents the burning-point of life. Childlike joy is life without thought or bitterness.

Standing stone 7: We must not be passive about life

The myth of 'Providence' is that happiness is something that *happens to you*. This myth suggests that 'the gods' will provide happiness for you because you are a good, loyal or self-sacrificing person. You want to believe that good things happen to good people and that happiness will be a by-product of your efforts in life. This is only partially true.

The impulse in you to transfer onto life the responsibility to provide for you is in grave error. You may abdicate your self-responsibility and hand it over to 'God' or 'life', but when life doesn't work out as you expected you may grow cynical, depressed or passive. This can become self-reinforcing. To the extent that life doesn't give you happiness you feel disappointed. As you feel more disappointed you are more inclined to seek relief from that frustration by wishing or longing for relief. You want relief from that frustration, and you waste away energy thinking about winning the lottery, getting out of your marriage, trying to earn more and more money or drinking your time away, waiting for the skies to open and for good luck to come your way.

What we know from the research on happiness and personal well-being is that what you actively do in the service of your well-being is the most crucial element of the happiness equation. It doesn't just happen: it's a by-product of the efforts and investments made in living a virtuous life.

There is not one shred of evidence to support the notion that happiness or well-being is provided for you, that happiness is separate from internal beliefs or that it can be found outside of oneself. Every therapeutic model, ancient religion, school of philosophy and piece of common sense forces you to look in the mirror to find the path to liberation. At one level this is annoying, because you and I want it to be otherwise. We want the answer to be provided for us. So we wait for it. Or else we look for it in all the wrong places.

The hard thing about life is that you are always left with, and stuck with, yourself. No matter what your history, life circumstance or relationships, you know in your heart of hearts that when you lie in your bed before you go to sleep you carry the lonely responsibility for your own destiny and well-being.

I also know that at times this is too much to bear. It seems unfair. There are times when, like a child, we want to cry out and ask for some relief, some rescue, some god to give us just what we need. Oh, there is a part in every one of us that wants to be rescued and saved.

However, the universe does in fact take care of us. It takes courage and a personal theology to realise that it has already given us the abundance we seek—that we don't have to wait passively for more to be given.

If you are a woman with children you love, and if you are trapped, terrified and imprisoned in the cage of an abusive and controlling relationship, these words may offer little solace. But even then you must hold on to the flickering light of possibility—you must have faith in your right and entitlement to the destiny of freedom. Never give up on that light that flickers within you, for that is what will guide you home. You are the expert and authority. Trust yourself deeply.

But if you are in a humdrum, depressing and passionless life, or feel imprisoned by your own depressiveness, anxiety, stress or low self-esteem, you also must really grasp the potential within yourself and reject the toxicity of passivity.

Scientific research consistently shows that the most powerful determinants of happiness and well-being are self-determined positive thoughts, attitudes and emotions. In other words, all the research tells us that our well-being lies within us, waiting to be uncovered or set free from the chains of negative thoughts and attitudes.

All great spirituality and philosophy encourages you to look within to find the solutions and relief from mental suffering. The kingdom of godliness lies within you.

You don't find relief in life by doing the right thing: you find it by being the right person. Therefore, all religions speak of virtue and living a meaningful life—not of self-sacrifice but of self-transformation.

Standing stone 8: You must find your lost voice

You are at your most inspired, at your best and functioning to your fullest potential when you have a meaning and purpose in your life.

You are probably thinking, 'I don't know what my meaning or purpose is, and I don't know if it's really necessary, because I have lots of meanings and purposes'. However, what I want to say is that most people *have* a meaning and purpose, but they haven't quite defined it for themselves. Most people have an inner myth that they follow and have a vague inner destiny that they imagine. They follow certain signposts and omens as they move in accordance with their subconscious purpose and meaning.

If your life story were to be written as a novel by an author who knew you intimately you would find a narrative in your story that progresses towards a particular destiny. You story would reveal the compass of your inner values. More than that, it would reveal the dialogue between the inner cast of characters that fills the stage of your inner life.

So don't let yourself off the hook by saying that your life has no meaning or purpose. You have no consciously thought-out meaning or purpose, but you have an unconscious emotional meaning and purpose that guides your life. Now, it's quite possible that this meaning and purpose is not altogether good for you. It's tragic but true that the purpose of some people's lives is destructive, depressive or defiant. In other words, the title of some people's novel of their life could be *Passive Self-Destruction: One Man's Effort to Defeat Life*, or *Searching for a Bleak Future: One Woman's Search for Justification*, or *Saying No to Life: One Man's Determination to Defy Love*. These are rather depressing and despairing stories—but you know people like this. Equally, however, your story could be titled *The Lifelong Pain of Childbirth: The Painful Joy of Motherhood*, or *Unexpressed Joy: The Secret Happiness of an Ordinary Person* or *Footprints in the Sand: Carrying God on My Shoulders*.

What is of considerable benefit here is the realisation that you author your own life. If you don't you let your subconscious do it for you, and that is not always good. The greatest gift you can give yourself in life is to become aware of whose story you are living, whose plot or narrative are you following and to what degree it's really your story. Is it really someone else's story that has taken over the plot of your life narrative? The greatest gift you can give yourself is to bring into your awareness the influences that are driving your plot. Most people don't do this. Many people are so set in their ways that they just let their story happen, believing that they have no choices or that they just accept who they are, never mustering up the courage for self-awareness, self-reflection and self-development.

As you are reading, I am hopeful that you are imagining your own title, getting a sense of your plot lines and considering the main characters in your story. Here, try this: If you like the title you thought of or wrote, stop for a moment and write a second one. If you don't like that, rewrite it from a different viewpoint into something you do like. Make sure it entices the reader into discovering what is fascinating about you! This could be the first baby step in authoring your own life. You have an inner dream, an inner map that is not conscious for you. Bring it into your awareness. Scribble down the plot of the next two chapters of your life as you would like them to be. Inhabit, then, your own story.

Standing stone 9: There are eight anxieties, compulsions and joys

The eight anxieties

There are eight core human anxieties that you have inherited. I have illustrated this in 'The Octet of Anxiety'. This diagram summarises the essential experiential effects or conditions of life itself. Human beings, by virtue of mortality and mystery, all experience these emotional realities. The consequence of our mortal human condition is that we experience a considerable amount of anxiety, inadequacy, helplessness, vulnerability, isolation, woundedness, 'shipwreckedness' and insignificance in life. These emotions define a very clear and unavoidable dimension of our emotional and spiritual life. It has been the role of ancient religions and rituals to give expression to these facts and to find solutions for them.

Not only have cultures and societies tried to give expression to, and found relief from, these human experiences—so too does each individual. You know the taste of these experiences and have found your own way to try to deal with them. You have your own private way of coping with this life. You have either sought to control life and each of these elements or you have learnt to integrate them naturally in ways that have released the natural joy that is within you. The traditional religions have all recognised the helplessness and vulnerability of humanity and have created imaginative ways to cope with this. The danger for positive motivational psychology is that it's fearful of these realities and seeks to deny them.

The mandala illustrated on the following page places the eight core existential experiences as the eight sides of humanity. All these experiences are known to you. Deep happiness and fulfilment integrates these elements in life. It doesn't take flight from them. Compulsive control does.

The octet of anxiety

ANXIETY
Feeling fear, worry, stress, terror, dread

INADEQUACY
Feeling imperfect, incompetent, confused

HELPLESSNESS
Feeling powerless, impotent, despairing

VULNERABILITY
Feeling unsafe or exposed

ISOLATION
Feeling alone, self-responsible, abandoned, rejected

WOUNDEDNESS
Feeling flawed, deformed, broken

SHIPWRECKED
Feeling cast-away, lost, without meaning

INSIGNIFICANT
Feeling unimportant, worthless, invisible

The unavoidable experiences of our mortal condition

The existential octet of natural anxiety

The eight compulsions

There are eight core negative and controlling human ploys that you use to imprison yourself. With this counter-phobic approach to life the person seeks happiness and security by denying or rejecting their human vulnerability and anxiety by overcompensating for them. This kind of person is then motivated by the need for ever-increasing control over, and success in, life. Therefore, this is the opposite of the octet of anxiety: the person chooses to oppose anxiety by becoming aggressive, to oppose inadequacy by becoming over-adequate, to oppose helplessness by becoming controlling and so on.

As presented in the octet below, this person is often aggressive, over-adequate, controlling, invulnerable, detached, perfectionist, self-directed and status-seeking. We all seek refuge in these positions throughout life or even throughout our day. However, this is problematic when it becomes a general attitude to life and to others. Some people will operate from this position in a consistent way. It makes genuine, deep and fulfilling happiness impossible, because the person is at war with life itself, and, in seeking to control life, they can never win. However, they can take hostages or victims along the way as false symbols of their success. An abusive, violent or controlling personality exhibits this pattern and often destroys or murders those close to them as one final act of 'godly' power, as if to show life and the world that they have been victorious.

The octet of control

AGGRESSIVE
Inhibiting fear by maximising power

OVER-ADEQUATE
Trying hard to overcome inadequacy

CONTROLLING
Counteracting helplessness by seeking control

INVULNERABLE
Coping with human vulnerability by maximising security

DETACHED
Avoiding loneliness and isolation by eliminating dependence

PERFECTIONIST
Trying to minimise brokenness by maximising self-perfection

SELF-DIRECTED
Dealing with lostness by maximising goal-orientation and driveness

STATUS-SEEKING
Compensating for insignificance by seeking status and importance

The unavoidable experiences of our mortal condition
The existential octet of control

The eight joys

Finally, there are eight core human joys that you have inherited. In seeking happiness through integrity a person embraces and fully inhabits the unavoidable conditions of life: its suffering and inadequacies. They integrate the dread of mortality with the joy of living. They don't take flight from such experiences as helplessness, vulnerability and anxiety but accept, tolerate and befriend them. In this way they calm the inner conflict, and, rather than trying to be victorious over the natural human emotions, the person of integrity displays a certain humility, grace, tolerance and flexibility. In assuming this attitude they find peace, competence, influence, openness, connectedness, capability, transcendence and self-worth. It goes without saying that this is not a constant state and that it's experienced to greater or lesser degrees by everyone. The path to a rich and fulfilling life demands this integration, this befriending of one's true self, this rising to the occasions of life, this rising above our fears and insecurities.

The octet of happiness

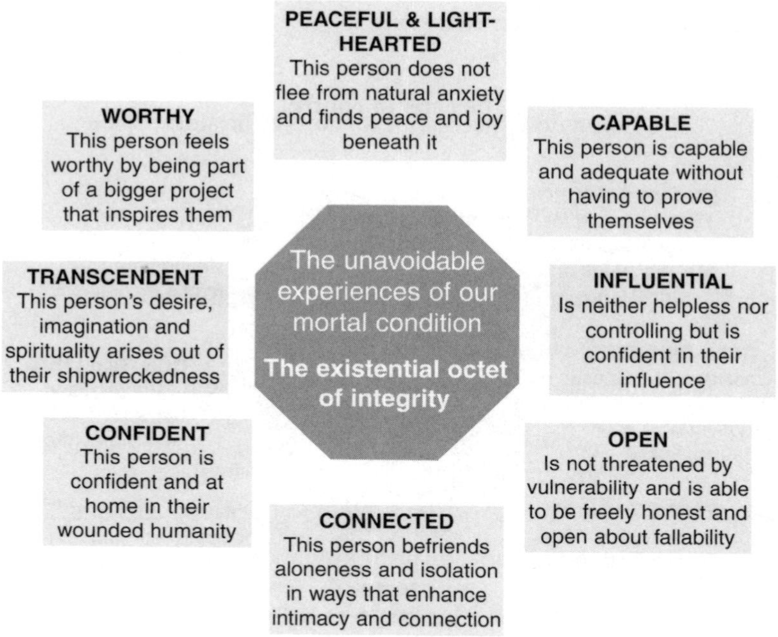

PEACEFUL & LIGHT-HEARTED
This person does not flee from natural anxiety and finds peace and joy beneath it

WORTHY
This person feels worthy by being part of a bigger project that inspires them

CAPABLE
This person is capable and adequate without having to prove themselves

The unavoidable experiences of our mortal condition

The existential octet of integrity

TRANSCENDENT
This person's desire, imagination and spirituality arises out of their shipwreckedness

INFLUENTIAL
Is neither helpless nor controlling but is confident in their influence

CONFIDENT
This person is confident and at home in their wounded humanity

OPEN
Is not threatened by vulnerability and is able to be freely honest and open about fallability

CONNECTED
This person befriends aloneness and isolation in ways that enhance intimacy and connection

Standing stone 10: You must remember who you are

There are a number of truths that we need to remember. These simple truths arise directly from existence itself. These are the essential burning truths about human life. They are the truths that counteract anxiety and helplessness. They are the truths you need to remember on a constant basis in life. They are truths you often reinforce for your children and for those you love, but they are so difficult to keep hold of for yourself. They are diamonds. They are truths of great clarity. They are not insipid affirmations: they represent who you are, because they have been mined from the ground of your being. They are from the pure uncomplicated pulse of your life. They are eternal.

Each of the following statements, drawn from the eight octets, is rooted in our human condition, is existential in origin, is prayerful in disposition and is psychological in intent. Our anxiety, stress and depression emanate purely from one source: the anxiety that sets in when we forget who we are. Here, then, are eight diamond-cut truths about you—about the you that has gone unseen, who has lost your voice and who waits patiently in the garden of your self.

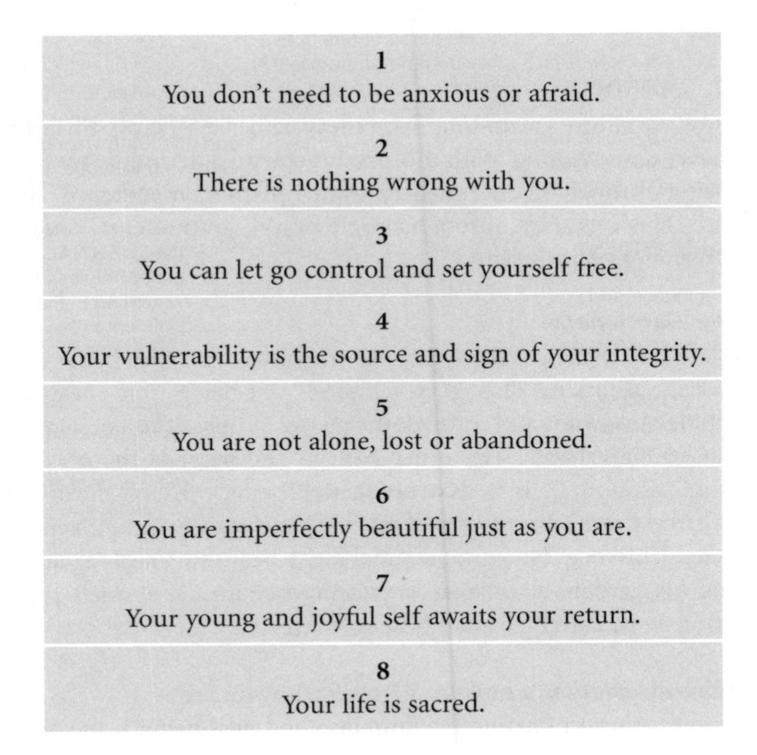

1
You don't need to be anxious or afraid.

2
There is nothing wrong with you.

3
You can let go control and set yourself free.

4
Your vulnerability is the source and sign of your integrity.

5
You are not alone, lost or abandoned.

6
You are imperfectly beautiful just as you are.

7
Your young and joyful self awaits your return.

8
Your life is sacred.

Standing stone 11: There are four solutions to happiness and twenty-one things to do

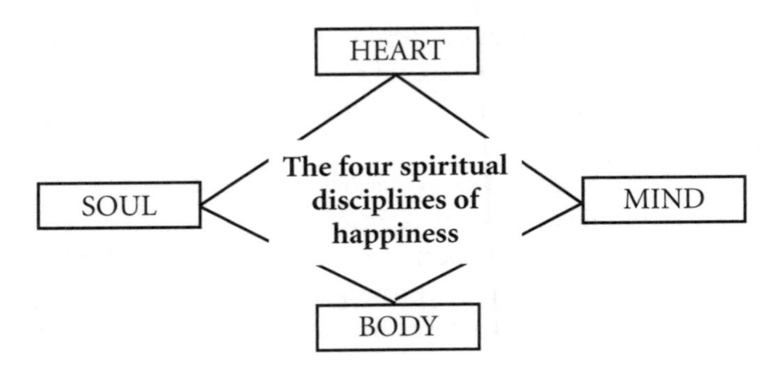

Broadly speaking, there are four solutions to the problems and contradictions of our human existence. There are four paths that point us towards happiness and away from unnecessary distress. These major solutions are the disciplines of the soul, heart, body and mind.

(1) *The soul solution*

The soul solution is finding happiness and well-being through *spirituality and meaning*. With this psycho-spiritual discipline we find well-being through transcendence, contemplation, meditation and purpose. This can come through simple prayer, gratitude, relaxation or uncomplicated joy in life.

(2) *The heart solution*

There are two principal disciplines of the heart. The first is the *love and service* solution. This is developing well-being and meaning through relationships and through the giving of oneself to one's loved ones as willing service. The other path of the heart is the *art and creativity* solution. This is developing well-being through creativity and artistry. I don't mean formal art, in this instance, but all acts of creativity. This may be a mother making a beautiful meal, a father keeping his garden, a teenager organising her music, a small child colouring or an elderly woman tidying her room.

(3) *The body solution*

The bodily solution for finding happiness and well-being is the *work and craft* solution. This is the experience of well-being through everyday work or the application of oneself to producing something through repetition, creativity or perfectionism. Again, I use these terms in the everyday, ordinary way. Work in this instance can be a homemaker caring for the home, a factory worker setting off for work in the early hours or a check-out operator at the shops. Craft involves application and practice at something such as mechanics, DIY, home crafts, cleaning a room perfectly, redesigning a home or painting a room.

(4) *The mind solution*

The *adventure and learning* solution refers to the cultivation of deep happiness through the love of learning, through reading, studying, travelling, exploration or whatever methods help broaden the mind and provide the experience of expansion. It can also include inner exploration and a love of one's contemplative interiority, thinking and introversion.

Standing stone 12: You need focus to counteract the diffusion of life

What you lack is the ability to focus. With focus you can decide to commit to something, and with commitment you can begin to practise self-discipline. However, without sharp focus your life becomes confusing.

It's necessary to develop discipline in order to stay committed to goals that are easily forgotten. On Monday you may be determined to get all the DIY chores done; on Tuesday that may have changed to improving your marriage; and by Wednesday you may be heading to the psychiatrist's office! However, when you have developed the habits of self-discipline you persist with what you want to do, even when you have forgotten why you wanted to do it in the first place.

Because happiness needs a focus it also requires a discipline. You have a life in which you can attend to any of twenty things that seem important and that are calling for your attention. While you want to do what brings you a sense of fulfilment, you aren't really sure what you should be doing. Should you be trying to be a better parent or spouse? Should you be going back to school to learn something new? Should you change your job? Should you go into counselling and work on your personality? Do you need to sort out emotional issues with your family? Should you escape and have an affair? Should you reclaim your lost youth? Should you separate and divorce or should you recommit and get on with life?

On any given day you will have an array of different thoughts. There can be so many that you don't really know where your happiness lies, because there are so many worthwhile causes. The effect, of course, is that you never quite commit wholeheartedly to anything. You give up on the diet, the treadmill remains unused, ten years have slipped by, and you're still unhappy in your marriage. Therefore, because happiness is so fluid and hard to hold it does require a disciplined approach.

With all this talk of discipline you may be afraid that if you did take this view you would turn into some sort of robot. Let me reassure you that, because our emotional lives are so fluid and are constantly changing, there is no danger of this happening. You will never fully tame the wild horses of your emotional life, but you can get them to work for you. You can get a foothold that allows you to ride them with a sense of direction and confidence.

The necessity of discipline recognises the disorder and diffusion of life. For this reason the disciplines and rituals presented in this book seek to narrow your focus from the grand to the specific.

Through practice and repetition, clarity is created. Some sense of order is created against the background of life's wonderful and often confusing disorder. Happiness is broken down. Your competencies are clarified, your failures identified, your limits understood, your knowledge accrued and your self-discipline and self-awareness achieved.

The specificity of your focus, and your commitment to significant actions, creates a particular discipline of your self-discipline. This is important, because so many of us have the will and the self-discipline to change but just don't know what to do. The following chapters define this in clear and challenging ways.

Standing stone 13: What you have to do will feel counter-intuitive

The things you must do to enhance and enrich your life are very often counter-intuitive. Things that you might imagine would not contribute to your happiness in fact do. For example, facing a challenge that stretches your abilities is better for your well-being than staying inside your comfort zone. A two-mile walk in the evening is better for you than an evening in front of the television, though your mind and body may want to choose the latter.

Therefore, being happy means doing things you don't like to do and that you imagine make you temporarily unhappy. We must not, however, mistake discomfort, reluctance, mild agitation or having to do something you don't want to do for unhappiness!

Our mental attention tends to be more concerned with immediate worries and anxieties than with long-term happiness and well-being. Research suggests that about eighty per cent of our daily thoughts are negative anxieties.

Almost everyone wishes they had more time to spend on considering their general direction in life and on making positive change. However, we invest most of our energies simply in coping with the present. We develop an array of habits that maintain this focus. Our daily habits relate more to daily survival than to long-term wellness. Few people slow down enough to fully experience, understand, evaluate and change their lives. Everyone would like to, but we say that we haven't got the time, money or support to do so.

After a lifetime, the habits you have developed around *not having enough time*, or *not having enough will-power* or *not having enough clarity* support this whole self-defeating lifestyle. The habits that support wellness are very different. And, yes, it's possible and essential to change many of them. This requires effort.

Because there is no immediate reward for behaviour affecting long-term well-being, we tend to avoid it. If you decide to do things that are in the service of your long-term happiness and well-being there is no immediate satisfaction—for instance, saving money for a rainy day. It's the same with most behaviour that is good for your long-term mental health. However, character, wisdom and courage correct this, because with these qualities we remember who we are and live not for immediate gratification but for a more distant destiny.

Standing stone 14: You must not use the 'I have no will-power' excuse

Many people believe they fail because they have no will-power. In many cases, nothing could be further from the truth.

Firstly, they 'fail' because they have grossly underestimated how their so-called simple decision to, for example, lose weight or get fit involves a host of other hidden decisions that are required to succeed. The person usually doesn't realise that it takes not one decision to lose weight but actually about ten additional ones. Most of the people I meet who say they have no will-power actually live lives that need extraordinary will-power. It's not that they have none; it's that they actually use so much of what they have. The problem therefore has less to do with will-power and more to do with preparation, focus and an appreciation of complexity. People have the will but not the know-how. The notion that you have no will-power is one that kills a lot of plans and dreams. Even the most slothful of teenagers has an area in life in which they apply self-discipline.

Secondly, people also fail because they haven't prepared themselves for self-discipline. Most of the failure happens before they start.

Self-discipline requires a mastery of your mind as much as of your body. The mastery of your mind enables you to prioritise, focus, simplify, commit, take action and form habits. Will-power and self-discipline must be applied to your mental life as much as, if not more than, to your behavioural life. You must have the will to direct your thinking, attention and moods in the direction you desire.

Clarify a pure intention

A lot of what you feel is a consequence of 'having no will-power' is in fact a consequence of you not having a 'pure intention'. A pure intention is having a very clear, uncomplicated goal that you wish to pursue (as distinct from a grandiose, oversized, confusing and poorly thought-through goal).

A pure intention is a goal that is small, simple, uncomplicated and easy to think about. It's fuelled by strong desire but not by histrionic emotion. Often, in response to certain situations, we suddenly desire to undertake a certain activity in the pursuit of a goal or desire, and we enthusiastically and emotionally embark on it. The problem is that after a while the emotions calm down and we quit what we started, disappointed that we seem to lack the will-power to proceed.

Things are not changed by emotion or passion alone! If you equate passion with will-power you will find yourself falling short very often. If you imagine that the person with will-power is able to do the things they do because they have built up an emotional intensity you miss out on the power of good habits.

Poor decision-making makes for poor will-power

We often make new-year resolutions and promises to ourselves to do something, but our new behaviour lasts only for a short while. We make promises with hopeful enthusiasm only for them to fizzle out weakly. The more often we do this the weaker we begin to feel, and our trust in our own will-power fades.

The truth is that most of our decisions to change are not decisions at all but merely emotional aspirations. We make these pseudo-decisions in response to some strong emotion or thought about wanting to change. We mistake our desire for a decision, so we suddenly and emotionally decide we will go on a diet, when the so-called decision has been little more than an impulse or wish with no considered or detailed preparation. The powers behind these pseudo-decisions are more emotional than they are reasoned and considered. However, building will-power, self-discipline and good habits must not be influenced by emotion, because one's emotions are in constant change. Though emotion can be part of one's initial inspiration, if it's deemed necessary for success you are doomed to failure.

So what can you do? How can you channel good intention into focused will-power and uncomplicated action. How can you make an *irreversible decision* to improve your well-being and happiness? We will examine this in the next chapter.

Standing stone 15: You must be a guardian of the whole of your life

'Grace' is a lovely word. 'By the grace of God' is an expression that hints at the humility of the human heart. You can substitute Creation for God in this phrase and have the same feeling. It means that there is a relentless spirit of strength and regeneration at work in you always. It's a condition of realising that, by your very life, you are in favour with all Creation, that you are in receipt of a freely given gift and that you are blessed by life and worthy of your place. It refers to the fact that you are graced by the life that is living you and not by your clever manipulation of life, your personal achievements or the approval of others. It's not by your achievements that you are worthy but by grace!

The idea of grace asks you to get out of the way, not to be in the centre and to allow the will, the joy and the natural well-being of life to blossom in you. A teaching of Buddhism, for example, is that when your controlling ego steps aside well-being is made possible. From this viewpoint you shouldn't really take too much credit for your achievements or accomplishments; you should see yourself as having been gifted, blessed or graced by Creation.

Every good thing we receive has been gifted to us by Creation. A spiritual view of life is to see how you are a minder of these gifts. You can see your whole life as a gift that you must shepherd and mind, and that this must be a discipline and a responsibility. You must be a guardian of your life—of your whole life through its many stages. In being a guardian of your life you take great care of what is given to you and accept your worthiness in receiving this gift; you experience a sense of the sacred when you do. The responsibility to be a guardian of one's whole life is a spiritual one that arises from a sense of grace and appreciation. It refers to the minding of one's story, the appreciation of the narrative of one's life and the desire to write yourself into your future in good, meaningful and passionate ways.

All these psycho-spiritual disciplines and things-to-do point us towards the sun and are gateways to appreciation, happiness and discovery. Practising spiritual discipline is a lifelong commitment, and we all need to commit ourselves to it again regularly. It gives us freedom from fear and self-absorption and shows us the path to happiness.

Your self-worth arises from your unique self that, in and of itself, is deserving of great respect and reverence. This is at the heart of our Western system of justice that recognises the dignity of each person, regardless of status. Our psycho-spiritual challenge is to remember the deep meaning of this truth: you are a person of great worth and are as valuable as any king or queen, any millionaire or celebrity. The disposition of humility, gratitude and surrender is, paradoxically, at the heart of spiritual discipline. It's not the discipline of accumulating and doing more that matters but the discipline of doing less and awakening yourself to the deeper mystery and to your real place in Creation and life.

For exercises related to this chapter please check out the book web site at

www.couragetobehappy.ie

Chapter 9

What to do

A psycho-spiritual approach

A SIMPLE 21-DAY CHALLENGE

What to do now

This chapter is about 'how to do it'. We now look at what has to be done and how to go about doing it. Here is where the book comes to land, with the integration of the science, the spirituality and the self-disciplines of happiness. There is an ancient Celtic prayer that asks us to have

> Honesty in our hearts,
> Strength in our limbs
> And deeds to honour our promises.

This is the spirit of this chapter: to recognise that our approach to living a full life culminates in 'deeds to honour our promises', that is, in action and self-discipline that makes our aspirations real. Our 'honesty' is to build the scaffolding around scientific research; the 'strength in our limbs' comes from our motivation and desire; and the 'deeds to honour our promises' are the self-disciplined actions that ensure that we honour our promise.

Preparing the soil of the self for the seeds of well-being

A great deal of the work associated with living a rich and fulfilling life is in preparing yourself for change. If you are to take the courageous path of taking your well-being and happiness seriously, and if you are willing to change your life to help this to happen, you need to prepare well.

What prevents you from achieving your goals is a lack of proper preparation. Our preparation for change is, regrettably, very often naïve. We tend to think that our enthusiasm will be enough to get us through. However, we tend to imagine our success without imagining the little ordeals involved. We naïvely think that an image of ourselves as thin and fit will get us to stop overeating, or that knowing that we want to get fit will be enough to get us there. This is all commonplace. But positive thinking is not enough. A bit of negative thinking and of anticipating the obstacles is vital.

You need to assess whether or not you have the necessary tools, beliefs, attitudes and skills to achieve your goal. Most people make naïve decisions and then fail.

If you want to be happier, to begin to enrich your life, to make some serious changes in your attitudes, thoughts, lifestyle, behaviour, values and purposes, you have a lot of reconnaissance to do. You need to scout the terrain ahead and within to assess whether or not you have what it takes to negotiate the many obstacles that you will face.

A failure to follow through on your decisions is often caused by an inaccurate assessment of what is required to persevere. Most people underestimate the nature of the obstacles and overestimate their ability to overcome them! You underestimate these obstacles because you only prepare for what you think are the big obstacles and don't see the many small obstacles that will be your undoing. These obstacles are the most difficult. The thorn in your shoe can cause your downfall more than the great weight on your back. What you find difficult is rarely the pure goals or objectives themselves.

It's the small, trivial and inconsequential things that you will find the most difficult. This will undermine your confidence. If you don't recognise this at the outset you are doomed to failure.

You must know yourself and honestly evaluate yourself.

> You will not fall at the hurdle of each action you have committed to; no, you fall before you get there.

Overcoming defensive well-being

The reason that you have such difficulty in getting yourself to act, think and feel in ways that are good for your soul is that your goal is not concordant with other everyday priorities. Your everyday goals may be that you—

- only consider your mental health when you feel bad
- are happy to go through life tolerating things
- are more reactive than active when it comes to your satisfaction with life.

Therefore, it's important to assess how defensive your lifestyle and thinking have become and to be aware of the force that might be working against your positive desire to change! Some of this has evolutionary and existential roots.

The psychology of downtime

Because the little things along the way can trip you up so easily, your inspiration and emotional commitment have to be accessible to you not when you are taking action but when you are inactive. In other words, your motivation to become fit has to be felt when you are not running; your motivation to eat well has to be felt when you are not eating; and your inspiration to develop your personal well-being has to be felt when you are engaged in the uninspiring activities of your day.

To lose weight, to become fit, to become happier, to improve your mental health are achieved by developing your 'downtime psychology'. Downtime psychology means developing the right thoughts, habits and attitudes during your everyday life so that you are fully prepared for your uptime, that is, when you have to do the things you have to do.

As this section highlights, such things as weighing-scales, exercise programmes, happiness activities and goal-setting will take care of themselves if you have prepared well. If you have assessed and realigned your everyday outlook to support your goal, success is impossible to resist.

You think that losing weight is about what you eat. It's not. Not eating bad food is actually the easy part. The reason you can't lose weight has very little to do with food: it's about what you are thinking, feeling and doing when you are not eating. The same applies to most of our life goals.

Closing escape hatches

In this section I want to talk about what it is that prevents you from following through on your intentions. To be able to follow through on decisions, you need to recognise and deal with your resistance.

Let's talk about 'get outs' and 'let outs': these are the small print of your commitments that represent the range of excuses, situations, conditions and feelings that you accept as legitimate reasons for getting out of the 'contract' with yourself. These are your escape hatches, as it were: the options you have left open for you to escape having to follow through on your decisions.

We are notorious for our ability to make so-called decisions to change and then to have a whole battery of small-print excuses that permit us to change our mind.

In psychotherapy I use a 'closing escape hatches exercise' for decision-making that requires the decision-maker to be fully congruent when making the decision. In making the decision, all let-offs, get-outs and escape hatches are closed. Excuses are explored and respected. The person makes the decision from the adult part and not the child part of the self. The decision is not made or accepted if the decision-maker can't state with conviction that all the escape hatches are closed off.

When it comes to your bad habits and need to change, you present yourself with the same tired old excuses for not being self-disciplined or following through, such as:

- I have no will-power.
- I try my best.
- I make a good effort.
- Circumstances work against me.
- The time has not been right.
- It's normal to give in every now and then.
- I am just like everyone else.

You might feel momentarily better about yourself when you offer these excuses, but you have a nagging awareness that you have let yourself off the hook—again. Don't believe the excuses. You don't need self-pity.

Symbolic action and happiness in the ordinary

It's through doing ordinary things with committed persistence that we begin to make changes. The thesis of this book is that deep happiness is found in the ordinary and not in the grandiose. Your goal, then, is to form habits that enrich happiness; it's not to develop a dramatic new personality or rebuild the foundations of your self. The stress of thinking that you need to change your personality is removed if you realise that your goal is changing habits through intentional repetition.

In doing ordinary things in an extraordinary way we act symbolically: the ordinary act symbolises and ritualises the extraordinary context. This is central to giving the approach its flesh and blood. Habits are trivial and meaningless if they haven't got deep symbolic meaning for the actor. We can then focus on the sub-skills of happiness and the genuine will to find pleasure in the ordinary—in washing the dishes, planting new bulbs or prayerfully vacuuming the front room!

It's not dramatic, but it is inspirational. It's the Zen realisation that the magic is in the ordinary, that the change is in the everyday. So when it comes to happiness you must break it down from the lofty to the commonplace. Your ultimate goal is to be without anxiety, stress and depressiveness; but your immediate goal is to relax into the self-discipline of repetition and to find meditative joy in the struggle that comes with it.

Instead of rebuilding your life from the top down, in the Zen-like way, do so from the bottom up: 'clean off your shoes and wash out your rice bowl'. Approach your happiness as a set of micro-skills to be practised. Don't see the acquisition of well-being as a consequence of some big breakthrough or discovery. To approach your self this way is to want to cheat, to want to find a magic potion. This is your attempt to cheat discipline and to find a solution that doesn't include real old-fashioned work

You can't find joy by dodging the obligations of practice and repetition

For a musician the joy of playing a piece of music is in knowing the effort that has gone into getting to the point of being able to perform it. It is the same with self-development. Your growth is dependent on self-application and self-discipline. If there hasn't been effort and persistence in the practice, there is less joy in the performance! While practising a piece of music every wrong note is not a failure: it's part of the success of the feedback process and the small incremental steps toward joy. You become happy working toward a goal with crystal-clear clarity of purpose, with deep inspiration and with repeated practice.

Goal is small, not big

Developing new mental and emotional attitudes and habits requires the repetition of small mental and emotional thoughts and behaviour. This insight should be interesting to you because of its emphasis on the repetition of small things and not on big transformation. This is incremental habit formation. The goal, then, is not to try to *be* happy but to '*do*' happy, by changing the thought or behavioural habits with clear and intentional repetition. The erasure of the small habits of stress, anxiety and depression, and the development of the small habits of relaxed, joyful acceptance, is achieved through intentional self-disciplined repetition. This is liberating. You are in control.

The 21-day challenge

Excellence is not an act: it is habit.

New behaviour is not achieved by doing something once a week but by doing it twenty times a week for three weeks! Therefore, repeating a true positive thought about your self five times a day for three weeks will change your self-image. Identifying and renaming a so-called negative feeling in a positive way, practised and repeated over time, can change that feeling. Repeating a sequence of thoughts many times a day for many days begins to have a profound and lasting effect.

All the important activities that have meaning have to be broken down into easy-to-do actions. When the action required to get fit, lose weight, reduce stress, overcome depression or stop worrying is too difficult, it doesn't get done. What you do has to be within your range of resources and competencies.

As I have repeated throughout the book, we are more symbolic than literal. Our thinking brain tries to operate on the literal level, but our emotional, behavioural, social and attitudinal self is a symbolic self. Our small everyday repetitive thoughts and acts can mean the world.

If you practice any of the things listed in chapter 6, you are giving expression to your philosophy, psychology and theology of life in symbolic ways. This is how we have to be.

A PSYCHO-SPIRITUAL DISCIPLINE FOR WELL-BEING

We need discipline because of our flawed nature. This is a vital point, because it goes to the heart of our human condition. Without the inner tension of human existence there would be no need for self-improvement, transcendence or an effort to rise to the occasion of adversity. There is an inner tension in humanity that sets the stage for our urgency. It's an impulse that has us wanting to improve, develop, refine and educate our children and ourselves. It has us wanting more happiness.

We can consider the spiritual disciplines of happiness as a way of life. We can see them as meaningful rituals that keep us awake to our true nature, our inevitable joy and our imagination. These truths are not the superficial avoidance of reality but the essential counterparts of the unavoidable anxiety and dread that are also part of life.

The disciplines and self-disciplines should take you out of yourself and keep you in touch with the true source of strength, wisdom and imagination in your life. You may be caught up in your past failures or inadequacies to such a degree that you lose all perspective and feeling for the extraordinary life that is living you. Or you may be caught up with your successes and accomplishments and feel so good about yourself that you also lose touch with the vulnerability of your life.

Self-discipline and discipline, then, is a spiritual walk, a pilgrim's journey towards health and well-being. We all need a corrective to our stress-oriented lifestyles, and we need to return to the roots of our authentic pilgrimage.

The disciplines must be relevant to the factory worker and the academic, the harried single mother and the office worker, the jock and the priest. The gentle disciplines of life can't be clever, strategic or sophisticated: they must be straightforward, challenging and accessible. The way of gentle self-discipline, although challenging and even arduous, can be ultimately joyous and liberating.

I have always guarded and revelled in *the treasures of a contemplative life*. The contemplative life encourages you to explore your inner life. This is not an indulgent introspection or a gloomy indulgence but a joyful practice that opens the door to one's deepest interiority.

Discovering the right practice and discipline of living is like meeting old friends who you haven't seen in many years and being delightfully surprised at the warmth of their company. The spiritual disciplines are a gateway to your abundant life.

> The disciplines themselves are valueless unless they are symbolic activities of a deeper truth.

The psycho-spiritual disciplines are simply a means to a greater end: deep satisfaction and inner freedom. Just as the laws of the wind enable a yachtsman to turn a headwind into forward movement, so do the spiritual disciplines allow us to turn our limitations and inadequacies into redemptive freedoms that benefit our family, work community and society. The disciplines can be practical and, at the same time, honour the great mystery of life. We will examine how to practise the disciplines in a detailed and concrete way.

They will not be a dull drudgery but a challenge to the self with the promise of redemption and discovery. It will not be for the sophisticated but for the ordinary. The disciplines will be easy to think about and easy to do. They will be resourced by an inspiration for creating a lifestyle and orientation that is simple and modest but deeply purposeful. The spiritual disciplines can be described as behaviour and rituals that facilitate psychological growth and spiritual awareness.

The traditional religions have identified a number of disciplines that are reassuring to us at this point. They prescribed various ways to achieve the purposes I am describing. The practices that are described in this book are based on traditional ritual, psychological research and existential need. The essential traditional ones, from our viewpoint, are prayer, meditation, service, celebration and grateful acceptance.

Psycho-spiritual disciplines and practices

Certain disciplines and practices help people keep the heart open and the soul turned towards Creation. These disciplines can't save you, but they can heighten your desire and awareness and love of life.

> A psycho-spiritual discipline, when practised faithfully and regularly, is a habit that repeatedly brings you back to the source of your life and opens you up to your deepest self.

Psycho-spiritual disciplines help to keep our relationship with ourselves in good working order. But no discipline is able to create one's desire for self-improvement and growth. That desire for growth and well-being comes from your heart.

Disciplines train you to stay on course when the moods swing. If you don't stay disciplined, you drift away. Contemplative spirituality helps make life simpler in another way. Chasing after a wealthy lifestyle is a rather complicated affair: the standards keep shifting and the worries are many. That's why contemplatives and mystics speak so often of 'detachment'.

By taking our focus off acquiring things such as wealth and status, we have more of ourselves available to focus on learning to love rightly. You can't attain well-being and chase status or wealth: most of the time the paths go in opposite directions.

The hero's path

Taking the hero's journey, the road less travelled, doesn't produce instant happiness or guarantee happiness; but it puts you on a road on which your heart can break open, on which the potential within you can be realised. The practice of psycho-spiritual disciplines is to take this road. The practice has many benefits and can open your mind, heart, soul and body to new life. If your present way of life is not bringing you deep happiness your way of life must change. It's as simple as that.

PREPARING TO BE HAPPIER

In the early chapters I mentioned that a great deal of deep happiness comes from overcoming small obstacles in the service of a simple goal. When you apply the four spiritual disciplines (mind, body, heart and soul) you will discover the self-rewarding gratification that comes with practice, repetition and learning. This is the satisfaction that comes from overcoming small resistance when working towards your goal. You actually let the goal slip into the background, and the activity itself becomes its own reward. Knowing this helps you to keep the right attitude of staying in the present rather than impatiently seeking the product: happiness or non-depressiveness.

If you make a decision to prioritise your well-being, and if you are willing to practise in a positive and good-humoured way, a crystal-clear focus will enable you to persist. The four disciplines and the twenty-one activities provide the framework for this. The model presented in the next chapter provides one simple and elegant method for helping you with this. You will hopefully develop your own.

Distractions

The difficult thing about caring for one's psychological health is that there are so many other demands being made on you. It becomes difficult to maintain focus, priorities and momentum. Distractions are everywhere. This is why habit-formation, repetition and practice are essential. This is a recognition that you need to develop automatic thoughts, behaviour and attitudes.

You live in an age of multi-tasking in which you expect yourself to be able to master many things at once: being a good parent, employee, spouse, friend, student, athlete, dietician, cook or volunteer. On top of that, you expect to be cheerful, happy, good company, mature, emotionally stable, non-anxious, worry-free and so on. While this kind of multi-tasking is good for coping and maintaining one's sense of self-importance, it's the enemy of personal transformation and change. You simply can't do everything! And when a lot of what you are doing is servicing your stress, status and security there is very little left over to serve your lasting well-being.

Focus

To make the inner transformations necessary for improving your well-being, and to practise happiness-enhancing behaviour, the first thing you need to be aware of is the power of focus, that is, the power that comes from being able to give your complete attention and energy to a very specific task or objective.

Assuming that you have set an appropriate goal, you often fail to achieve it because you don't give it your full attention. When you can't give it your full attention you get distracted, lose your focus, forget your exact intention or allow circumstances to overtake you. If the task is not specific enough your efforts become confused, inconsistent, hard to measure and generally 'all over the place.'

If you are like a lot of us, when it comes to your general efficiency in life you are for ever at war with yourself over your inability to get on top of things. This is because you have a number of different priorities that are inevitably in conflict with each other, which creates internal distress and tension and a feeling of being ineffective, unhappy or inadequate. Your good values can be in conflict with each other.

However, the person who has developed the self-discipline 'muscle group' is able to focus and single-task when necessary. Amazingly, when this happens a sense of serenity and clarity can emerge.

Being able to focus on a single specific task, and knowing that it's your first priority, can bring real clarity and a self-perpetuating energy. This doesn't mean that you haven't got other priorities, but you are crystal clear about what will get your primary attention and focus. If you are to make an effective decision it will require the strength and self-discipline to say No to many other good things in life. This is the hard part.

Can you give your emotional well-being your priority? Can you undertake a 21-day de-toxing, reframing and rebuilding of your inner life in a simple, elegant, evidence-based and psycho-spiritual mental training?

LEARNING TO 'DO' HAPPINESS

We are what we repeatedly do. (Aristotle)

No magic pills: The importance of practice

In the practice of any new skill, if you are focused only on an ultimate goal, like being stress-free or generally happier, you will become very frustrated with your slow and tedious progress or with how inconsistent your feelings are. However, if you are focused on the practice of the many small sub-skills involved, you will find joy in the learning. If any student only tolerates impatiently the boring rituals of practice, they will not last long at all. Rather than simply tolerating practice, if one's attitude towards learning is driven by the desire to grow and develop, the disciplines necessary are their own reward.

Therefore, the commitment to personal growth and to the *practice* of personal development gives its own positive feedback. This, in turn, produces psychological wealth. Personal development can be exhilarating for this reason. In fact, it provides us with the experience of being alive, of not being stagnant or decaying. Engaging in personal development over time works because the goal is not really the final product but the process.

The wonderful thing about learning and practising anything new, particularly in the second half of life, is that it enhances *the experience of being alive*. The application of oneself through self-discipline in order to grow and learn as a person is surely the most noble of applications and the most fulfilling of endeavours.

The greatest sense of self for a child comes from the mastery of some small task through practice, such as walking, drawing or even drinking from a cup. The relationship between well-being and practice is self-evident. Learning requires practice. You will appreciate, therefore, that the desire to be happier only gets us to the starting-line. Many of us, however, like to think that this is enough to get us through the race. Many a diet falls flat because of the assumption that all one has to do is start the race.

Without an awareness of how to persevere and practise new habits, your initial desire and inspiration runs into the ground. It's all very well knowing what your ultimate goal is, but if you don't know what exactly it is that you need to do it gets confusing and disheartening. Running your race requires hundreds of small steps. It is not one big leap.

Therefore, you need drills, as it were—the drills and exercises that isolate the mental muscle groups that need to be challenged, pushed and surprised. It's likely that some of your emotional and thinking muscles have atrophied, and it will be your task to begin to exercise that which has all but wasted away. Now, you will probably not like this exercise, like any workout, but if you are serious you will find yourself surprised, if not exhilarated, by the results. Your workout can be built around the twenty-one things already identified.

Mental repetition and sets

If you repeat a particular motion ten times a day for twenty-one days you will form a new habit that will be ingrained in your mental muscle memory. You can't train your mental muscle to perform in a certain way without repetitions, sets, workouts and practice.

For example, when you are ready to work on your *self-image* it will require you to do a mental workout every day. In it you will have to repeat a particular thought over and over again. You will have to flex your imagination, stretch your mental muscles and push against the resistance of old, lazy thinking. With it comes the exhilaration of having done it, and it will be its own reward. You will gain momentum from the strength that you have built up and the mental endorphins that follow. The mental workout, like the physical one, requires corrective feedback, adjustments, refinements and pain! There is no joy in learning without struggle against a resistance that you overcome. This is essential. Boring repetition is necessary. The overcoming of your negative self is exhilarating.

Conscious repetition

If you understand that the method presented in the next chapter involves practice you will accept that it involves intentional and deliberate repetition of behaviour, mental exercises and rituals that have been shown to have positive effects. Self-discipline in the development of happiness means that your behaviour must be a deliberate repetition of seemingly unremarkable behaviour. It is uninspiring if isolated from meaning, purpose and personal ethics. But, at the end of the day, self-discipline in the practice of well-being involves some perseverance and tedium.

However, it's the willingness to engage in what are superficially tedious tasks that distinguishes the ambitious student from the lazy student. The apprentice carpenter will spend hours trying to shape wood into natural curves; the golfer will spend hours trying to manage taking their club away from the ball correctly; the artist will spend weeks trying to master the consistency of acrylic colours; the musician will practise scales on their instrument over and over again. In this way, the true student, who grows and develops, finds joy in the process of practising. The attitude of discipline is transforming.

Enjoying the practice, not anticipating the outcome

If you wish to develop your wellness you must be willing to participate in the learning more than in wanting the outcome. Practice needs present-centred awareness. Your awareness and attention will need to be the simple task at hand. You are in the present. However, if you are focused on measuring your level of progress or the degree to which your practice is helping you, you become less focused on what you need to do. If, when trying to lose weight, you stand on the weighing scales every day, you are driven more by seeking success than by participating in wellness.

When you are present, in the moment, with what you are doing in the 'now', you experience calm and non-anxiety. If your goal is to focus on the present there are no mistakes or bad feelings. You need a goal as your reference point and destination, but it should remain out there in the hazy future. In practice there is no profit and loss, no good and bad, no 'I'm not good enough' or 'what's wrong with me.' There is only feedback—a fascination with learning through practice.

Mental practice

Research shows that if you mentally practise swinging a golf club it has positive effects on your swing. In other words, disciplined and focused mental rehearsal of a physical activity enhances the ability to perform that action. This applies to the happiness exercises also. For example, if you are unable to thank someone in your life for what they have done for you, a five-minute meditation in which you imagine yourself thanking them can create some of the same good feeling.

When it comes to being happy, we need—like a recovering alcoholic or an athlete in training—to maintain our conditioning at a high level. Without practice our mental fitness will diminish and disappear. The recovering addict must say their serenity prayer and their twelve steps all the time. The athlete must stretch, warm up and go through their drills every day. The monk must pray at morning and evening every day. The pianist must play their scales repetitively every day. Changing our experience of life is well within our grasp, but we have to rehearse core ideas and practices again and again so that everyday life doesn't steal them away.

For exercises related to this chapter please check out the book web site at

www.couragetobehappy.ie

Chapter 10

A 21-day method

ELEVEN MINUTES PER DAY: A 21-DAY PROGRAMME

1. Complete the daily book of lines (five minutes).
2. Do fixed-minute attention for thirty seconds three times a day.
3. Think 'One pure thought' (one minute).
4. Rehearse 'One pure act' with coffee (one minute).
5. Do the 'One pure feeling' exercise each toilet break (twenty seconds).
6. Do the 'One Pure Prayer' at bedtime (thirty seconds).

Teaching your brain new habits

Maxwell Maltz, in *Psycho-Cybernetics*, claimed that it took a minimum of twenty-one days before the brain of a patient suffering from the amputation of a limb set up new neural pathways to prevent the feeling of phantom sensations in the amputated limb. He used that as a rough estimate for how long it takes a person to learn a new habit so that it's integrated in the brain. While the number of days is arbitrary, really, what is essential is the realisation that the learning of new habits—not ideas—takes time to be integrated in everyday movement and thinking. Whether you are practising a scale on the piano, adjusting to the subtleties of a new car or learning any new skill, it takes time before there can be a change from conscious deliberation to automatic response.

My own estimation of this time, from my experience playing rugby, painting with acrylics, drawing and meditation, is similar. It takes three weeks to turn a behaviour into a good habit: one week to get started, another week to get comfortable and a final week to consolidate.

The learning of any new skill has three stages, starting with practising something and being aware of your incompetence and awkwardness, such as awkwardly learning a scale on a piano. The second stage begins with the very conscious and deliberate mastery of the skill. The third involves the ability to practise the skill automatically and unconsciously. This is the stage at which you can do it without thinking, because it has been integrated in your autonomic system. Our three-week method follows this model, recognising the time needed to embed thoughts, patterns of feeling and actions in the brain and body.

The necessity of anchors

It's of vital importance with whatever habit you try to build into your life that you use what are called 'anchors' or triggers to remind you of your commitments and decisions. Anchors are small items that act as reminders of who you have decided to be. They symbolise your decisions and new discipline. When you commit to doing something it's important that you create an anchor that symbolises that decision and that it's something you see or have contact with regularly. It could be a wristband, a ring, a credit-card size summary card, a little notebook, a poster on your wardrobe door, a symbol on your key-ring, a night-light in your room, an automated text, a set of prayer beads, a new pair of shoes or coloured stickers on your kettle. It's important that they are physical and visible. These things or signs then anchor down your behaviour and are a symbolic focus for your mind. They help you not to forget, which is very easy to do.

Buy yourself a new pair of shoes

Here is a simple anchoring exercise: If you are to create a new attitude and programme for yourself buy yourself a new pair of shoes. Wear them for the twenty-one days. They will remind you every morning and night that you are walking a new path. That you are standing on new ground.

21-Day Discipline

Exercise 1 of 6:
The Celtic Book of Lines

Five minutes per day

EXERCISE 1: THE 'CELTIC' BOOK OF LINES

This is a very simple exercise. However, like many good exercises, its simplicity will be deceptive. The Celtic Book of Lines is a simple technique in which you write out repeatedly, over a period of twenty-one days, core thoughts that repair and encourage your mind. I have based this on my successful experience with clients, who have used this method to embed core thoughts and attitudes. The method is simple, uncomplicated and non-taxing. It's not unlike when you had to write lines at school saying 'I must not . . .' But in this exercise it's more of a clarification and declaration of what and who one is. The results of this uncomplicated and simple exercise can be quite significant.

To return to narcissism and escape hatches, please don't think that this is beneath you, because, if you can do it, you will find it has emotional effects. It requires a humility and modesty of self to begin.

The aim of writing out your lines is based on the realisation that changing negative thinking patterns and introducing new thoughts only happens effectively through practice and repetition. Positive and negative thinking don't change as a result of occasional and random efforts at thinking positively. Mental habits are like behavioural habits and require disciplined focus to change.

You need to introduce a new positive thought stimulant that initiates its own cascade of positive feelings. The thought that needs to be practised has to be carefully selected and have a pure application to your area of need. Not just any positive thought will do: each thought needs to have an existential foundation and be applied in a very specific and deliberate way towards your area of need. The short-term tedium and repetition associated with writing out one's lines is actually an essential part of meditative practice, as it allows a quietening of one's mind as one focuses and concentrates on the specific task. The repetition has subconscious benefits, because it permits the writer to *feel* the thought in different ways, to *hear* the thought in different ways and thus to draw out the nuances and implications of this seed declaration. That is, a declaration that becomes the seed from which good things can grow.

The self-discipline of the repetition is also critical as a symbolic acknowledgement of the vital importance of this thought. The thought must also have a purity and simplicity that is good for the writer. The writing must be done with artistry and consideration.

The thoughts should have a direct link with our core existential anxieties and realities and be literal and symbolic reference points for growth. Therefore, your practised new and pure thought should be refined and sculpted roughly (not obsessively) into a mental 'brushstroke' that you will, like a musician or artist, practise over and over again. You will enjoy and appreciate the meditative tedium of it, and you will be inspired by how it creates a cascade of associated thoughts that wash through your being.

Finally, I call this your 'Celtic Book of Lines' to encourage you to decorate your lines with Celtic lettering, knots and little designs in order to develop an affection for your book. I would suggest you buy yourself an attractive spiral-bound notebook or journal in which you can artistically and purposefully write.

By doing this most simple and humbling of tasks, you reject your narcissism, which suggests that you are entitled to do something more exciting than this ritual. You sidestep self-rejection and self-doubt. Finally, you will observe your self-defeating self along the way with good humour and wisdom. With a smile, you can be aware of your self and practise, through repetition, some profoundly uncomplicated and pure thoughts.

Instructions

Using the 'Emancipations of the heart' in the appendix and your 'One pure thoughts', as developed in the following section, write out your one-line thought declaration twenty times twice a day. This line may be 'No harm can come to me' or 'There is no need to be afraid.' Write the same line for the first day and then sculpt it into a modified one on the second day in order to personalise it. *It takes only two-and-a-half minutes to write twenty lines!*

Buy the attractive spiral-bound hard-covered notebook and give it the title 'My Celtic Book of Lines'. Your page would look something like this.

My Celtic Book of Lines

There is no need for me to be afraid.
There is no need for me to be afraid.
There is no need for me to be afraid.
There is no need for me to be afraid.
There is no need for me to be afraid.
There is no need for me to be afraid.
There is no need for me to be afraid.
There is no need for me to be afraid.
There is no need for me to be afraid.
There is no need for me to be afraid.
There is no need for me to be afraid.
There is no need for me to be afraid.

21-Day Discipline

Exercise 2 of 6:

Three minutes per day of fixed-minute attention

FIXED-MINUTE ATTENTION

The practice of fixed-hour prayer is common to Judaism, Christianity, Islam and Buddhism. In the context of the themes covered in this book—such as our search for meaning, our need for disciplined practice, the importance of meditation and the necessity of symbolic ritual—the practice of fixed-minute attention can be a powerful method of self-orientation. Such meditation, attention, prayer, urgency and focus are essential to psycho-spiritual practice.

Since ancient times it has been a mark of spirituality to set aside certain fixed times during the day for meditation, thanksgiving and prayer. Taking time out of one's day to express thanks, experience gratitude or turn one's heart toward the deeper movement within one's life is exactly what we all need. Buddhist and Christian monks spend many hours a day in such prayerful meditation! The practice of fixed-minute attention need not be the same as that of Buddhist monks, but the form and intent of this practice must be the same.

In meditation groups the form I have used for the past fifteen years has been similar to the traditional structures: begin with body and mind focusing; follow that with structured meditation; then finish the mediation with a declaration by the self.

Therefore, your fixed minute should be confined to three times a day, during which there is, for one minute, a focused repetitive attention on one of the declarations or emancipations of the heart (see appendix).

In order to heighten focus, deliberateness and discipline this needs to be done at the exact same minute every day. These three fixed minutes should be at 12:01, 3:01 and 6:01.

The structure of the one minute

1. Take twenty seconds to calm the body and to stop thinking, with deep breathing and physical relaxation.
2. Take twenty seconds to repeat over and over one of three 'declarations'. (Use the other two for the other fixed-minute attentions).
3. Take twenty seconds to imagine joy.
4. Breathe deeply and stop.

It's as simple as that.

21-Day Discipline

Exercise 3 of 6:

Practise one pure declaration

PRACTISING ONE PURE THOUGHT FOR YOUR SELF

Having considered the three dimensions of well-being—science, self-discipline and theology—I was faced with the real challenge of considering how best these findings could be converted into meaningful practice. My conclusions were very clear and compelling. It became clear to me that—against the background of one's stressful daily life, one's subterranean existential life and one's uplifting spiritual life—we need ways in which to practise well-being that are simple, elegant, symbolic and deeply meaningful. Once I had crystallised all the necessary words, it was clear and consistent to me that what we need in life is a psycho-spiritual discipline that, very simply, helps us to have uncontaminated thoughts, feelings, actions and meditations.

Our minds are busy with a frenzy of thoughts flitting through our brains every day. Because of life's complexity we think many different things about our lives and ourselves. We often get 'quick-sanded' in confusion. The great religious traditions, as well as the research we have looked at, point us towards simplicity of thought as a central life-affirming quality. It's central to meditation, action, consistency and well-being.

We need many pit-stops in life to be able to *know* some very simple but often forgotten truths, as highlighted in the standing stones of happiness. As I have hopefully illustrated, we forget who we are and we forget some essential truths because of our physical and anxious preoccupation with survival. We can't help ourselves.

As a consequence, we need simple disciplines to navigate us through the dark valleys of our lives and to keep us moving towards True North. To assist us in this we need to return to some essential personal truths about ourselves. We arrive at these truths through the octets of existence. We arrive at the truths by examining which of the eight pure anxieties most affects us and which of the eight joys we most need to reaffirm for ourselves.

These, very simply, become the skeleton of our pure thought. As we shall see, around the skeleton of that thought we can place some of the flesh of our unique feelings. Our discipline is to make this declaration a repetitive practice, until it becomes embedded in our consciousness. The effects of this are profound. That is it.

Your goal here is to develop simple, honest, inspirational, meaningful and encouraging 'declarations of the self' that become stable reference points in your mind. They are developed and grown like any habit—through practice and repetition. Once embedded, they can be sculpted and shaped. The thoughts should be grounded in science, philosophy and existence. In relation to science, this thought can easily have elements that counteract over-thinking, promote optimism, inhibit comparisons with others, and are goal-oriented, image-enhancing, enemy-defeating and self-accepting. They can counter the core symptoms of anxiety, stress and depression.

Self-statement to say to yourself

As part of practising pure positive declarations, you should read the following statement each day:

> *I have committed myself to developing the self-discipline of good thinking. I realise that a few core negative thought-clusters can easily direct my attitude towards negativity and self-rejection. Therefore, I willingly and optimistically commit to practising a few core seed thoughts in a repetitive, consistent and persistent manner. I am committed to the repetitive practice of good thinking, because it's essential to my well-being, self-image and happiness.*
>
> *I realise fully that many of the core thoughts I have about my self and my life are not objective but have emerged from a hodgepodge of my emotional impressions, subjective interpretations, genetic temperament and my brain's ingenuity and enterprise.*
>
> *Therefore, I choose to develop my core thoughts about myself in active rather than passive ways. I realise that developing new seed-thoughts requires the development of thought-habits and that this will require my modesty and self-discipline. I realise that the benefits of beginning to learn good thinking can be powerful, because what I think of myself and my life will influence everything else. My simple declarations point my heart, mind and soul towards a personal integrity, courage and heroic struggle.*

My method

> *Because my thoughts are not objective facts but subjective punctuations it's essential that I discipline my thinking in ways that stimulate happiness. I commit to practising and rehearsing new thoughts repetitively. The thoughts I will declare are symbolic of a family of associated thoughts that stimulate my well-being. I will*

make these declarations as a mental exercise, knowing that they will gently create a domino-effect in my thinking.

I will envisage my thoughts as pure. Without such refined purity my thoughts are left open to contamination by self-doubt and over-thinking. My approach to this thought is one of simplicity and acceptance. A pure thought is any thought that has clarity of focus, is true, is simple, and has a clear intention that promotes my well-being. It's pure in that it's grounded in good research, spiritual wisdom and common sense. Therefore, it doesn't represent a naïve or childish wish. It's not a free-floating affirmation but a grounded declaration that is not naïve about my inevitable suffering.

The thought will also be small. The beauty of building any artistic ability is in the practising of small skills that are a fractal of the larger art. My small thoughts are symbolic of what is necessary in my larger life, and, at that level, they will succeed gloriously.

It's a specific and literal habit that must be learnt. My commitment to the process of learning will, in and of itself, enhance my well-being.

My one pure declaration can become the anchor point, or still point, of my thinking world. This pure declaration is based on existential truths but is unique to me. I will refine it. It will be written and rewritten until it has been, like a piece of sculpture, refined to a spotless and pure perfection that I adopt fearlessly.

I will undertake the self-discipline of thinking and repeating this declaration for twenty-one days, at which point it will be suspended. I will write this thought in the form of twenty lines per day using the Book of Lines.

There can be 'One pure thought' if I am anxious and afraid, despairing or depressed, stressed and overwhelmed. It will be the declaration that, like a laser, cuts to the core self-beliefs that defeat me from time to time.

It's not enough to be able to embrace my mortality. I will also connect with my immensity, my eternal and infinite source. This pure and spotless thought will be a consequence of my courage—the courage to be hopeful. This appreciation of life and Creation, of my inherent worth and goodness and of life's beauty and immensity, will take courage—the vulnerable courage to be happy in an unsafe world.

My 'One pure declaration' becomes my sword of courage, my shield of protection, my beam of light into the dark, my prayer of thanksgiving.

An existentially inspired thought

Most of our anxious, depressive, stressful and self-doubting thinking emerges from the core conditions of existence. These negative thoughts are not pathological or a sign of mental disturbance: they emerge from some of the harsh facts of life that we all face. However, over time and through mental habit they can become solidified and crusted. They then have secured a foothold in our mental self-image.

Human existence generates negative, survival-oriented thoughts; but it also inspires life-enhancing and hopeful ones. As has been explained, there are eight core existential conditions. These conditions inspire eight clusters of thoughts that influence our well-being in profound ways.

Each of the following declarations is linked to an existential-spiritual reality that goes to the very core of our mortal existence. Look through each of the thoughts and carefully select the two thoughts that point, in a simple way, towards the burning-point of your well-being. (You will have some sense of this from your 'Me at my best' assessment on the web site).

Each of the following declarations counteract your anxious predisposition towards decay with a spiritual declaration that prompts you towards growth. The thought is located beautifully on the third and elevated point in the triangle, between the extremes of acquiescence to, and denial of, mortality. Therefore, select the two statements that come closest to what you know you need to inhabit and declare.

Rough life declarations that awaken confident joy

Anxiety
There is no need for me to be afraid.
Everything is and will be okay.
I have nothing to lose except the symbols of my status.
My infinite and eternal self can never be harmed.
I am a good person and am at peace with myself.
My future is hopeful.

Adequacy
I am divinely perfect.
I am a heroic person.
I am a good person.
I am equal to life; there is none better.
I can be the kind of person I want to be.
I can make my life the kind of life I want it to be.

Significance
I am worthy of joy.
I am unique and special.
Before I was ever born, I was being prepared.
I am worthy of receiving life's gifts.
I matter.
I have a right to respect and to my unique view of life.
I am connected to a deeper meaning that gives purpose to my life.

Belonging
I have a special place in the universe, in the world. I belong.
I have been chosen and blessed with life.
My God watches over me.
Like all created things, I am at home in this life.

Helplessness
I can't control everything.
I can 'let go'.
I am free.
My future is bright.
I can influence and shape my life.

Isolation
I am not alone.
Invisible hands support me.
I lay down the burdens that are not mine.
I am accompanied in my life.
I am free and unburdened.

Vulnerability
I am safe.
Nothing can harm my real self.
I remember that the fountain of my being is joyful.
My world is rich.
Nothing bad is going to happen to me.
I can claim my confidence because I can cope.

Woundedness
I am perfectly beautiful.
The wound of my life is my brokenness.
Behind the veil of my self-doubt I blossom effortlessly.
I am not responsible for the happiness of others.
I am naturally beautiful and wonderful.

Worthiness
I need not worry; I am entitled to joy.
I am important, worthy and significant.
I have been blessed.
I am free.
I am beautiful.

Sample negative declarations that heighten your existence-based anxiety

- There are so many problems I must solve.
- I am limited and small.
- I must be vigilant and careful.
- I am on my own.
- I am anxious and afraid, because bad things will happen.
- My worst fears may well be realised.
- I am inadequate and incompetent.
- I am powerless to control my life.
- Joy comes to those who deserve it, and I don't think I do.
- I am not really important.
- There is no special place for me in the universe. I am forgettable.
- There is something wrong with me.
- I don't belong or fit in.
- I have heavy burdens and responsibilities.
- Life has laid a heavy load upon me.
- I am trapped and imprisoned by my life.
- I am deformed and ugly.
- Unless I worry, plan and take anxieties seriously, bad things will happen every day.
- Because I am inadequate as a person I must work hard to keep myself up to scratch.
- I must compensate for my inadequacy with control, anticipation and work.
- I don't deserve much, if anything at all, and I must earn everything, prove myself at everything and gain little bits of satisfaction through my accomplishments.

- I am exposed and will control, monitor and be vigilant about everything I do.
- I am not important and am largely insignificant. The world and others pass me by almost unnoticed. Therefore, I must work hard at being bigger than I am.
- I am powerless and helpless to really change myself, my life and my circumstances. Therefore, I must accommodate myself and acquiesce in what I have. I must expand myself to deal with the demands made of me.
- I can let go of worries and anxiety that I can neither control nor prevent. I accept.
- I let go of perfectionism, keeping people happy and trying to control everything.
- My world is rich, fulfilling and full of potential. The future is bright.

21-Day Discipline

Exercise 4 of 6:

One pure feeling

ONE PURE FEELING: THE POSITIVITY OF LIFE

One pure emotion

All our psychological problems are related to *feeling and emotion.* Most of our psychological disorders are about emotions, for example depression, anxiety, stress, addictions, bipolar disorder and psychoses. Feelings and emotions are the medium through which we experience life. Therefore, what we feel and how we feel define the quality of our mental health.

Feelings and emotions are often complex. Usually we have cocktails of feelings that are unique responses to any situation. Feelings are also complicated, because they are fluid and never fixed. They seep, mix, ebb, flow, fade and intensify as our perceptions change. We are affected by sensations, feelings, emotions, memories and images, all of which affect what we experience about ourselves at any moment.

The purpose of this simple discipline, *the discipline of one pure feeling*, is to practise the distillation, reframing and identification of one pure uncomplicated positive feeling in oneself. The one pure feeling to be found in the body is *positive emotion.* This discipline doesn't ask you to name that positive emotion but, very simply, to find it and *feel* it.

The science of this is interesting, because some theorists have postulated that all feeling and emotion can be reduced to two feelings: a positive feeling, which makes a person feel good, and a negative feeling, which makes a person feel bad. The two different feelings are then identified by their intensity, from very mild to very intense. In simple terms, negative feelings are warning systems for the body that something is not right. Positive feelings are indications to the body that one is safe and well. Classifying your feelings as positive and negative is a simple and very effective way of developing your awareness.

Our feelings can become limited by the degree to which we are prompted by anxiety and self-doubt. When it comes to the positive emotions we can lose touch with them. We make them secondary to our exterior life and allow our feelings to be determined by what is happening in our life. We don't take the time to sink into the deeper truths about ourselves. Nor do we take the time to sink into the ground of positive emotion and pure feelings that lies at the foundation of the self. This is why meditation and psycho-spiritual practice are so essential. The horizontal emotions of stress, anxiety, distress, dread, anger and guilt consume us. These are acutely intense feelings that demand our physical and mental attention. They are feelings prompted by our sense of danger, that is, by our evolutionary survival mechanisms.

Beneath these attention-grabbing feelings and emotions there is something more pure. Behind the anxiety of the self there are the existentially derived feelings of simple joy and uncomplicated happiness. Meditation as a discipline helps people to get in touch with these deeper-layered feelings and emotions. Beneath your stress and worry lies a hidden and repressed joy!

Behind the complexity of our emotional lives we have only four basic positive emotions: joy, interest, surprise and affection. On the other hand, we have about nine different types of negative emotions: anxiety, fear, anger, disgust, sadness, helplessness, shame, loneliness and frustration. However, as I have indicated above, the negative and positive emotions are gradually funnelled and distilled into positivity or negativity. It's not difficult to imagine how easily we get entangled in negative emotions and their consequences.

The pleasure of being alive

We must realise that the purest emotion is not caused by the external world but arises from the fact of life itself. You don't exist in an emotionally neutral state, just waiting to be triggered into action. While this happens to a considerable degree, we do have an emotional resting-state of positive well-being. It's that sublime quality in all beings of just enjoying being themselves. It refers to that delight that is a consequence of being alive that you see in an infant. The happiness of the child is not a consequence of thoughts, circumstances or achievements. The cooing of the baby in the cot is pure positive emotion. It's the smile of the infant at moving objects. It's the little kicks of delight simply at being alive.

The purity of these feelings is always accessible to us—it's just harder for us to clear away the debris of our stressful lives to access the simple, uncomplicated pleasure of being.

We need to bypass a lot of negative feelings so that the primary pure emotions of joy are detected and cultured. Our psycho-spiritual discipline is to touch this deep personal emotion until it flows through our hearts.

Self-statement to say to yourself

Because my negative feelings are not objective facts but subjective experiences it's essential that I discipline my emotional life in ways that stimulate honest and good feeling. Based on scientific research and philosophical wisdom I commit to reframing and uncovering my natural joy.

I will envisage my emotions as pure. Without such refinement my emotions are open to contamination by thoughts and attitudes. My approach to pure feeling is one of simplicity.

It's an emotional habit that I must learn. This is achieved through focusing, meditation and deep awareness of the joy, surprise, anticipation and contentment that is dormant within me. My awareness of my physical well-being will enhance my emotional state.

I have committed myself to developing the self-discipline of good feelings. This includes feelings about my past, such as contentment, fulfilment and pride; feelings about my present, such as happiness, pleasure, engagement and peace; and feelings about my future, such as anticipation, hope and optimism. Any trace of these feelings I will define as positive.

Each day, for twenty seconds, after I complete my Book of Lines, I will let myself feel the emotional well-being of my heart. I will imagine how the emotional ground on which I travel in life is one of positivity: of joy, love, hope, anticipation, delight and light-heartedness. Each day, for twenty seconds, I will feel how life itself, as experienced through my pulse and breath, is a good and positive feeling. The feeling of life is inherently good, and, for this reason, all life, from the tiniest insect upwards, feels good about itself. Without this positive feeling life would lose its desire to continue. This positive feeling, in its simplest form, defines my very existence. I must not for one instant allow passing negative feelings or mental cynicism to diminish or erase this profound emotional truth:

My very life is evidence of my positive emotion. Beneath my worry and self-doubt my heartbeat and breath work away in unending self-belief and ceaseless good feeling. I must notice my natural well-being. It is my inheritance.

Each day, my heart beats about 80,000 times on my behalf. Each day, my lungs breathe about 17,000 times on my behalf. These are

100,000 unrecognised positive efforts made on my behalf, because the very essence of my life is simple, non-intellectual hopeful desire.

Each day, for thirty seconds, I will notice the life that is living me. I will suspend the cascade of cynicism that colours my life, and, for just thirty seconds, I will coo like an infant, dance behind my eyes and kick my imaginary legs in delight, after which I will be free to return to my everyday worries and efforts that anaesthetise my joy!

Bathroom bliss

To make this simple discipline of being aware of your body's physical optimism and hope easy, every time you go to the bathroom during the 21-day method allow the relief of taking a pee be an anchoring reminder of your inherent wellness. Drop a plumb-line into your soul and get a simple reading of your irresistible but unconscious physical joy. Draw it up into your awareness and force yourself to feel it! Aside from your thoughts and feelings, your body feels good in its very existence. Every breath is an intake of physical hope and possibility. Your stress, worries or even despair don't thwart your body's inherent optimism. You have an entitlement to coo like an infant!

21-Day Discipline

Exercise 5 of 6:
One pure act

Doing one of the 21 things to do
on each of the 21 days

ONE PURE ACT
(Two minutes per day at a fixed minute)

With this simple discipline your goal here is to practise the simple activities presented in the 'Twenty-one things to do' in chapter 6. These can become stable reference points in your life.

The *actions* are grounded in science, existence and theology. In relation to science they have been shown to have a positive effect on our well-being. In relation to existence they counter the core existential symptoms of inadequacy: the actions are literal and symbolic reference points for growth. In relation to experiential theology the simple acts can symbolise your heroic engagement with Creation. The act can be big in feeling but small in expenditure.

The experience of being alive

It's no surprise to find that ancient societies and cultures used physical ritual as a means of celebrating existence and enhancing the experience and meaning of being alive. These were developed as existential actions to enhance the experience of life, to savour it, to give it meaning and to draw from life every last drop of exhilaration. It was passionate living.

The 'list of things to do' and exercises

Each day, do one pure act from the list of things to do. This act shouldn't be complicated or drawn out: it should be brief and focused. It may build into something else and grow of its own accord or it may simply be itself for those few moments. Select one of the core activities listed and spend two minutes doing what it prescribes. Or spend two minutes doing one of the exercises on the web site.

When we think about the spiritual activities, the discipline of service may be the easiest to visualise. The spiritual value in acts of service is very important to contemplate and understand. Service reveals the individual's heart and life. It's the overflow that pours from a life filled with love. Service is what you bring to a relationship, and it's the reflection of your identification with the nature of life.

Your self-statement to say to yourself

It's essential that I discipline my ACTIONS *in ways that stimulate my well-being. I commit to practising and rehearsing new actions repetitively. The behaviour that I will practise is symbolic of a family of associated activities that stimulate my well-being. I will practise these rituals, knowing that they will gently create a domino-effect in my being. I will envisage my action as* PURE. *Otherwise I leave them prone to cynicism and self-doubt. My approach to this action is one of simplicity. A pure deed or act is any action that has clarity of focus and intent that promotes my well-being. It's pure in that it's grounded in good research, spiritual wisdom and common sense. It therefore doesn't represent a naïve or childish wish.*

I have committed myself to developing the self-discipline of good acts. I realise that negativity and cynicism can easily push me off course. Therefore, I willingly and optimistically commit to practising a few core deeds in a repetitive, consistent and persistent manner over the next twenty-one days. I am committed to the repetitive practice of good acts, because it's essential to my well-being, self-image and happiness.

I have a responsibility to develop my core deeds in an active rather than passive ways. I realise that developing behaviour requires the development of habits, and this will require modesty and self-discipline. I realise that the benefits of beginning to learn good acts can be powerful. The consequence of not doing this is the repetitive cycle of acts that have defined and limited me in my growth and development.

Your two-minute, small-action coffee break

Therefore, once a day, at the fixed time of my first coffee or tea break, I will spend two minutes doing, or preparing to do, one of the twenty-one activities of mind, body, heart and soul.

21-Day Discipline

Exercise 6 of 6:
One pure prayer

Gratitude and hope at bedtime

ONE PURE PRAYER

Of this I am certain: the purest discipline is the discipline to pray. To pray is to take an attitudinal position towards one's life within the round of a great mystery. The mystery of our unique and mortal life that allows us to experience the wonder of a magnificent universe, the ache and sorrow of life, the specific and touching narrative of our own story and the stormy experience of love. When we experience ourselves fully within the essentials of all life we cannot but take a position of humility, if only for a brief period. We cannot but *pray*. I don't mean prayer as attached to any religion, nor do I mean to pray to a specific god, but to pray in a way that is common to our ancestors, from the dawn of humankind. A prayerful disposition is one of deep gratitude, exhilaration, terror of death, freedom and love. By 'praying' I mean looking toward the sky with gratitude.

When we pray we can stop our endless self-rejection. When we pray with our ancestors we can let go our self-obsession and our fretting over trivialities. When we pray we can experience once and for all that we are safe, that we are held, that there is no need to be afraid, and that our worry, stress and bad anxiety are disproportionate.

Bad anxiety is the anxiety of a life over which we have no control. Bad anxiety is related to fear, which is related to our fearful attempts to be little gods in our mortal bodies. Good anxiety is the feeling that you are not quite worthy of your life, that you are concerned about the fact that you are not living it fully, and that you are not appreciative of the gifts you have been given.

When you pray you remember that your worries, anxieties and stresses are about everything other than your life: ego, status and security. Your life is not really about these things. Your life is about the life that is living you. This is the simple truth that everyone who faces death realises. This is the simple truth that everyone in later years comes to regret not savouring enough. Your life is, very simply, a glimpse of what God sees. In fact, for the passing moment of your life, you are God's eyes.

Prayer and meditation

I love the *idea* of prayer. I love the *humility* of prayer. You don't have to believe in God to pray. Belief or non-belief in God suggests that your spiritual reflexes are reasoned or intellectual. Prayer is an existential cry of praise, fear and thankfulness. You don't pray because you believe in a god or because you think you should but because some part of you has no alternative. Prayer is a reflex of our natural sense of awe, our sense of being in the presence of a majestic Creation, our terror, our sense of unique isolation, our sense of gratitude and our experience of love. Prayer is a natural reflex to cry out into the mystery, to allow us to imagine a god, to allow us to acknowledge the intimate relationship we have with Creation, and to cry, sing, scream, dance or rejoice before we translate it all into religion!. Prayer gives expression to one's deepest isolation and one's deepest intimacy.

I recommend that you imagine your god. Meditative prayer can change your position relative to your life, the world and your sense of control. It's a way to feel the heartbeat of Creation. When we allow ourselves to have a god-feeling we are different. The universe graciously reveals itself to us while we pray, and it's during those moments that we can breathe in deeply the invisible love of Creation.

Meditation is prayer's twin. It comes from the same part of your heart; but in meditation, rather than it giving expression to your life-experience, you find a state of stillness, mindfulness and deep acceptance of your bodily self. Through the stillness of your body your mind and emotions become soothed and you get in touch with the rejuvenating and reassuring stillness within you. In the discipline of meditation you are not so much acting as opening yourself to be acted upon. You open your heart and clear your head to allow the pulse of life to awaken you, to work through you. Meditation gives you the glorious opportunity of dwelling completely in the goodness and perfection of your difficult life.

The wonderful thing about prayer and meditation is that, when you begin to find a position like this, Providence moves in to support you. Life comes to meet you at the points where you shed your preoccupations with horizontal things. Invisible hands lead you into a deeper, more real relationship with your self, with the source of your being with happiness.

The prescription

Every night, for twenty-one days, kneel by your bed for fifteen seconds and repeat a simple prayer. These are my rewritings of some old children's prayers.

Guardian
Spirit of Life
That guards me tenderly
And comforts me lovingly,
Be with me this night
To soothe my thoughts
And remind my anxious heart
That I am safe and loved.

Dear Father of Creation
You are the nameless one
Who makes my future bright
And my life sacred.
Thank you for caring for me this day.
Forgive my cynicism and negativity
And let my heart be open.
Give me courage and hope
And make me worthy
of this beautiful life.

Your summary 'happiness credit card'

This card represents a summary of the simple, easy-to-think-about activities suggested in this chapter. Use it! And don't forget to get an *anchor* for each of these six activities.

The eleven-minute disciplines

1. Write twenty *lines* twice a day for two-and-a-half minutes each time.
2. Set your phone alarm so that at 12:01, 3:01 and 6:01 you do '*Fixed-minute attention*' for one minute: twenty seconds calming, twenty declaring and twenty imagining joy.
3. Use 'Life declarations' to think *'One pure thought'* for one minute every day.
4. Rehearse *'One pure act'* from chapter 6 with coffee for one minute every day in your notebook *or* do a simple thought stimulating exercise from the web site.
5. Do the *'One pure positive feeling'* exercise for twenty seconds every time you go to the bathroom.
6. Do *'One pure prayer'* at bedtime for thirty seconds.

Refusing to take yourself too seriously

In today's hectic, stressful and violent world, how can we experience the true joy that comes from life well lived? Can we have freedom from anxiety and care, which form the basis of a thankful celebration? We cause ourselves stress in our preoccupation with productivity, wealth and security. We forget the joy of simple celebration. The spontaneity of celebration is essential in our lives.

If you are ever in a dead end of problems and stress, remember this simple declaration: don't take yourself too seriously! Despite the seriousness of this book, it has to be put in perspective, and we must remember the need to recharge the batteries of life with craic, holiday breaks, celebrations, spontaneity, a few pints or a song. There are times when our brain shuts off and we let go of whatever we believed was holding us up. We discover in times of craic that most of the things we fret about are just symbols of our insecurity. They matter not a whit. So drink up. Tomorrow we set sail!

For exercises related to this chapter please check out the book web site at

www.couragetobehappy.ie

Appendix

The emancipations of the heart:
Soothing our existential anxieties with everyday truths

Negative octet **Because of mortality and your human condition, as realised through evolution and existence, you inevitably feel all of the following**	**Positive octet** **Because of the gift of life and your human condition, as realised through the evolution of your awareness and imagination, you inevitably feel all of the following**	**Core affirmation-truth** **Because of the predominance of your anxiety and your negative octet it's important that you support your positive disposition with reality-checks and encouragements that remind you of the ultimate spiritual truths—truths that are remembered when you let go of fear. These are necessary because of self-amnesia and forgetting who you are.**
Anxious and afraid	Peaceful and content	Don't be afraid: Everything will be okay.
Inadequate and useless	Capable and essential	You have a special gift.
Insignificant	Valued and important	You have great worth and value.
Helpless	No need to control, cared for	Let go: I will care for you.
Vulnerable and weak	Confident and strong	Be strong, for invisible hands support you.
Isolated or alone	Connected and belonging	You are not alone.
Responsible and burdened	Burden-free	Lay down your burdens.
Rejected or ignored	Blessed and loved	You are holy, blessed and loved.

Trapped or imprisoned	Free	You are meant to be free.
Weak, depressed and despairing	Energetic and hopeful	Your positive energy is dormant within you.
Ugly and deformed	Beautiful and perfect	You are beautiful.
		Things will work out.

Self-rejection **In your attempts to cope with the negative octet (above), which is inevitable, you can be at war with yourself. You turn this into the following negative attitudes towards yourself**	**Self-acceptance** **In your acceptance of life and the positive octet (above), and in your ability to inhabit the joy and suffering of life, you experience your potential and your self with a loving kindness and joy. You develop the following positive attitudes towards yourself**	**Self-encouragements** **Because your self-rejection can begin to predominate, as a consequence of your evolutionary preoccupation with surviving rather than thriving, it's of extreme importance that you soothe your fretful mind with simple, uncomplicated truths and encouragements to yourself**
Self-imprisonment	Self-emancipation	I set myself loose from my bondage.
Self-monitoring	Self-freedom	I set myself free to be who I am supposed to be.
Self-control	Self-spontaneity	I let myself express myself without inhibition.
Self-obsessiveness	Self-forgetfulness	I set myself free of my obsessiveness.
Self-accusation	Self-affirmation	There is no fault in me, for my motives are perfect.
Self-blame	Self-encouragement	Be who I am supposed to be: I am deserving.
Self-guilt	Self-forgiveness	I am forgiven for all my failings: I forgive myself.

Self-punishment	Self-rewarding	I am deserving of applause and reward.
Self-rejection	Self-acceptance	I accept myself just as I am and have been.
Self-doubt	Self-approve	I am perfect just as I am and have been.
Self-loathing	Self-love	I am deeply loved.
Self-hatred	Self-affirm	I am pleasing to Creation.
Self-neglect	Self-care and protection	I will not neglect my emotional life; I will take care.
Self-trivialisation	Self-taking-seriously	I take myself seriously and don't doubt myself.
Self-denial	Self-honour	I honour myself, for I have a deep wisdom.
Self-ignoring	Self-see	I see myself just as I am, for I am wonderful.
Self-detachment	Self-trust	I trust myself.
Self-cutting-off	Self-drawing-forward	I come forth from the shadows.
Self-withdrawal	Self-approach	I am befriending and getting to know myself.
Self-separation	Self-inclusion	I include myself.

Select bibliography

Baumeister, Roy F., and Vohs, Kathleen D., *Handbook of Self-R*... ork: Guilford Press, 2004.

Becker, Ernest, *The Denial of Death*, New York: Simon and ...

Ben-Shahar, Tal, *Happier: Learn the Secrets to Daily Joy an*... New York: McGraw-Hill, 2007.

Campbell, Joseph, with Moyers, Bill, *The Power of Myth*... hor Books, 1991.

Caspi, Avshalom, and Moffitt, Terrie E., 'Genes and depres... 3.

Clarke, Peter (ed.), *The Oxford Handbook of the Sociology o*... ord University Press, 2008.

Diener, Ed, and Biswas-Diener, Robert, *Happiness: U*... *of Psychological Wealth*, New York: Blackwell Publishing, ...

Gilbert, Daniel, *Stumbling on Happiness*, New York: Rando...

Haidt, Jonathan, *The Happiness Hypothesis: Finding M*... *ient Wisdom*, New York: Basic Books, 2006.

Hong, Howard, and Hong, Edna, *The Essential Kierk*... (NJ): Princeton University Press, 1995.

Kahneman, Daniel, et al., *Well-Being: The Foundations of H*... *hy*, New York: Cambridge University Press, 2003.

Linley, P. Alex, and Joseph, Stephen (eds), *Positive Psycholog*... Hoboken (NJ): Wiley, 2004.

Lyubomirsky, Sonja, *The How of Happiness: A Scientific Approa*... *ing the Life You Want*, New York: Penguin Press, 2008.

McAdams, Dan P., 'The psychology of life stories,' *Review of General Psychology*, 5 (2003), 100–22.

Maltz, Maxwell, *Psycho-Cybernetics*, Chatsworth (Calif.): Melvin Powers Wilshire Book Company, 1967.

Nolen-Hoeksma, Susan, *Eating, Drinking, Overthinking: The Toxic Triangle of Food, Alcohol, and Depression and How Women Can Break Free*, New York: Henning Holt, 2005.

Peterson, Christopher, and Seligman, Martin E. P., *Character Strengths and Virtues: A Handbook and Classification*, Oxford: Oxford University Press, 2004.

Seligman, Martin E. P., *Authentic Happiness: Using the New Positive Psychology to Realize Your Potential for Lasting Fulfillment*, London: Nicholas Brealey Publishing, 2003.

Teilhard de Chardin, Pierre, *The Phenomenon of Man* [1955], reprinted New York: Perennial Press, 2002.

Vaillant, George E., *Spiritual Evolution: A Scientific Defense of Faith*, New York: Broadway Books, 2008.

Yalom, Irvin D., *Existential Psychotherapy*, New York: Basic Books, 1980.